I0824155

SOMETIMES WRONG BUT NEVER IN DOUBT

HOW A CUBAN KID FROM QUEENS TRANSFORMED WWE

GEORGE ALDO BARRIOS

Peakpoint Press books may be purchased in bulk at special discounts for sales promotion, corporate gifts, fund-raising, or educational purposes. Special editions can also be created to specifications. For details, contact the Special Sales Department, Skyhorse Publishing, 307 Fifth Avenue, 4th Floor, New York, NY 10016 or info@skyhorsepublishing.com.

Peakpoint® and Peakpoint Press® are registered trademarks of Skyhorse Publishing, Inc.®, a Delaware corporation.

Visit our website at www.skyhorsepublishing.com.

10 9 8 7 6 5 4 3 2 1

Library of Congress Cataloging-in-Publication Data is available on file.

Cover design by Rodrigo Corral Design Studio

ISBN: 978-1-5107-8655-4
Ebook ISBN: 978-1-5107-8713-1

Printed in the United States of America

Contents

Dedication

To my mother and father, whose courage in fleeing Cuba gave me the chance to grow up American. They taught me the virtues that matter most: love, an unrelenting spirit, laughter, and the unbreakable bonds of family and friendship.

To Carol, my wife, lover, and best friend for over forty years. You were responsible for the most important pivot of my life, and every good thing that followed.

To Jorge Gomez-Quintero, my brother in all but blood—confidant, guardrail, and constant encourager.

To Michelle Wilson, the best business partner anyone could have, without whom this book's tagline would never have been possible.

To my daughters Alayna, Katrina, and Celia, who taught me more about myself than any business school ever could and made me the father I never knew I could be.

To the extended family who helped raise me: Adolfo Gomez-Quintero, Aristedes and Ana Amador, Dr. Ela Gomez-Quintero, Marta Gomez-Quintero, Juanita Salas, Raysa Amador, Marian Mendoza, Anarosa Sande, and Aristedes Amador. You created a warm and loving space amid the turbulence that engulfed us all. For that I will be entirely grateful.

To my UCONN family ("The McConaughy 16"), who became my brothers and sisters for life: Taylor and Arianne Beerbower, Kevin and Maria Casalveri, Alan and Michele Hankin, Josh and Chris Hawks-Ladds, Tom and Kris Russo, Russ and Elsie Siegel, Chas and Kim Turecek, and Ken and Beth Young. We've shared the fun of young adulthood, the joys of adulthood, and now we get to relish the past and the future together.

And to all the friends, family, and colleagues whose names don't appear on these pages but whose impact on my life has been immeasurable—thank you for being part of my story.

Rock musician Joe Walsh once said: "You know, there's a philosopher who says, 'As you live your life, it appears to be anarchy and chaos, and random events, nonrelated events, smashing into each other . . . and later, when you look back at it, it looks like a *finely crafted novel.* But at the time, it don't.'"

This is for everyone who helped me write my finely crafted novel.

Prologue: Called Back into the Ring

When you're in business, if you're doing things right, sooner or later you'll have to risk moving against the herd. Some people call this having vision. They prize it as a rare thing. From my point of view, lots of people have vision but few have the guts to act on it. It's the action that's the key. Without action, all the vision in the world amounts to talk and wishes and nonsense.

A question I get all the time: *Why don't more people act on their vision?*

A fine answer has been given to us by Jerome Lawrence, the great American playwright who wrote *Inherit the Wind*:

> It's the loneliest feeling in the world to find yourself standing up when everybody else is sitting down. To have everybody look at you and say, "What's the matter with him?" . . . I know what it feels like. Walking down an empty street, listening to the sound of your own footsteps. Shutters closed, blinds drawn, doors locked against you. And you aren't sure whether you're walking toward something, or if you're just walking away.

This loneliness—and the courage to push through it—is what this book is about. It tells the story of how I stood up when most other people sat down, and how my willingness to take risks and put my neck on the line helped me pull off the largest transaction in sports history. It's about the challenges I faced and the prices I paid along the way. Bottom line, it's a story I hope will inspire you to believe in your own vision, to push through whatever obstacles arise, and to bet on yourself when no one else will.

Before we get started, I'll make a deal with you. These pages contain no bullshit. I won't sugarcoat anything or skirt the unpleasant parts. In plain language, I'll tell you about all the times I miscalculated and fucked things up. In my view, that sets the stage for you to learn from these incidents so that maybe—just maybe—you won't have to go through what I did. Does that sound fair?

Wait. One last thing. Spoiler alert. Sometimes, if we're lucky, life gives us a chance to rewrite our unhappy endings. This book tells that story too.

***

Late November, 2022. I was visiting my mother, who was ninety-eight years old. To the world, she was Erena Gloria Barrios. To me, she was Mami. Always had been, always would be. (Here in this book, I'll just call her Mom because, in English, it means the same thing.)

My wife, Carol, and I had just moved Mom into a beautiful one-bedroom apartment at a top-of-the-line independent living facility down in Florida called the Palace at Coral Gables. Picture an elegant high-rise whose old-world interior was ripped from the Waldorf Astoria. Sumptuous furnishings. Lavish salons. Scroll mirrors. Hand-woven carpets. Chandeliers dripping with crystal. Marble statues gazing down from niches carved into the walls. The place had no chairs, only Renaissance thrones with high backs, carved inlays with lots of gold paint, and cushions upholstered in red and blue velvet.

Like most palaces, this one cost a fortune. So fucking what? It's strange what happens when you finally make real money. The important stuff in life doesn't change. You still love your wife and your kids. You still have your friends. But certain shit becomes untenable, like watching your mother pace back and forth through the same two-bedroom rent-controlled apartment where she raised you in Flushing, Queens, a block from the 7 train.

That place is still burned in my mind. We lived close enough to LaGuardia Airport that if you climbed to the roof of our building and stretched out your arm, you could almost scratch the belly of a Boeing 747 as it took off or landed. Plus, we had a firehouse right across the street, with hook-and-ladder trucks howling day and night. The streets were choked with people of every race, every ethnicity, a bouillabaisse of New York (and therefore America) yelling at each other 24/7. On top of all this, the Long Island Rail Road ran directly behind our building, so every five minutes or so, ancient trains would rattle and clatter east or west, a thunderous din.

Overwhelming noise and confusion. To the out-of-towner, it felt like chaos. To me, it was soothing. I loved it. How could I not? I grew up as a child of chaos.

Mom had lived in that neighborhood for the last five years. It was now home. Her sisters lived in the same building; they were my surrogate parents. Hell, the whole neighborhood was. Flushing is home to working-class people with solid working-class values. Maybe you've heard the saying that you'll always be your first zip code. I believe that, which is why I'll always be 11354.

But as time passed, Flushing didn't suit Mom anymore. By the time she hit ninety-five, most of her friends had passed away, including two of her sisters. Another sister, my Aunt Marta, had moved to Miami. Carol and I had to face facts. We approached Mom and told her we'd like to bring her closer to us, and she agreed.

We thought the apartment we got her in Shelton, Connecticut, was perfect, a nice two-bedroom place in one of those new yuppie buildings that pop up everywhere now. Mom was only seventeen miles up Route 8 from our home in Fairfield, which meant we could visit whenever we wanted. She enjoyed her new digs with the fancy lobby, having her son stop by every weekend for lunch, plus our regular family dinners at the house where she could visit her three granddaughters, the joy of her life. Then COVID hit and we all became shut-ins. No more lunches with me, no more dinners with Carol and the girls. I'm sure you remember that time. It was awful for everyone, but particularly for the elderly who were more isolated and vulnerable.

So, Carol and I started talking again. We agreed that Mom shouldn't spend her golden years like a prisoner in a supermax penitentiary. She should feel right at home, like the old days. That's why we moved her to Miami. Cubans created that city. We chose the Palace at Coral Gables because about half its residents were Cuban. The other half were snowbirds, mostly New Yorkers on the north end of eighty, but even they spoke a little Spanish. This meant that Mom could stroll the facilities, hearing familiar Cuban phrases:

"¡No comas mierda!" A quaint expression, it literally means "Don't eat shit" but translates to something like "Don't be a dumbass." Or:

"¡No tiene pelos en la lengua!" Literally, "He doesn't have hair on his tongue," meaning he has no filter. Whatever he thinks, he says it out loud. And lest we forget:

"Él es un zero a la izquierda." "He is a zero to the left," which implies he's worthless and should be ignored.

The effect all this had on my mom was amazing. She sprang back to life! Suddenly, she was dressing up again, putting on jewelry, making sure that her hair was just right. Finally, after so long, I began to smell Must by Cartier whenever she was with us—Mom's signature scent. She became a staple at the Palace's daily happy hour. She visited old friends who lived close by while making new friends in the building. The look in her eyes was as if someone standing close by was shining a bright but gentle light in them. And she was smiling again.

Mom's sister, my Aunt Marta, lived just a few miles away in Miami, and every now and then they'd get together, along with some old friends, to talk and swap memories. When Mom confessed how she missed seeing me so often, I began booking flights to Miami every month so I could visit with her for a few days. All in all, I'd never seen her happier.

Now: Imagine Mom and me sitting in the lavish main lounge at the Palace. Happy hour was underway. White-haired folks were grabbing seats near the bar, which was big enough that you could land a two-seater Cessna on it. The grand piano was humming. The player spoke fluent English and Spanish and switched back and forth between Celia Cruz and Frank Sinatra—"Guantanamera" with a side order of "Come Fly With Me" sprinkled with hits from the fifties and sixties. All while mini spring rolls, cubes of cheddar, pigs in blankets, and toothpicked stacks of prosciutto and melon got lifted off bright silver trays zooming past us as butlered hors d'oeuvres.

Everything I've just described was the daily pregame ritual leading up to the night's main event, the Palace's gourmet dinner. Table service if you wanted, buffet available if you didn't. You could get chicken Francese or eggplant parmigiana on Italian night, beef bourguignon and stout-braised lamb shanks when the chef was going heavy on red meat. And there were regular nods to the Cuban clientele. Congrí. Pan con lechón. Masas de puerco. The list went on.

A young lady came by to take our drink order. Everyone knew Mom, who made friends fast when she wanted. This particular young lady was Cuban and knew Mom well. She put Mom down for a virgin tequila sunrise. She looked at me, smiled, and raised her eyebrows. I ordered a white wine. Because it was Florida. When in Rome.

When the server left, Mom and I sat on a couch that swallowed us whole, but I didn't care. The look on her face said it all. She was in heaven, which meant I was too. We'd made it to this place together, against all odds. In my chest, my heart started swelling. But then, as so often happens in stories, the other shoe dropped. My phone started buzzing. Cue the theme song from *The Twilight Zone.*

I picked up my phone off the little end table where I'd left it and checked the screen, which said VINCE McMAHON. Above his name was a headshot of Vince with his hair slicked back. He didn't have his new mustache, just that impish grin on his face; it looked good on a guy who was six foot two, weighed 250, and could bench press a Chrysler on an off day.

I was not expecting that phone call and it must have shown on my face. I'm a shitty poker player.

My mother narrowed her eyes at me. "¿Quién es?"

I tilted the phone so she could read the caller ID and see the picture. Her mouth fell open. "Vincent?"

She never let go of her old-world manners. He was always Vincent to her. She'd never met him in person though of course she'd heard all about him. From the papers, from the TV. From me. Some people got fooled by Mom's walker, but that was a big mistake. At ninety-eight, she was sharp as a tack.

She arched one eyebrow at me. "¿Por qué te está llamando?" (Why is he calling you?)

I shrugged. "Yo no sé."

This was true. I had no idea why Vince would call. He and I texted once in a while, but we hadn't spoken in quite some time. Not since everything happened.

The lounge was too damn loud so I sent the call to voicemail, patted Mom's hand, got up, and went to the adjoining library. It was a big space, beautiful mahogany paneling, lots of bookshelves. And empty right then. Perfect. I closed the French doors, took a seat, and thumbed a reply call.

I was nervous. This was Vince McMahon, one of the most successful entrepreneurs of the last hundred years. We'd worked together for twelve years, but I can't say we'd ever been chummy. More like generals planning a battle, then leading our armies from the front. That was our style. Still is. We always led from the front. So no, we weren't pals. More like brothers-in-arms. A powerful, complex relationship.

When I worked for Vince's company, World Wrestling Entertainment, he would call me 24/7, and he never asked how I was doing or how my family was doing. Well, okay. He did that twice in twelve years, so infrequently I couldn't help but notice when it happened. Mostly, we didn't waste time on such things. There was always too much at stake. We plowed all our energies into moving the business forward. And boy, did we ever.

I signed on as company CFO in 2008. At that point, WWE was primarily a North American live event business that in the preceding years had averaged $400 million in revenue, $70 million in profit, and a stock price of $15. When I left in 2020, I'd been promoted to copresident alongside my friend and colleague, Michelle Wilson. WWE was approaching $1 billion in revenue and more than $200 million in profits. Our stock had peaked at $100—more than anyone had once thought possible.

But then Vince fired me, very publicly, very abruptly. So, yeah. Things felt a bit delicate.

Two rings and the line picked up. "Hey, George. How you doing?" That familiar gravelly chuckle that came from somewhere deep in his gut.

"I'm good, Vince. You?" A loaded question.

In March 2022, it came out that Vince had had extramarital affairs, at least one involving a female employee. Since this potentially put the company at risk, the WWE board launched an investigation. By June, they discovered that Vince had paid out $12 million to four women who'd all signed NDAs to restrict them from talking about their relationships. The blowback from all this was large enough that in July, Vince stepped away from his duties.

He was replaced as CEO by his daughter, Stephanie, and another executive. Not that it mattered. Regardless of his role, Vince retained a controlling interest in the company. But the timing could not have been worse. WWE was on the brink of negotiating global media rights, which were its largest source of revenue. No one knew what kind of impact Vince's situation would have on those talks, but in my opinion from the outside looking in, the optics weren't good.

If all this sounds like I was paying attention to Vince's life or life at WWE, I've offered the wrong impression. By that point, I was too busy. Months after being let go from the company, Michelle and I founded our own investment advisory firm. Isos Capital had already scored our first big win with a $2.6 billion go-public deal with Bowlero, the largest bowling center operator in the world. More on that later.

In typical fashion, Vince got right to the point. "Big changes are coming," he said. "The industry's shifting." He meant the sports entertainment sector. "So, George . . . remember how you used to say that thing?"

Of course I remembered. When you spend twelve years in the trenches with someone, you develop a shorthand. It was one of the many pleasures of working with Vince, the way we practically read each other's minds. "Yup," I said. "In the media sector, scale can drive value." We'd had this conversation many times over my last two years at WWE.

"That's it, yeah." Vince paused. I could practically hear the gears turning in his head. "Right now, that's all I'm thinking about."

For the record, Vince is not your typical billionaire entrepreneur. Most of the ones I've met have an incredible grasp of their business and its economic fundamentals. Vince is no different. What makes him unique is his proprietary blend of three qualities: work ethic, optimism, and his uncanny ability to read people. Vince is a student of human behavior. He observes people, gets to know them, then uses this knowledge to stay at least three or four steps ahead of the game.

Actually, let's make that four qualities. I forgot to say that Vince has deep instincts for showmanship. Take his onscreen persona. That tough guy image he's cultivated? The madman? The muscle-bound, swaggering villain? That's not the guy I worked with. In truth, I'd always found Vince to be somewhat introverted, almost shy, and definitely tough to read. But underneath that exterior there was always a lurking intensity. He was always listening, parsing information, filing it away, reviewing it from all angles. It took Vince a long time to trust anyone, but over our more than twelve years together I felt like I'd earned that trust.

I think one of the things Vince appreciated about me was my hard-scrabble upbringing. We used to one-up each other about who'd had a rougher time growing up. We never gave each other shit in the open; that kind of comedy routine would be too obvious, too easy for guys who appreciate gamesmanship. Instead, we found ways to insert references about our backgrounds in conversations.

For instance, every once in a while, during one of our many meetings, I'd figure out a way to remind Vince I'd grown up fatherless. Or that after my dad died, my bedroom had been a cot in the living room of our tiny studio apartment. If I'm being honest, I never felt poor growing up, though technically Mom and I were. Still, I admit I wasn't above dramatizing my upbringing so that the people I found myself speaking to felt I had chops. I didn't go to Harvard Business School, play lacrosse at boarding school, or wear nifty blue blazers. What I had instead were brains and an edge. I was grittier. Tougher. More real.

Vince would hear me go on about this and say nothing. But the next day, we'd be in another meeting and he'd casually mention, "You know, I grew up in a trailer park, North Carolina. The water was so damn brown and smelled so bad, we figured they'd piped it out of a cesspool." Glancing at me with that sly look out of the corner of one eye. Point taken.

A couple days later, I'd find an opportunity to say, "You know, my dad died when I was nine. He had a stroke. Growing up without him was hard."

One day, Vince's son-in-law, better known by his wrestling names, Hunter or Triple H, picked up on this and he groaned. "We get it. Both you guys grew up poor. For crying out loud, can we get back to business?"

I'm saying that Vince was a complex guy with a complex background working at a complex company in a complex sector. He was easy to misinterpret. But when he spoke again on the phone that day in the library at the Palace, his voice had altered, gone soft and vulnerable. It occurred to me then how hard it must have been for him to pick up the phone and call me. Something big must be up.

"Listen," Vince said. "I've discussed this idea of yours with some of the folks on the board and I don't think they get it." There was that chuckle again. This time it sounded more nervous, more real. "It's a different team since you left, George. Don't get me wrong, they're a good team. They're just . . . different." He paused. "I've decided I want to do this. Your plan. And look. This is the last thing I'm going to do with the company. I only get one shot at it so I want to do it right. I need the A-Team. So . . . if I asked you to come back as a member of the board, to figure out the right thing to do, maybe even sell the company . . . would you think about it?"

I was not expecting that. Not at all. I sat still, trying to process it.

Vince heard my silence loud and clear. "If you need time to think about it . . ."

Then I heard myself say, "I don't need any time, Vince. You're thinking about this the right way. Look, I love the company. I love the people. I love you. One question, though. The things they're saying about you in the press—"

"Not true."

He said more than that, but that's not important I'd known him a long time. I felt I had a sense of the man. I believed him. "Then let's do it," I said.

Once, long ago, I had a boss who wrote this about me in a performance review: "George is an amazing leader. People will follow him into a burning building. One small problem he has is that he's always running into burning buildings."

Another boss wrote this: "George is sometimes wrong but never in doubt."

Was I doing the right thing? Jesus, I had no idea. All I knew was that it felt right in that moment. I had to trust that. So I did.

The line went quiet. I think Vince got a little choked up. I surprised myself, too, getting teary-eyed.

When he spoke again, there was a rasp in his voice. "Thanks, George." Another pause. "How about Michelle. You think she'd do it?"

I shrugged. "If you're asking me what my gut says, I'd be shocked if she wouldn't come back."

"Do you want to talk to her first?"

"Sure."

"Alright. Talk soon?"

"You got it."

I clicked off the call and sat staring at the phone. It was one of those moments that lasts ten seconds but feels like it easily goes on for years. Then I got up and went back to the lounge. Mom hadn't moved but her drink was three quarters empty, ice cubes smaller than when I'd left her. The piano player had switched to "Cielito Lindo." *Fitting*, I thought. That was my mom and dad's favorite song. I sat down beside her again and she turned to me.

"¿Qué quería, Vincent?" I told her what he'd wanted. Mom was surprised. "¿La Junta Directiva? ¡Oye!" She whistled.

Like I said, everyone's the hero of their own story. There are no bit players in the passion play of life, unless that's how you cast yourself. You can play any role that you choose, but be warned: The moment you start thinking this way, you take on tremendous responsibility. Because once you're the hero, you can't let yourself off the hook for anything, big or small. Whether you win or you lose, get caught in the swamp of despair or make it all the way to the promised land . . . the burden is yours to bear, and yours alone. Because that's what heroes do.

They are sometimes wrong but never in doubt.

I wrote this book to tell you my truth in the hopes that it helps you discover something about yourself. I'm living proof that you can start with nothing in life. You can get punched in the face, ridiculed by the media, fired from a job that you love. So what? Life sucks sometimes. That's a fact. But if you're willing to get back up each time, to punch back . . . if you've got good people around you—people you love and who love you back . . . if you keep moving forward, ever and always . . . then you are a hero. Which means you win. Just by doing all that.

And if there's a chapter to your story that ends on a low note, you can change it.

Bottom line, it's all up to you.

PART ONE

The Apprentice

CHAPTER ONE

Strangers in a Strange Land

I've already told you that as far as zip codes go, I'll always be 11354. Or rather, George Barrios, the only child of Cuban immigrants who grew up in humble circumstances in the steel and concrete jungle of Flushing, Queens.

My mom was the third of five daughters. Her family didn't own land in Cuba, but they were educated and lived in the northwest or urbanized part of the island. Which meant they were culturally rich. Mom earned her EdD from the University of Havana. As a young woman, she taught at a regional college. She was a scholar and a professor.

By contrast, my father, Aldo, grew up in a family of subsistence farmers. His people were deeply poor, which prompted Dad to leave school before he'd completed eighth grade. This could have proved crippling for anyone else, but luckily Dad had an insatiable curiosity. A lifelong autodidact, his passion for reading filled in the gaps that were left by his lack of formal education.

While still barely into his teens, Dad went to work in a shoe leather factory. Picture a tall man, about six foot one, with curly dark hair that started to thin as he aged. He was loud and gregarious in the style made famous by Cubans. Laughter and smiles were his typical masks. When he walked into a room, his powerful presence commanded attention. By nature, he was a backslapper and a joker, but he wasn't above calling you a motherfucker if you got on his bad side. Few people did. He could fit right in on a loading dock, but he could also put on a business suit and fedora and enter a boardroom.

In my mind, he often appears this way now: dapper and regal, a leader of men. I remember he always wore Guerlain cologne, and to this day its woody, earthy, animal spice is inextricable from my memories of him. He was a chess player, a boxing and baseball fanatic, a pragmatist by nature. A self-made man in every sense of the term.

Through hard work and savvy combined with his natural charisma, Dad worked his way up to become the leather factory's manager. A job like that was a plum gig for someone with little formal education. But Dad wasn't satisfied. He got very involved in Cuba's labor union, Central de Trabajadores de Cuba, or CTC. Like our modern International Brotherhood of Teamsters, CTC boasted members in various trades. Dad rose to become their number-two man. His boss held titular power; he'd been elected to his office. Dad was more like the right-hand man of the king, the equivalent of a chief operating officer, someone who got things done. He met with union clients, both internal and external, and gave them the good news, the bad news, the stuff in between. For this, he became known throughout the country.

He became relatively well-off while still in his early thirties. He had two cars, each with its own chauffeur, a nice house, and plenty of marvelous suits. He ate very well, which was something none of his family members could boast of, and he had an 18-karat gold Longines watch that he prized. He bought it in the mid-1950s on a pleasure trip to the United States during which he fulfilled his dream and saw the Yankees play in the World Series. Not bad for a kid who'd grown up barefoot and poor in the island's sugarcane fields. Today, I wear that watch on special occasions.

My mother was Dad's third wife. They must have made quite a pair, coming from opposite sides of the tracks as they did. Mom's people were educated, well-bred, and cosmopolitan. Dad's people had dirt caked under their fingernails and showed missing teeth when they smiled. Mom and Dad married while both were in their late thirties.

"Meeting your mother and marrying her," Dad told me once. "That was maybe the luckiest turn of my life." But it turned out his luck wouldn't last.

In the late 1950s, Dad's affluence and union connections made him a target of Castro's regime. At the height of the revolution, Castro's thugs arrested my father and threw him in jail. He was stripped of his clothes and held in a large room crammed with hundreds of other naked men who'd all been told that they could be executed before dawn. Indeed, some were taken outside every night to a plain dirt yard and shot. But my father got a reprieve and, later, a trial.

He was saved by a family connection. His niece had married a man who supported Castro. According to family lore, this man arrived at Dad's hearing and testified glowingly on his behalf, after which Dad was released with the firm admonition that he behave himself. Read: do whatever the new regime tells you to do or you'll probably end up dead.

Dad promised he would comply, then fled to Mexico. From there, he made his way north to the United States.

Arriving in New York City, he discovered that a vibrant community of Cuban expatriates had taken root in the borough of Queens. This community included members of my mother's immediate family who had also escaped Castro's persecution. Dad got settled and sent for my mother, who had to flee Cuba through Spain. It took a few years to arrange things so she could legally join her husband, but once this was done, they were no longer Cubans but Cuban Americans: proud and committed, joyful but centered, with eyes fixed firmly on the new life they were determined to carve from the old.

I was born to this happy couple in 1965.

***

After a brief stay in the Sunnyside neighborhood, north of the Long Island Expressway, my parents and I moved to Flushing, across the bay from LaGuardia Airport. We rented a two-bedroom place in a building called the Glen-Ora, on the corner of Roosevelt Avenue and Union Boulevard. Two of Mom's sisters already lived in the building. Ela and Marta shared an apartment with Marta's son, Jorge, who was two years younger than me, plus the sisters' wheelchair-bound widower father, my grandfather Adolfo, whom I grew up calling Abuelo.

If our family wasn't traditional, you could still call us nuclear. Our energy output was tremendous. It helped that my mother's eldest sister, Ana, lived less than a mile away with her four kids in Woodside and, later, Elmhurst. My Tía Juanita, their youngest sister who had settled in Miami, visited us a few times a year. She always brought her smile, her infectious laughter, and a suitcase full of ripe mangos, which were like gold to us in New York. We were a loud, loving, dynamic clan of upwardly mobile Latinos. We supported each other, made fun of each other, uplifted each other, and loved each other beyond measure.

Ela was our matriarch, the yellow sun blazing at the center of our family's galaxy. She was childless, unmarried, indomitable, and did not suffer fools. Before fleeing Cuba, she'd worked as a corporate attorney for the island's Coca-Cola bottling company. She delighted in telling anyone who would listen—and many who didn't—that Fidel Castro had once been her law school classmate.

"He was the tallest, best-looking, most charismatic guy in our class!" Ela would say. Then her face would always grow dark as realizations set in. Castro might have cut a charming and handsome figure back in her youth, but that hardly forgave what he'd done to Cuba. As it happens, "charming" and "handsome" are two qualities many dictators share.

Ela's Cuban law degree was worthless in the States. Undaunted, she cobbled together resources, took classes at NYU, and earned her PhD in Spanish literature. Soon after that, she got a good job teaching at Iona College, which later became Iona University, in the bedroom community of New Rochelle, about half an hour north of the city.

Marta finished high school in Cuba and never went to college. She worked as a clerk in the shipping department of a factory in Queens. Not that you would have known that by talking to her. This was a funny thing in our family: Everyone was so vocal, so well-spoken, you could never tell which of us worked with our hands for a living and who had advanced degrees.

Like Ela, my mother's degree was basically worthless in the US. Her PhD from the University of Havana was less marketable than mud pies at a dirt convention. It didn't help that Mom's English was poor at that point. And so this woman who'd once been a scholar and a college professor took a job at the jewelry counter at Woolworth's, a department store two blocks over from our apartment.

Woolworth's turned out to be a great opportunity for Mom. It helped her learn the language of her new country. Later, following in Ela's footsteps, she went back to school and earned her master's degree in Spanish from NYU. This allowed her to teach high school. But I think she regretted not following Ela's path and returning to the life of a tenured professor that she used to have, back in the day.

***

Then there was Abuelo. Not long after I was born, a stroke had taken the use of his legs. I remember he sat in an elegant old rocking chair that was parked in Ela and Marta's living room. Picture a stately, handsome, elderly man with alabaster skin, a sign of royalty among Cubans. His nose was patrician and aquiline. He had a full head of thick white hair swept back from his forehead. His gaze was formidable, brooking no nonsense, though his smile, when it came, could be easy.

He had been a newspaperman in Cuba. He understood politics, economics, art, and culture. His thoughts were the thoughts of a writer—curated, organized, carefully vetted. Everyone who met Abuelo assumed he was some sort of authority. My father called him El Senador, which was fitting. He had that powerful air.

Many people found my grandfather imperious. I knew better. As a child, I would watch how he joked with the home health aides who stopped by to attend him. Mi abuelo had dignity, yes, and authority, true. But I also saw how soft he could be, how charming and self-effacing he was when someone helped him sit up or use the bathroom. Being dependent can be hard for anyone. It was especially hard for him.

He was a proud man who knew he could no longer provide for his family. A man of the world who understood that his condition was not getting better. Time and illness had already taken his legs. What would be next? I took stock of the way he deferred to his daughters. He knew what a sacrifice Ela and Marta were making to house him, bathe him, dress him, and feed him, all while pursuing their separate careers and, of course, raising Jorge.

***

One time, I asked my mother, "How come all your family is here—Tía Ela y Tía Marta y Abuelo, claro que sí. But where is the rest of Papi's family? Other than Tía Berta and La Rubia."

"Some came," Mom said. "But many stayed back in Cuba."

"Why?" I was young back then but I still understood that staying in Cuba was bad.

"When the communists came, lots of people thought things would get better." Mom folded a pair of my tiny underwear, freshly washed, and stacked it on top of a pair just like it. "Your abuelo, my sisters and I . . . we saw things differently. So we left."

That was all she would say on that subject. My father was also quite stoic about the past, uncharacteristically for him.

To be clear, none of my relatives—my parents, my aunts, or Abuelo—ever looked back with anger or regret. Self-pity and victimization were foreign to our clan. Rather than gripe about what we had lost, we looked to the future. It was like we were saying: Life can never be lived in the rearview mirror. Don't even try it. Life's not in the past, it's right here in front of us. We have plans, and in order to get where we're going, we're willing to work very hard, right here, right now. Despite all odds, we will prevail.

And God help anyone who tries to stop us.

***

The love my father and Abuelo shared could be measured by how much they needled each other. In a model typical of Hispanic men, they could be merciless with each other. Dad, as I mentioned, called Abuelo El Senador, but he also called him a "blanco de laguna." This special Cuban curse referred to my grandfather's ivory skin. It was also a nod to the massive gulf in their backgrounds. Abuelo was worldly and educated whereas my father was swarthy with curly black locks and the rough manners of someone who'd grown up with nothing, and sometimes less.

The two men discussed world events almost daily. Their individual views were filtered through vastly different lenses. One man had formal schooling while the other had graduated with high honors from the university of hard knocks. One had made a good living as part of Cuba's intelligentsia; the other had made an even better living through narrow, committed exertion of hard work, intellect, and savvy.

When I recall their daily debates, Abuelo is always seated in his rocking chair with my father standing over him. Dad holds the latest copy of *The New York Times* and reads aloud from it, in English, though he frequently switches to Spanish to clarify terms or draw comparisons. Dad's English was better than Abuelo's, a point which provided more fodder for their ribbing.

I remember them discussing the Nixon impeachment. Abuelo took the view that it was better to leave Nixon in office despite his transgressions. "Removing a leader leaves a vacuum in the power structure," he said. "And who fills a vacuum in power? Dictators do. Just ask Fidel Castro."

My father disagreed. "Nixon is either incompetent or he's lying. Either way, he has to go."

I think it's fair to say that neither man was so firmly entrenched in his own views that he couldn't be swayed. This talk took place after the Bay of Pigs, an event that soured many Cubans against America's feckless leaders. At core, my dad was a capitalist while Abuelo was an institutionalist. Neither man gave a fig about party affiliations. They found common ground in upholding what each considered to be commonsense principles of governance. In the end, I think they liked to argue because they loved each other so much.

"Will you have a glass of wine with me?" Abuelo would ask. "Or are you running off to your night class at the kindergarten?"

"I'll drink with you." Dad would grab the bottle and two glasses and plop himself down in a chair beside his father-in-law. "You know," he would say. "Despite how different we are, at least we have one thing in common."

"What's that?" said Abuelo.

"We're both Americans now."

At this, they would both roar with laughter.

***

Our apartment was on the Glen-Ora's first floor. Ela, Marta, Jorge, and Abuelo lived on the fourth floor. Like us, they had a two-bedroom, only theirs was slightly bigger. Ela and Marta shared one room, Jorge and Abuelo shared the other.

Boundaries came to mean little for us. We were always wandering in and out of each other's spaces, sharing everything, talking, arguing, trading opinions, singing, and shouting. But we also looked out for each other and inspired each other. If this sounds like the makings of a sitcom—*Cubans in Queens!*—you're getting the proper idea. Looking back, I can tell you for certain there are far worse ways for kids to grow up.

These days, not many people can say that as children they saw their relatives a lot. I saw mine every day. Though technically my cousin, Jorge was—and still is—spiritually and emotionally my brother. Over the years, I've called him by many names: Jorge, Jorgito, Primo, and Little George. Today he goes by GGQ. While the names have changed, there has always been one constant: He is there for me and I am there for him. Whatever the situation, we'll always have each other's backs.

My Aunt Ana, my mom's oldest sister, had four kids who were ten to fifteen years older than me: Raysa, Marian, Ana Rosa, and Aristedes. Their constant presence in my life paid unexpected dividends. For instance, before I was five, I could read in both English and Spanish.

My Aunt Ela once brought me as a guest to the college class she was teaching. "Look here," she told her students. "This is my nephew. He's not in first grade yet and he reads better than any of you."

In front of everyone, she had me read a selection from *Don Quixote*. I remember how stunned everyone looked. How proud that made me feel.

From that point forward, I read everything I could get my hands on. I plowed through comic books and kids' books and remember feeling bored. They weren't fulfilling enough.

***

My cousin Raysa was the oldest of Ana's children. Energetically, she was patterned after Aunt Ela, a force of nature. Whenever she walked into a room, Raysa owned the space. I remember thinking she was one of the most beautiful, powerful women I'd ever seen.

Raysa seemed to sense that I needed more elevated literary challenges. I'll never forget how she got me a copy of *Bulfinch's Mythology* for my fifth or sixth birthday.

"Stop reading those comic books." Raysa waved the mythology book. "These are the original stories, the ones those comics are based on. Always go back to the source, George," she told me. "The source is where all good things lie."

God, how I loved that book! It was packed with everything I could want. The myth of Prometheus. The Twelve Labors of Hercules. Ovid's descent to the underworld. Tales of Charlemagne and King Arthur. I was in heaven!

Looking back, that book prepared me to leverage the power of story in speaking to stakeholders inside and outside of all the companies I've worked for. Business is built on products, of course, and products generate sales. Which generate revenue. Which can be shuttled this way and that.

But the one thing I find most people forget is that businesses are also built on stories. In business, just as in life, it is the storyteller who wins.

***

I remember asking my father one time how it was that he and Mom got along so well. He gave my question serious consideration before saying, "I've got her right where she wants me."

My parents had a pretty good relationship despite—or perhaps because of—the fact that they were so different. Physically, Mom was small and compact while Dad was tall and gangly. My father's personality—gregarious, extroverted, even brash at times—seemed the perfect antipode to my mother's stoicism, her quiet thoughtfulness, her intensity.

Dad leaped high but Mom was the grounding force. You could say that he was the extrovert and she was the introvert, but that would be missing the reality of their relationship. In fact, they were different expressions of the same primeval force. Externally, he was the yang and she was the yin. His white fish appeared to follow her black fish round and round the pond of life as she followed him, and vice versa. Internally, they were both driven people who never let anyone stop them.

My mother's dream was that I would one day be a success at whatever course I chose to pursue. She put a lot of stock in financial gain. My father dreamed of this too, so long as his dream also included a brand-new Lincoln Continental—which, he told us over and over again, was the most beautiful car in the world.

For all their differences, both my parents were strict with me. They believed that if you spared the rod, you would spoil the child. Dad had his infamous strap, his preferred instrument for corporal punishment. I got the strap only twice, but once you got it, you never forgot it, and you sure as hell made sure to avoid getting it again.

They argued so rarely that the times when they did stick out in my memory, thorny and sharp. The topic of my schooling was one such occasion. Unimpressed with the quality of public schools in Flushing, my parents invested in sending me to St. Michael's Catholic Academy on Forty-First Avenue, due south of the tracks for the Long Island Rail Road.

***

I liked being Catholic, although, truth be told, I went through a period where I rebelled against it. The uniforms, rituals, and pageantry quickly lost interest for me. What eventually kept me in it was how much I liked being part of a team.

For instance, at one point, Jorge became an altar boy. I remember him telling me how much he enjoyed it, and that got me thinking. I liked the idea of helping the priests. I liked the idea of playing an integral part in a mass celebration. Even then, the notion of winning was a driving force in my life. I thought, *If the priests and I work closely together then maybe we can win one for God.*

I went to my parents and told them I wanted to be an altar boy. Dad nixed the idea. He never told me why, but years later Mom explained that he was concerned about child abuse and buggery. He'd shot down my joining the Boy Scouts for the same reason. However, knowing I'd taken an interest in mass, my parents would send me to Sunday services all by myself. They always gave me cash to put in the collection box. It never arrived there. I used it to buy baseball cards and never got caught. Even back then, I was learning to do what I thought was best for myself and my interests. Even then, I guess you could say, I showed a contempt for most forms of authority.

Now and again, my attitude backfired. For instance, once, when I was in second grade at St. Michael's, I got in a fight with one of the boys in my class. I can't remember what the whole thing was about, but I remember I yanked the lid off one of those old Oscar the Grouch–style metal garbage cans and beat the kid with it.

The beating was serious enough that the school tried to expel me. The nuns in particular were deeply pissed off. Since there was no email back then, they sent me home with a note for my parents. I never delivered this note. Instead, when I got home, I took it into my bedroom, tore open the envelope, and quietly read it to myself.

It said there was only one way I could stay enrolled at St. Michael's. My parents had to write back with a note of their own, and this note must describe the various ways they were dealing with my violent misbehavior, as well as personally guaranteeing that it would never happen again.

Well. This sounded too easy to me. I went into our kitchen, grabbed paper, and wrote a note in what I still believe was exceptionally mature handwriting. At the end of this note, I signed both my parents' names after taking time to practice the peculiarities of their signatures. I remember holding up the finished piece and reviewing it for accuracy and style.

Yes, I remember thinking. *This will work. I'm in the clear!*

My mistake (I reflect on this often) was that I underestimated my opponents. The priests at St. Michael's had been lied to by countless generations of sinful miscreants. Despite my perfect penmanship, immaculate spelling, and nonpareil grammar, I'd written my note in pencil. In the end, that damn pencil was what tipped the priests off.

The priests called my parents, who went to their office and quickly emerged with a brand-new concept of their son's capabilities. My mom was beside herself, by turns irate and mortified. Dad was angry but, tellingly, he didn't give me the strap. Instead, I watched him soften. He shook his head, then stared into space like there was some answer lingering there. Then he snorted and threw up both hands like, *What can you do?*

Holding my pencil-forged letter up, he read it silently again before chuckling to himself. "Not bad for a seven-year-old," he said. "Este niño es un genio."

***

Despite such incidents, I showed promise. I'll never forget this one time when my report card came back with straight A's. Dad kept gushing about it. He was so proud, he insisted on taking me shopping at our neighborhood corner store, Genovese Drugs. The Genovese chain was a forerunner to the CVS or Walgreens stores we find all over America today. We had little money, but Dad told me I could buy anything I wanted. Because I was such a meticulous organizer, I chose a bunch of little containers I could use to store my tiny green army men and my baseball card collection, plus all the weapons and paraphernalia that came with my GI Joe action figures. It felt like a second Christmas to me. I was in heaven!

Not long after that, the priests and the nuns of St. Michael's gave me an aptitude test whose results suggested I skip ahead two grades. This decision was up to my parents, of course. My mother said yes, my father said no. He was concerned that my social growth would be harmed if I took classes with older kids.

I remember lying in my bed, hearing them argue in the kitchen. "Is that what we want for our boy?" Dad asked Mom. "To be ostracized? A freak? I don't think so."

I drifted to sleep knowing that, whatever the outcome, at least I had parents who loved me enough to argue over my well-being. It was all the same to me if I stayed where I was or went on to a higher grade. So long as I got to read books and play games and talk baseball and boxing with my father. More on that later.

When I woke up, I found the decision was made. I would stay in the grade I was in and all would be well.

"Keep doing your work, Georgie," my father told me. "Wherever you go in life, no matter what you do, keep doing the work and all will be well."

***

Often, when all the adults were out working, Jorge and I would sit with Abuelo and watch TV. One of our favorite programs was professional wrestling.

I wouldn't say we were huge wrestling fans, but I loved how much fun the three of us had watching it together. Our little community. And while I had no vocabulary for this at the time, I felt there was a certain poetry to it all. I liked watching the absurd gymnastics of these muscle-bound athletes who dressed up in bright-colored spandex to operatically beat the shit out of each other.

The ring announcer back then was this snarky muscle-bound madman, Vince McMahon. He was always causing trouble, the evil manipulator pitting contestants against one another. His antics were hilarious and sometimes dark but always entertaining.

I remember sitting for hours watching characters like the Iron Sheik, Sgt. Slaughter, Greg "The Hammer" Valentine, and "Nature Boy" Ric Flair smash each other with folding chairs and 2 x 4s. But my favorite wrestler was Ricky "The Dragon" Steamboat. He had this martial arts vibe going on and a black belt to prove it. Ricky was badass. I often fantasized of being just like him.

If I get to be big and strong like Ricky, I thought, *one day I will beat the shit out of Quinn.*

***

Michael Quinn (not his real name) was our building superintendent and, at that point, my greatest antagonist. He had pale skin and freckles. His eyes were rheumy from liquor. His beer gut hung over his belt. He had short dark hair, slicked back off his forehead like the gangster wannabe that he was. Picture an overgrown alcoholic leprechaun with a giant chip on his shoulder and no love in his life. That was Quinn.

Reliably drunk and surly as hell, he loved to enforce the signs that he'd posted in the playground area of our building. No Ball Playing Allowed! the signs said.

I remember thinking, What the hell else is a playground for if not for playing ball?

Growing up an only child meant that I sometimes played alone. Often, I amused myself by throwing my ball at the side of the building and catching it when it bounced back. But when Quinn told me not to do that, I figured the next best thing was to try my hand at hitting those stupid signs he'd put up. I got pretty good at hitting them with my fastball. And since I've always been interested in skill building, I kept backing up to see if I could peg those signs from farther and farther away.

One time I ended up hurling my ball through somebody's bedroom window. Quinn came out right away, and boy was he pissed.

"Ya liddle feckin idjit!" he screamed. "Don't yer know why I put up dem signs that say no feckin ball playin?!?"

Don't ask me how but my father was suddenly there. He put himself right in Quinn's face and the men started shouting at each other. I remember staring at them, thinking one of them was bound to take a swing at the other. It was that kind of argument.

Dad had boxed as a kid, and of course he was Cuban. He knew how to handle himself. Apart from me and my mom and reading, boxing and baseball were Dad's greatest passions in life.

I remember him trying to teach me what I've since come to think of as the Way of the Cuban Fist. "Never throw the first punch," he would tell me. "Only cobardes start a fight." Cobardes means "cowards." Dad would always pause before adding: "On the other hand, don't walk away from a fight. Okay? I don't want you ever to start a fight. But don't walk away from one. Okay?"

"Sí, Papi."

"You walk away from a bully, they'll only come after you. Bullies won't stop. So if that happens, you deal with it. Entiendes?"

"Sí."

"And look. If a bully comes after you, get the first punch in. Things tend to go better if you do that."

"But you just said—"

"And never hit a woman," my father continued. "That goes without saying. In fact, if I ever hear of you hitting a woman, you and I will have problems. Do you hear me?"

"Sí."

Naturally, almost as soon as he'd said this, the universe sent me some bullies to test my grasp of this philosophy.

***

Our kitchen window faced out on a little courtyard playground area to one side of the Glen-Ora. One evening, four boys from the neighborhood who had a low opinion of me started pressing their faces up to that window, licking the glass and blowing their cheeks really wide so their buck teeth were clearly displayed. This would have been embarrassing in its own right. But my father happened to be home. He came into the kitchen and saw these boys making fun of me.

"What's going on out there?" he demanded. "Who are those boys?"

"No one," I lied. "They're just friends."

One boy flipped me the bird and laughed.

My father shook his head. "Friends, huh?" he said. "Okay then. Let's go talk to your friends."

He took me by the hand and led me outside to where the four horsemen of my personal apocalypse were still on the playground, raising hell.

Dad marched right up to them. "You there!" he called to them. "Yes, you! Did anyone ever teach you boys how to box?"

The look on their faces said no one had. They were half-terrified of my father, half-intrigued. In other words, ripe for the lasting impression made by a good coach.

"Well, come on," Dad said. "Let me show you how it's done!"

He lined us up like a drill sergeant working with pint-sized green recruits. Made us stand with our legs spread, dukes up, shoulders dropped, and our heads hanging loose.

"Like this." Dad demonstrated a jab. "You see how it works? The waist moves first, the hand follows. No no." He corrected one boy's form. "That's too much shoulder. We don't use the shoulder when jabbing. Let go of it. Swing your hip forward and . . . yes! That's it! See the difference? Now do it again!"

Looking back, it was a masterful display of parenting alchemy. My father had taken lead—a bad situation where his son was being taunted by peers—and turned it into the gold of a teachable moment. And he wasn't finished.

After drilling us several times, he threw down a gauntlet. "Now then. Which of you wants to fight my son?"

Dead silence.

"Come on. You think you can take him? Let's see what you've got!"

When all was said and done, Dad made certain that each of the boys and I boxed with each other. Lips got swollen. Noses got bloodied. One or two boys got kicked in the balls and went down.

Dad was an able referee. He made certain that no one truly got hurt. If it looked like one fighter was too much for another, Dad would pull him off and give him a shake so he remembered his place.

"Okay," he'd say. "Next!"

Oddly enough, from that day forward, those four boys and I became very good friends.

I'll never forget how wise Dad was. How generous. How committed he was to raising me. He was a very good man. A good father.

When he died, not long after this, it felt like my world had completely collapsed.

CHAPTER TWO

Books and Boxing Gloves

Eventually, my mom got a job teaching Spanish at a Catholic high school in Bridgeport, Connecticut. Without a driver's license, she threw herself into a punishing daily commute via public transportation. Every Monday through Friday, she was up and out the door by 4:00 a.m. She took the 7 train into Manhattan—that leg of the journey alone took forty minutes—then Metro North from Grand Central to Bridgeport, and buses from Bridgeport to work. In the final tally, she traveled three hours each way or six hours a day, thirty hours a week.

Meanwhile, Dad worked a full-time job at Doubleday Publishing, where he ran a computer room filled with IBM mainframes. This was the early 1970s when you programmed computers by feeding thick stacks of punch cards into a slot for hours on end. Dad worked the night shift because my parents didn't want anyone else raising their child, they wanted to do it themselves. Mom watched me during the evenings, and every weekday morning, it became Dad's job to get me ready for school.

Word to the wise. If you can help it, do not try to get one over on your tough-talking, boxing aficionado Cuban father while he's getting you ready for school in the morning.

I would wake up, rub sleep from my eyes, and sit on the toilet in our tiny bathroom, watching my father shave or trim his goatee when he wore one, which was often. I would shower, then he would shower. This became our manly routine, capped off by my father's idea of breakfast.

Cod liver oil to prevent rheumatism, stiff muscles, and rickets. Rickets! Even then I knew this was ridiculous. He also made me eat plenty of raw eggs, which he mixed into chocolate milk because, he said, I needed the protein. To this day, I'm still not a big fan of eggs. In fact, I learned to hate them so much that whenever Dad jumped in the shower, I'd dump out his mixture and make my own chocolate milk, which I always drank it in front of him, throwing in plenty of *mmmms* and *ahhhhhs* to make him think I was in egg heaven.

This worked until, one day, he didn't step into the shower but watched from the kitchen while I dumped his concoction down the drain. My dad was pissed. Not so much because I wasn't eating the eggs or that I'd wasted food, but because I had lied to him. Lying was a cardinal sin in the Barrios household. That occasion was one of the two times I mentioned I got the strap. I'll never forget it because I couldn't sit down for the next three days.

I've never given corporal punishment much thought. I can tell you that I've never hit my own children. But I'm not convinced, prima facie, that it's a bad thing. Children need boundaries sometimes. At least I certainly did.

Dad and I had a great relationship. Whenever Mom was out of the house, it was just the two of us, one older man, one younger, one bigger, one smaller, sitting around talking sports or playing catch. Dad taught me to add, subtract, multiply, and divide by practicing with formulas used to calculate the batting and earned run averages of our favorite players on the New York Mets.

For instance, I learned that an earned run average, or ERA, is the most common statistical tool for evaluating pitchers. ERA measures how many runs a pitcher allows per nine innings of play.

"The formula is ERA = (ER/IN) * 9," Dad said. "Where ER is the number of earned runs—that's the number of times a team scores against a pitcher—and IN represents the number of innings pitched. Okay? As an example, an ERA of 3.0 means that, on average, a pitcher gives up only three runs for every nine innings they pitch. Not bad. Now you try it."

One of my favorite calculations Dad taught me was a player's slugging percentage, or SLG. This measure quantifies a batter's power, meaning their ability to hit the baseball a long way. I still find the equation poetic: $SLG = 1B + 2B(2) + 3B(3) + HR(4)/AB$, where 1B equals the batter's number of singles, 2B equals his number of doubles, 3B equals his number of triples, HR is the number of home runs, and AB is the number of at-bats.

Note the weighting system at play here. Because of the multiplicand (the numbers in parentheses), each batter's doubles count twice as much as singles, a triple three times as much, and so on. So a player who hits forty-two singles, seventeen doubles, six triples, and six home runs in a season with 280 at-bats would have a slugging percentage of .421. That's pretty damn good. For the sake of comparison, an SLG of .500 means the batter averages one base every two times he's at bat, while an SLG of 4.000—which is impossible—means he gets a home run every time he's at bat.

Because of Papi, I could work out calculations like this before I started first grade.

***

These days when I think of my dad, I recall his personality as a three-legged stool.

The first leg, the part most people saw, was his big gregarious presence. If you asked nine out of ten people who Mario Aldo Barrios was, I bet they'd think of his loud laugh, his perpetual grin, his warm inviting eyes. And sure, he was all that. But he was also more.

The second leg was his temper. Not many people saw this but when they did, they never forgot it. I've already mentioned this but it's worth repeating. I share this quality with him. And just to clarify, having a temper isn't all bad. It can be useful. For instance, it keeps you from suffering fools, which tends to increase the amount of stuff you can get done in life. My advice, however, if you share this trait, is to learn to control it as early in life as possible. In my case, it took me a while, but now I own it; it doesn't own me.

The third leg was the one I don't think anyone outside my immediate family knew about. This was Dad's affectionate side.

For instance, when I was a boy, if I had a nightmare, I would go to my parents' room, straight to my father's side of the bed.

"¿Qué es, Georgie?" he'd murmur.

"Estoy asustado." (I'm afraid.)

Without a word, he'd pull up the blanket. I'd crawl into bed with him, snuggling in while feeling his power, his warmth, the evenness of his breathing.

"Está bien," he would say. "No te preocupes. Todo va a estar bien." (Don't worry. Everything's going to be fine.)

Within moments, I'd be asleep.

His caring could take many forms. He was physically affectionate, meaning he was a kisser, a hugger, and a cuddler. But he was also intellectually affectionate.

For instance, he made it his mission to take time every weekend and teach me Spanish. By "Spanish," I mean the formal written language. Dad refused to imagine a world where his mother tongue, with all its beauty, passion, and poetry, could not be written masterfully by me, his son.

He bought a book on Spanish grammar. After that, every Saturday or Sunday morning, after the breakfast dishes had been cleared, I'd hear, "Georgie, ven aquí." He'd tap the seat of the kitchen chair beside him.

I would always sigh. Working on verb conjugations wasn't my favorite part of hanging out with my dad. He knew this. He accepted it. He was gentle but also firm as he coaxed me through warmups, vocabulary drills, and the proper scripting of prepositional phrases. He always made sure I understood the material and he never pushed me too hard. Best of all, he knew when it was time to close the book, go outside, and throw a baseball around.

Small wonder this has become an essential component of my definition for manhood. A real man is someone who knows when to work. But he also knows when it's time to relax and have fun.

***

Dad took courses and earned his associate degree to become a 1970s version of what, today, we call an IT manager. One of his school assignments asked him to write a vignette from his life. After he died, I found this essay.

In a voice distinctly his own, Dad talked about how, back in Cuba, Castro's troops would barge into people's homes every night, pull them out of their beds, and execute them in front of their families. He talked about spending time in jail, sitting naked with other terrified men, waiting to take a bullet between his eyes, and wondering what would become of his wife and family. He told the story of how he fled to the US by sneaking first into Mexico. How his wife, my mother, fled to Spain and later joined him in New York City where, against every type of odd, they started over with practically nothing.

I remember crumpling that paper in my fist and weeping into it like it was a handkerchief. I remember being appalled by what he had written, then thankful for what he had gone through—what both of them had gone through—so that I could be born where I had been. That I could grow up an American.

***

Dad took me to visit his job one time. I forget what age I was, but I was small and very excited to see where my father went every night, what he did to earn money.

I remember the big room filled with goliath computers all clicking and churning away in a manner that's long since vanished into the past. Computers are smaller now, sterile, lifeless. I remember him showing me the little office area where he sat and oversaw everything. Well, okay. Not an office. It was more like a desk in one corner of the room fenced in by one of those fabric-lined cubicle walls to give him some privacy. He brought me into this alcove where he proudly showed me his books.

I remember staring at them. They were everywhere, dozens of them, all shapes and every size, on every topic. His employers at Doubleday were publishers, after all. Books were their stock in trade. The company ran a program where its employees got some books for free while paying for others at massive discounts. My father took full advantage of this.

"¡Papi!" I said. "Wow! How many of these books have you read?"

He shrugged but I saw him look proud. "All of them," he said.

I picked up the book closest to me. It was heavy and thick, a real doorstop, close to a thousand pages long. The title, in English, said: *The Warren Report*. With a subtitle: *Report of the President's Commission on the Assassination of President John F. Kennedy*. I opened this book—which took some effort, it was so big—and stared at my father's neat pencil script choking the margins of every page. Close-written lines in English and Spanish.

"What are you writing here?" I asked.

Dad got very excited. He took the book to his desk and we both sat down. Then he started to teach me. "This is a very important document," he said. "And I want to make sure I understand it. Spanish and English are different languages. They use different expressions, convey different meanings in different ways. I'm studying why certain words were chosen in certain contexts. Here. Listen to this."

He picked out a sentence and read it aloud to me in English. I can't remember what the sentence was about but I'll never forget how his face lit up.

"Do you hear that?" he said. "How eloquently the sentence conveys a meaning? Now look. They could have said it this way . . ." He plucked a sharpened pencil out of the coffee cup on his desk and started writing in the margins of the book. Finished, he read his sentence aloud. "That would basically mean the same thing, but it allows for different interpretations of the writer's intention. Or they could have done it this way . . ."

He wrote another sentence and read it to me.

"You see?" he said when he was finished. "A man who knows how to speak, how to write, is a man who knows how to think. Critical thinking! That's what I'm getting at, Georgie. They say that common sense is uncommon? I say that critical thinking is the rarest thinking of all, a valuable skill. The man who knows how to think critically controls his brain, and therefore his destiny."

I will never forget the image of my loud, gregarious father bent over a still and silent book. How his face twisted up as he struggled with parsing a sentence. For all his bravado and bluster, he was exacting, meticulous, and thoughtful, reading and rereading, getting things right. This is how he madc it through life. With no education to speak of, he'd taught himself to wade into details, honoring one before moving on to the next. And the one after that. And the one after that.

It occurred to me many years later that I approach my own work precisely the same way. And this approach is what made me successful.

Ironically, my well-educated mother, who was so proud, used to tell me, "Georgie, tu mama es muy inteligente pero obtuviste tu cerebro de tu padre." (Your mom is very smart, but you get your brains from your father.)

Maybe. The way I see it, I simply lucked out. Both my parents were smart. More importantly, they were disciplined. In their own ways, neither of them could be stopped when they set their sights on a goal. That might be the most important life lesson I ever received.

***

I stayed with my father that whole day. When his shift was finally over, we left the building and walked through the employee parking lot. I remember we passed this long, heavy, two-door car with a fairly rectangular body, a tall metal grille, and rectangular headlights that only flipped open when the car was turned on. As we passed it, I read the name scrolled into the metalwork on the front. "Con . . . ti . . . nen . . . tal. ¡Papi!" I pointed. "This is that car you like! It's your car!"

His eyes grew bright and he grinned. "That's it, Georgie! ¡Sí!"

"So?" I said. "Why don't you buy one?"

"We can't afford it," he said. Very matter of fact.

"Well, who has a car like this?" I asked.

"The boss of the company does, I guess. And you know what? Tú vas a obtener un carro como este, Georgie. If you work very hard, you can be the boss of a company someday." He laughed. "And then you can buy a car like this! For me! How does that sound?"

I thought it sounded perfect. I told him right there that someday I would buy him that car and he gave me a hug and then we went home.

I slept through the next morning, dreaming of being the boss of a company, making great money, and buying my father the Lincoln he'd always wanted. It was a beautiful dream and it got me very excited. But then, a few months later, Dad was dead and so was my dream.

Or part of it, anyway.

***

It was just before the holidays, at the tail end of 1974. I was nine years old and midway through fourth grade. I was home one day when the phone rang in our apartment. Mom grabbed the receiver and listened a moment. I still remember the way she said, "¡Ay! ¡Dios Mío!" That plus the pain in her face.

To this day, if the phone rings and no one's around, I panic. Inside, I'm always wondering, *Who in my family is hurt?*

This got so bad that I sought out a therapist. We're working through it together.

Someone had called from our neighborhood supermarket to say that Dad had collapsed there while picking up groceries. A stroke, we were told. He just dropped to the floor and went into a seizure.

An ambulance came and picked Dad up, took him to Booth Memorial Hospital in nearby Flushing, Queens. He was fifty-four years old.

He'd had a heart attack in 1969, when he was still in his forties. He got through that by making a bargain with his doctor. "Aldo," the doctor said, "you can only watch baseball if you promise not to get too excited." The Mets were playing the Orioles in the World Series that year. Dad wouldn't have missed that for the world. He loved the Mets. And so he made his doctor that promise and bounced back quickly, Aldo-style.

"Better than ever!" he liked to tell people who asked. And he would grin.

His cholesterol might have been high and maybe he drank just a little too much the way some Cubans do. Hell, the way many folks do. But this time, he wouldn't be better than ever. This time, life had my father locked in the chokehold of death. And it wouldn't let go.

***

My mom went straight to the hospital to see him. When she came back home, she looked very relieved. She reported that Dad was awake and cogent. "We talked," she said. "Your father is weak, but I think he'll be fine."

But that night, he got hit by another stroke, bigger than the first. Nowadays this almost never happens. The art of medicine's come a long way. Doctors and nurses have new medications and follow new protocols.

Back then? We had nothing but hopes and prayers, and these were doubly needed since Booth Memorial had a so-so reputation.

The second stroke put Dad into a coma. This time, his own body finished what Fidel Castro himself could not. Dad lingered for two or three months in the bardo, that curious threshold that isn't quite life and isn't quite death, while all his loved ones gathered around him.

Well. Not all of his loved ones.

This is one of my most painful memories. I have trouble talking about it but I'll try.

At one point, knowing my dad was close to death (he was in and out of consciousness, vital signs dropping, the end was near), my relatives took me to see him. I guess they thought they were doing Dad a favor, letting him see his son, but it didn't work out like that.

I remember getting off the elevator on the floor that housed his intensive care unit. I remember holding somebody's hand as we walked down a corridor, straight to his room. The door was open. I remember peeking inside and seeing Dad lying in his hospital bed, the feeling of shock when I saw how weak he looked, how much weight he had lost. From his lean fighting trim of 160 pounds, he was probably down to 120. Maybe lower.

No, I remember thinking. *This isn't right. This isn't my Papi, this is a poor imitation of him that somebody threw in a clothes dryer, shrunk down to size.*

I stared at the tubes running into his body. The wires taped to his skin. And why was that stupid machine going *beep-beep-beep* all the time? None of this made sense to me. It scared me so I rejected it.

Looking back on my career, I've visited some of the most high-tech manufacturing facilities in the world. These are places where they make semiconductors, which demand the highest standards for cleanliness, precision, and orderliness that human engineering has ever devised. It's amazing how a plant like that works, what a marvel of engineering it is. But then you visit most hospitals where actual human beings are sick, where the stated intent is to help them get better. And what do you find?

Total chaos. Random people walking the hallways. Equipment shoved into corners, unused. Paper charts dangling from clipboards, filled with hurried, illegible writing. Nurses and doctors hanging out laughing about their escapades from the previous night while, around them, people are suffering, people are dying, and nobody seems to care.

It's one of those anomalies that's intrigued me all through life. We're so diligent about fabricating inanimate objects to run our machines but we can't devise a similarly elegant and efficient system to care for members of our own species.

Give me carte blanche and I'd fix this.

***

Here is why I find all this so hard to describe: I never went into Dad's room. Instead, I tore my tiny fingers out of whoever's hand I was holding, turned, and ran back down the hallway to the elevator, where my family eventually cornered me.

They tried to get me to go back and talk to my father, but I refused. I couldn't accept what I was seeing. I couldn't accept how he'd been diminished. I've always regretted this.

To this day, I feel like I let my father down, I let my family down. That I was a coward.

Dad died a few days later on February 28, 1975.

***

The day of his funeral comes back to me sometimes. I see it in snapshots. Impressions. I remember donning the suit my mother picked out for me. I went in the bathroom, combed my hair and brushed my teeth. I remember glancing at the tub, expecting my father to step from the shower, the way he always had. But this time he didn't. I was alone. Dad was gone and he'd never come back.

We held Dad's service in St. Michael's Catholic Church. Mom and I sat in the front pew, holding hands. I remember feeling guilty, as if somehow I'd done something wrong.

Yes, George, a voice in my head said. *You have done something wrong. You're a bad kid. You get into fights and you call people names. You misbehave. Your father tried teaching you how to get better, to grow up and be a good man. But did you listen to him? No, George. I think you did not. You forged your parents' names. You made Quinn, the superintendent, hate you. The kids at school all hate you too. You're nothing special. You're just a smart-ass who's destined for problems that one day will break you. And now the one man who might have protected you, who could have saved you, your Papi, your father, he's dead.*

I remember twisting around in my pew and staring behind me. St. Michael's was packed, as if we were there to celebrate Christmas, Easter, or my very first Holy Communion. I saw a confusing mosaic of faces staring back at me. Tía Ela was there, and Tía Marta, and all of my cousins. Abuelo was there, looking stone-faced, plus plenty of people I didn't recognize, people from our building, our neighborhood. People Dad worked with, I think.

The organ started to play. Up to that point, I'd always liked organ music, but right then I hated it. I have hated it ever since. I heard the rustle of clothes and the clatter of bodies as everyone turned in their seats and watched the pallbearers walk the coffin down the aisle. They came closer and closer.

You see? that voice in my heart said. *No, don't do that. Don't look away, George. You already did that, back at the hospital. Look at his coffin. Your Papi is dead but you know what the worst part is? He will never drive that car, his precious Lincoln. Never ever. He never lived out his dream because all he dreamed about was you and you did him wrong, George. You are not worthy of him.*

I remember I tried to distract myself by running my mind through equations.

You find a player's slugging percentage by using this formula: SLG = 1B + 2B(2) + 3B(3) + HR(4)/AB, where 1B equals the batter's number of singles, 2B equals his number of doubles, 3B equals his number of triples, HR is the number of home runs, and AB is the number of at-bats . . .

Looking back, I think I only cried twice in my childhood. This was the first time, and the worst, because now there was one less person to hear it. To tell me to stop. To tell me to buck up and act like a man.

No child should ever grow up without a father.

Adding insult to injury, mere months after Dad died, Ana's husband, my Tío Aristides, passed away unexpectedly. And a few weeks after that, Dad's best friend, Evelio, also passed. I took each loss like a blow to the head. They left me reeling, stupefied, punch-drunk, fighting for balance in the ring of my small life. The sorrow and pain I felt was immeasurable.

Suddenly, I wasn't just missing a father, I was missing all my male role models.

It would be an understatement to say that this changed the dynamics of my childhood. In fact, today, writing these words, I have to pause and wipe tears from my eyes.

***

Not long after Dad passed away, I got in more trouble with Quinn. I was still young. Still grieving. Still scared. Acting out. The details of what I did escape me now. Maybe it was another ball through a window, or maybe graffiti I'd painted on an outside wall of the Glen-Ora. Not with spray paint, I was too young for that. I used Magic Markers instead.

I remember the tag I developed for myself. La Piedra, meaning "The Stone." It was an homage to one of my father's favorite boxes, Roberto Duran, who went by the name Las Manos de Piedras. The Hands of Stone.

Regardless of how it all happened, I'll never forget what Quinn said to me. "Ya feckin spic. Yer gonna end up in a box, just like yer old man."

Maya Angelou once famously said, "I've learned that people will forget what you said, people will forget what you did, but people will never forget how you made them feel." She was right. Quinn made me feel lower than I ever had in my life and I've never forgotten that. Nor will I ever.

***

After Quinn said his piece, I walked into our apartment and sat in the kitchen, alone. I remembered the time when Dad saw those four boys pressing their faces up to the window, making fun of me. How he'd turned that potentially bad situation around by teaching us how to get along.

My mother came into the kitchen. "How are you feeling?" she said.

I just shook my head.

She sat down beside me. "Georgie, I know this is difficult. But we're going to get through this. That's what your father would have wanted."

"It's not that," I said. And I told her what happened with Quinn.

She listened. Then she muttered "hijo de puta" under her breath. I noticed her lip was quivering and her hands were shaking.

A few days later, our extended family got together, same as always. Except it wasn't the same. How could it be? Dad wasn't there so everyone struggled to fill in the gap that he'd left. But nobody could.

My Mom told everyone what Quinn had said to me. I remember my aunts were outraged. They railed against Quinn in Cuban Spanish, a particularly colorful language for cursing. I also remember how the young men in our family, my cousins' husbands and boyfriends, just sat there and listened. The way they said nothing. The way they looked at each other. They were all in their twenties at that point, strong proud men who knew how to get things done.

A couple of days later, I bumped into Quinn. His face was swollen and he had a black eye. The moment Quinn saw me, he flinched. His pale face grew paler than its customary Celtic tone. Turning, he got out of there fast. From that point forward, we never said another word to each other.

To this day, I have no idea what actually happened. But I can say this with confidence: If you know what's good for you, don't fuck with a grieving Cuban boy. His family probably has his back.

***

Before I close this chapter, there's something I have to mention. My mother never remarried. She never even went out on a date. She considered my father the love of her life. She told me this once—like I hadn't already figured it out. It was obvious to anyone who'd ever seen them together. What they had together, that was the real thing. And once you've had the real thing, nothing else will ever come close.

But there was another reason I think that my mom stayed single. She did it for my sake. She understood that she had a son who was still just a boy and who missed his dad, a man whom no other man in the world could replace. In fact, it would likely have caused me great harm to have someone else, a stranger, some counterfeit father, enter our family. Especially at a point where the awkward specter of puberty was about to possess my body and, through that vector, my mind and my soul.

Not that Mom would have ever expressed those things in such a fashion. She'd have employed her colorful Cuban, a strain of Spanish rich in idiom. For instance, I once overheard her telling my aunt that I was "comiendo un cable," which literally translates to "eating a cable" but which, in practice, means "having a very hard time." After my father died, she began saying, "Cantó el manisero" or "He sang [the song about] the peanut vendor." Meaning, he'd passed.

The idea of Mom dating again was "va a terminar como la fiesta del Guatao," or "going to end like the Guatao party." Meaning tragically. She wasn't wrong.

Now that I'm a parent myself, I understand the commitment my mom made to me. I still feel guilty that she sacrificed her own security and happiness for mine. Especially considering how badly I behaved. More on that soon.

For now, just to give you a clue, here's another Cuban saying. "Éramos pocos y parió Cantana." Literal translation: "There were a few of us, then Cantana gave birth." Meaning: "Shit was bad but then it got worse."

It got much, much worse.

CHAPTER THREE

Spic on a Bus

The Christmas after my dad died—December 25, 1975—I was ten years old and I asked for some toys. I remember I wanted a Matchbox Steer-n-Go car, GI Joe twelve-inch action figures with the super-cool kung fu battle grip, plus some vehicles they could ride in, like the GI Joe giant helicopter (over two feet high!) and the patented, ass-kicking Amphicar, which could roll over enemy soldiers in two terrains, by land or by sea. And—again, if memory serves—I also asked for a portable cassette recorder. They were all the rage back then. I fantasized about carrying mine around so I could tape record . . . well, everything. Conversations. Songs on the radio. Traffic roaring by on the street in front of our building. Abuelo's snoring. That last one was especially important because my grandfather insisted he never snored and, more than anything else in the world, I wanted to show him he wasn't just wrong but seriously, super-duper, egregiously wrong.

Cut to the chase. I got none of the presents I asked for. On Christmas morning, the first box I pulled out from under the tree and tore open contained . . . a basketball! Cool! I loved playing basketball. What city kid doesn't?

The next box I opened contained new pairs of Fruit of the Loom jockey shorts sealed in their thick, clear retail plastic. So did the next box. And the next.

I opened another box that contained a pack of tube socks. By then, it was dawning on me that I would not be sharing a cup of Christmas cheer with GI Joe. Nor would I have the pleasure of watching him roll over enemy bad guys in his ass-kicking Amphicar. And the notion of recording Abuelo's snoring? Kiss that notion goodbye.

At ten years old, I knew that Santa Claus wasn't real. Or rather, I knew that my parents were Santa Claus. But it didn't sink in until after I'd opened the tube socks that half of my Santa Claus was now dead. Which meant that Santa's elves weren't just having a hard time handing out toys that year. They were having a hard time making rent and buying food.

When Dad was alive, and both my parents were working, our lifestyle had been modest but sustainable. With Dad gone, we'd lost more than half our income and I was still growing. I needed more food, more clothes, more supplies, more amusements than ever before. Mom and I were in dire financial straits until her sisters stepped in.

To this day, I don't know the specifics of what they worked out. I just know that my aunts would never allow my mom or me to go without. That's how it always was in my family. Still is. If one of us falters, the others always take up the slack.

In fact, after Dad died, I was raised in practically equal measure by Mom and my aunts. As I sit here writing, it's clear this was probably one of the greatest gifts of my life, to be raised by these stunningly competent, caring, and driven women. Few people can imagine possessing such a fortune, let alone being gifted it willingly.

***

With or without this assistance, Mom's long commute was grinding her down. It made more sense to live near her job. We moved to Bridgeport in the autumn of 1976, just in time for me to start middle school there.

In those days, few Latinos lived in New England or Bridgeport specifically. To call Mom and me fish out of cultural water would be like saying icicles feel right at home in a pottery kiln.

Don't get me wrong. There were plenty of fine things about moving to Connecticut. The most obvious win was how much apartment we got for our rent money. Prices in Bridgeport and prices in Flushing weren't just on different planets, they were in completely separate universes. Mom and I got an immediate upgrade on space in a really nice apartment building while saving money. And then there was Mom's commute. Instead of traveling six hours a day for her job, she was down to twenty minutes. Nor was she pissing away so much money on train and bus fare.

If we weren't exactly rolling in dough—and trust me, we weren't—at least we were breathing again. We were still in an urban environment, but Mom had picked a place in Bridgeport near the Fairfield border, a leafy, peaceful town that gave our lives a semblance of rustic New England living. That mattered to Mom. She was trying to make sure every dollar she spent mattered, meaning it would make my life better and keep me safe.

For anyone who's never visited the towns along the Connecticut coast, don't get fooled by all that Yankee doo-dah, country-fried New England crap. Those little places can be citified as shit. From west to east you've got Stamford, Norwalk, Bridgeport, Stratford, Milford . . . all the way out to New Haven. Each of those towns has an inner city. If Bridgeport wasn't Queens, it felt like home to me nonetheless.

Mom enrolled me in another Catholic school, St. Peter's in Bridgeport. This was attractive for a number of reasons. First, I'd been attending Catholic schools the whole time, so the cultural consistency was appealing. Second, back then Bridgeport's public schools weren't exactly renowned for their academic rigor; any substitute would have been preferable. I suppose it helped a bit that I had abandoned my beefs with the priests and the nuns at St. Michael's of the Immaculate Handwriting back in Flushing.

But the thing that intrigued me the most, I recall, was the size and composition of my cohort. If memory serves, my sixth-grade class had five boys and twenty girls. The key word there being "girls." Classes at St. Peter's were coeducational. So I would learn, walk the hallways, hang out at my locker, eat lunch, and take gym class with members of the opposite sex. The possibilities of this seemed endless.

For those of you taking notes, this is the part of my story where things started going off the rails.

***

If you asked Mom why I went astray, she would have given you a succinct answer. A dark angel of Satan himself had turned me toward the dark side. My tempter was my classmate, a kid named Billy Theobald.

Now before you start to snicker, I get it. That name isn't just quaint, it's a nineteenth-century novelist's wet dream, a character straight out of Melville. "Captain William 'Billy' Theobald thumped up the steps from the hold of the *Pequod* and stared at the vast sea heaving and churning through fathomless currents."

Despite how archaic his name might have sounded, Billy was twenty times cooler than anyone else at my school, cool in the way of the mid-1970s. Picture a young Peter Frampton or Leif Garrett. (Look them up if you need to, I'll wait. There. See what I mean?) The long blond hair. That "nature-boy-leaning-androgynous" vibe. Billy was our little school's basketball champion, and since I loved basketball too, he was one of my idols.

Billy and his family lived in a little house right across the street from St. Peter's. They had a basketball hoop out back in their tiny yard. It wasn't a ton of room to play in, but enough for two-on-two if everyone held their breath and didn't mind getting a face full of elbows.

Billy was taller and more athletic than me. As a latchkey kid, he always had the house to himself. His parents were always out, which made it easier for him to access copious liquor and drugs. He had already been initiated into the pleasures of marijuana. Which is why, when the final class bell rang, we almost always went over to Billy's place to get high and shoot hoops. I always looked forward to this, particularly because Billy's sister, Melanie, was often about.

Ah, Melanie! I worshipped the ground she walked on. I was twelve and just hitting puberty. She was probably sixteen, and I would have given my right arm to have her make a man out of me. She was every image of teenaged feminine loveliness that you've probably seen while flipping through ancient issues of *Teen Beat*. She had long brown hair, which she wore in a feather cut like Farrah Fawcett did in *Charlie's Angels*, complete with a set of feather earrings (a nod toward earthy spiritualism or possibly sympathy with Native American cultures). She wore those wide-brimmed, floppy hats that Carly Simon made popular on the cover of her *No Secrets* album. In fact, I often compared Melanie Theobald to

Carly Simon (Melanie was prettier) and another popular singer I liked back then, rock star Ann Wilson from the band Heart. In terms of looks, Melanie had Ann beat, too, but Melanie had that kind of spark, that kind of pizzazz.

Good God, even now, whenever I see a woman with feather earrings . . .

To be clear, I didn't stand a chance with Melanie Theobald. Not. A. Chance. She was so far out of my league that if she'd hit a pop fly, I couldn't have caught it using a parachute draped on the infield. The closest I got to making out with her was the first time I ever got high. I'll never forget how that happened.

***

Billy and I had spent the afternoon hanging out in his room. He produced a joint and asked if I wanted to smoke it. I think I said, "Whoa." I'd heard of marijuana. Remember, this was the 1970s. Of *course* I'd heard of marijuana. But I'd never tried it. The thought of doing so made me nervous.

"What if we get too high?" I asked.

"No problem." Billy knelt and pulled out a bottle from under his bed. "The vodka will ground us."

Sold.

We smoked. We drank. Profound life questions arose and a lot of them got answered, just don't ask me how. Even now, I consider the process of chemical enhancement somewhat mysterious. Regardless of what you put into your body, you're always you; you can't ever escape that. To my credit, I didn't puke and neither did Billy.

I was having the time of my life when God, the universe, or fate upped the ante. Someone knocked on Billy's bedroom door, then it opened. Melanie stuck her lovely brunette head in. Sniffing the air, she grinned. "You idiots. What are you doing in here?"

Picture Billy and me sitting on his bed, grinning like a pair of stoned monkeys, the bottle of vodka hidden behind us. "Nothing!" we said.

"Uh-huh." Melanie's grin got bigger. And right then? At that precise moment? The Carly Simon comparison held. Melanie had very big teeth.

It could have been the pot, but I suddenly felt I could picture her singing "You're so Vain" in a see-through negligee. "You guys wanna come hang out in my room?"

Be still my heart.

Our Father, Who art in Heaven, hallowed be Thy name . . .

Thank you, Lord Jesus, and thank you, St. Michael (I'm sorry about the whole forgery thing).

Thank you, Mother Teresa of Cal-friggin-cutta and all the angels seated at the right hand of God the Father, forever and ever, amen.

I didn't wait for Billy. I hopped off his bed and shot forward. "Let's go!"

***

It probably won't surprise you that Billy's reaction was different than mine. After all, Melanie was his sister. He had (ahem) different feelings for her than I did. He'd also been in her room many times. He was over the seventies classic rock–inspired decor. But me? I thought I'd died and gone to heaven.

At that moment, the only thing more important to me than making out with Melanie Theobald was getting Billy out of the way so that Melanie would *let* me make out with her. Sadly, this didn't happen.

The pot kicked in, then the vodka kicked in, then the pot kicked in even harder. I remember lying supine on the hand-woven Afghan-style carpet in Melanie's bedroom. I remember wishing my head was in her remarkable lap when it most certainly was not. I remember Melanie playing Led Zeppelin's *The Song Remains the Same* album. Robert Plant was singing "Whole Lotta Love" while I was thinking, *Yeah, man. That's me. I get what you're saying 'cause I got a whole lotta love . . .*

Melanie had her own joint, which she shared with Billy and me. Which meant I was suddenly no longer high but alarmingly high.

I'm gonna kiss her, I thought. *I'm gonna kiss Melanie Theobald!*

Nope. Didn't happen.

That night, I went home and I think Mom figured out right away what was up. From that point forward, Billy Theobald—actually, anyone named Theobald—became persona non grata in our apartment.

"Melanie Theobald? Ay Dios mío!" Mom knew Melanie because she was a student at Kolbe-Cathedral, the Catholic high school Mom taught at. In fact, Melanie was a student in one of Mom's classes. "¡Aléjate de ella!" Mom told me. (Stay the hell away from her!)

"Don't worry, Mom. I will."

I was lying, of course. That kicked off a trend.

Suffice it to say that from that point forward, drugs, alcohol, and mendacity became somewhat normalized in my life. And if my encounters with Melanie Theobald left me with a bunch of unrequited preteen fantasies, so what? I finally had my first kiss.

No, not with Melanie. It was another girl. I don't remember her name. That's all beyond me now. But let me tell you about it.

I remember we were hanging out down the block from where this girl lived, right out in the open, the way kids do in urban environments. I'd come equipped for the event with a 1970s-era boom box. Remember when I didn't get that radio for Christmas? Well, by that point I had my first job (more on that later), which meant I had money. Which meant I didn't need gifts. I had money so I could buy what I wanted. Lesson learned. If you want something, don't depend on others. Figure out how to get it for yourself.

At any rate, the song "Dreams" by Fleetwood Mac came on. I still love that song and probably always will. Though once I made the mistake of telling my wife why it's near and dear to my heart. After almost forty years of marriage, let me advise you. Some things are better left unsaid.

***

Eventually, Mom finally got her driver's license and bought a car, after which she moved us from Bridgeport to Stamford. The plan was for me to start eighth grade at Greenwich Middle School, which was associated with Mom's new high school, St. Mary's in Greenwich.

Moving meant that I had to make new friends, but I did this pretty quickly. Soon, I was up to my old tricks. Different crowd, a different location. Same bad behavior.

Compounding the problem, it was summer. Without any classes to keep me grounded, I was a young bull dancing to salsa tunes in a china shop made out of sugar glass. Things were breaking all over the place—including my mother's heart when she saw what I was getting up to. Without going into detail, some of my antics would have made Billy Theobald blush. Maybe Melanie too. And so, Mom being Mom, she came up with a plan to save my Catholic soul.

***

It was later that year. We were at a family birthday party in Flushing. Mom had called my cousin Raysa's husband, Rufino, and told him about the trouble I was getting into. Rufino was a real character, as many Spaniards are. A man of great gusto and hustle, he had a couple of restaurants going. His flagship establishment was called Los Porches. It was located in Great Neck, Long Island, an affluent community about ten miles east of Flushing. But it might as well have been 10,000 miles away given the different lifestyles.

Rufino had recently opened his second restaurant, La Mansion de Goya, in Southampton, Long Island, where New York City's rich and famous spend their summers. "You'll come out to Southampton this summer," he told me at the birthday party. "It's a beach community. You'll like it. The people who come to the restaurant spend tons of money, so you can make a lot of cash, say about $200 for three days' work. What do you think?"

That sounded fine to me. "What will I have to do?" I asked.

"Bus tables."

It was the first time I'd heard this term and it confused me. I imagined me picking up tables with my bare hands and hauling them down to the corner where I would jam them onto a bus.

"It's easy," Rufino explained. "Like, suppose someone's finished eating an appetizer or an entree. You take their empty plate. Then, when they're done with dinner, you take away glasses, silverware, everything. Change the tablecloth. Put out new napkins, new settings." He gave me a serious look. "It's hard work but I think you'll do well at it. You'll have to live in Southampton, but I have a house next door to the restaurant. All of my workers stay there. They speak Spanish. You'll feel right at home."

We were speaking Spanish while discussing this, so I just shrugged to prove he was right. "When can I start?" I said.

I was only thirteen, so even back then my working a job was a flagrant violation of every child labor law on the books. But I had no problem joining the workforce. No one ever questioned my age. Puberty struck me early, so I was taller and looked older than most of my peers. Being Cuban, I had a mustache starter kit plus the requisite gold jewelry and the attitude to match.

Also, I never gave anyone any reason to doubt my work ethic or performance. I'd always been a super-motivated kid. The idea of getting hired, making cash, and standing out from a crowd by doing an excellent job . . . those notions appealed to me. Still do.

***

I enjoyed many things about working at La Mansion de Goya. The menu was high-end Spanish fare. We served paellas, gazpacho, a lot of jamón, and gambas al ajillo. The guys running the kitchen let me eat whatever I wanted. Though tall at thirteen, I was still growing like a weed. To be able to eat so much of whatever I wanted, whenever I wanted . . . it was like being in heaven.

Happily, Rufino had underestimated how much money I'd make. I raked in about $400 a week, all cash, and this was at a time when the minimum wage was about three and a half bucks an hour. At thirteen years old, I was making more money than Mom was.

How did I end up making so much? Simple. I learned how things worked, came up with a plan to make things fucking better, and worked my ass off.

For instance, it was a busboy's responsibility to shuttle desserts to tables that ordered them. I soon realized that if I set up certain desserts at my station before my shift got started, I could move faster, cover more ground, and be more efficient. I always had three coffeepots in service instead of two, and I systematized rote duties like carrying bus trays back to the kitchen in batches. My life at the restaurant became a series of performance hacks.

It was the policy at La Mansion de Goya that tips for the serving and bussing staff got pooled. At the end of each night, waiters got two shares, busboys got one. But I was so good at my job, the waiters and bartenders I worked with issued me bonuses far and above my take every night. I was proud of that. The drive to be better than everyone else led me to break down the systems by which our restaurant operated and optimize them.

In fact, years later, I overheard Rufino telling my oldest daughter Alayna at a family gathering, "You know, your father was the hardest worker I ever hired. I've never seen anyone work like him, before or since."

That's still one of the greatest compliments I've ever received, better than any of the thirty or so performance reviews I got at various points throughout my career. To understand why, you have to consider the source. Rufino was a maniacal worker. To hear him talk up my work ethic was like hearing Santa Claus compliment someone on their generosity.

I've been skipping the obvious here. The best part about being a busboy was the lifestyle. If my mom thought the Theobalds led me astray, she would have been appalled to learn what the kitchen staff and I got up to in our spare time.

Picture a younger me living with older guys, mostly South American, mostly career kitchen staff. That's a hard life, in case you don't know it. We were drunk and high all the time and we were constantly scoping out chicks in a beach town where most of the bars didn't card me. *And* I had a lot of cash on hand. I mean, a *lot* of cash.

I was in heaven. Small wonder that somewhere around this point, I stopped giving two shits about going to school.

***

After that summer, I started eighth grade. What a shit show.

Greenwich is a wealthy community. Mom and I couldn't afford to live there, so we rented a little place in nearby Stamford on the second floor of a two-family house at 77 Coolidge Avenue. It was the wrong side of the tracks and we were the people the train ran over. Most of the kids in Greenwich drove better cars than my mom's shitty old Toyota Corolla. The family who owned the house we lived in was Italian, an immigrant couple, Mr. and Mrs. Angelo Ritorto. Their daughter, Adrianna, was a girl about my age and maybe the only one I didn't date throughout this period. Even then, despite my indulgences, I knew you never shit where you eat.

So. Mr. Ritorto. God, what a pain in the ass.

His gut was round as a bowling ball and his head was nearly as bald. He had one of those heavy paisano accents where you barely knew what the hell he was saying. His English was almost incomprehensible. I remember how he and Mom used to communicate using their mashup of Spanish-Italian, the no-man's-land where those languages meet. To this day, I feel certain that neither of them ever fully understood what the other was saying, though they liked to pretend they did.

Mr. Ritorto was always complaining about us. "You-a puddah the air-a conditionin' uppa too high!" he would say. Or, "Mamma mia! Why-a you gotta flush-a the toilets so many times? It a wastin the watah, capisce?"

I found it odd that Mr. Ritorto kept going on about noise when he kept about two dozen chickens and roosters in our backyard. Which meant that each day, at sunup, we heard a fanfare of avian cackling that rattled my brain like dice in the cup of my skull. This racket wasn't fun to come home to when I was hungover, which was always.

By that point, I was staying out late every night, getting drunk and high, and going out with girls. And in case any clarification is needed, I wasn't taking them to the movies. In short, I had lots of potential—I think that's a blunt and honest assessment. But I was undisciplined. Misdirected. Although I misbehaved with a certain flair, you could call me a deeply talented fuckup in danger of running my life off the rails.

The weird thing was, my grades didn't suffer, or at least not at first. I mostly found middle and high school easy. I did okay just by going to class. It helped that I liked my history and literature courses. I found that I would engage whenever I found a teacher engaging. If I thought they weren't giving me much, I had no qualms about flunking their course because I was bored. Besides, I had other things on my mind at that point.

When the school bell rang at the end of each day, I was like a werewolf kissed by the light of a bright full moon. The hairless human grew claws and long sharp fangs, and a new beast emerged: George Barrios, party animal.

Music became my constant companion during this time. I was always carrying that boom box, or I had headphones on. The songs that spoke to me weren't exactly hymns. My favorite bands included Led Zeppelin, Black Sabbath, and Alice Cooper.

Years later, one of my high school teachers introduced me to Carl Jung's concept of the Shadow archetype—the repressed parts of our personality that we hide in our unconscious minds. Jung theorized that exploring our Shadow and making peace with it can make us more effective and release incredible creativity.

Over the years, I've given my Shadow different names, all borrowed from the rock music that soundtracked my teenage rebellion.

"Problem Child."

"The Unrepentant."

For the last few years my Shadow has been "The Wolf."

***

To keep up my partying lifestyle, I needed to get an after-school job. Taking a page out of Mom's former playbook, I went to work at the local Woolworth's. They hired me on as a stock boy, but I had grander visions than that. At first, I was responsible for hauling boxes of product to the back of the store and stocking them on the shelves. But, just as I'd done at La Mansion de Goya, I developed a system to optimize the process. Cue my immediate conflict with management.

About a month into my employment, my boss confronted me. "What are you doing? That's not how we stack boxes here."

"Why?" I said. "What's wrong with how I'm doing it?"

He moved some boxes around. "You get more inventory on a shelf if you do it like this. See?"

I shook my head. "You're going for volume per shelf. I'm going for volume per cart, which decreases the number of trips I make overall, creating backlogged time I can then use to keep inventory organized. See how you're just sort of randomly throwing stuff on the shelves? Using my system, I know that there's eight wholesale boxes worth a total of $240 on each shelf. Each wholesale box is worth $30 and breaks down into six units sold at $5 apiece. So if you stack the boxes just so—would you mind if I showed you . . . ? Just step back there and . . . thanks—Okay, see? This allows you to rotate stock, which helps folks in Procurement, especially during the holiday sales. They can tell what goods are moving at a glance and order more on demand."

My boss looked at me for a long and terrible moment. Then he turned, left the stockroom, and went upstairs to complain. But instead of firing me, his own boss came down to inspect what I'd done. He shook his head. "This kid shouldn't be hauling boxes. Train him to work a register, front of the store. One day we'll all be working for him."

My first promotion.

Looking back, that's sort of how my entire career went.

I was doing so well at my job, and school was so easy, I started skipping class to work at Woolworth's. Very quickly, I got promoted again to register supervisor. At sixteen. Meanwhile, I was dating multiple girls who also worked at Woolworth's.

God, I loved that job. If I wasn't a Big Man on Campus, I was sure as hell Big Man at Woolworth's.

***

When high school started, I enrolled at St. Mary's. Of course I did. Mom was a teacher there, which meant my tuition was free. It also meant that, every day I went to school, I could carpool to classes with her. But I didn't.

It was hard enough being the new kid in town and the only Latino in a twenty-five-mile radius. Bad enough that my mom was on staff at St. Mary's. On top of all that, I had to drive to school with her? No thanks. Instead, we'd get in the car and I'd have Mom drop me off where the school bus stopped, in Greenwich, about a mile from my school.

The first time I got on the bus, I got heckled. It was awful. A kid called me a spic. I'm not saying that Greenwich was racist. In fact, I'm not even sure that kid knew what the word "spic" meant. He was just trying to get under my skin. He succeeded.

After I got hazed that first time, I went home and told Mom what happened. Not long after that, her friend Jennifer, who had taught with Mom at Kolbe-Cathedral, visited our apartment. Mom asked for advice. Jennifer was half-Italian, half-Irish, all blunt.

"Who called you a spic?" she asked me. "What was his name?"

I told her the kid's name was Larry and mentioned his last name, distinctly Irish. He was Larry McSomething.

Jennifer rolled her eyes. "So here's what you do," she said. "The next time you see him, go right up to him, get in his face, and call him a mick."

Basically, the advice I got was for me to get back on that bus and escalate tensions. So that's what I did.

The next day, I walked right up to Larry McSomething and told him off in front of everyone. And the next time I climbed up the steps of our bus, the first thing I did was assert dominance by picking a fight with a Polish kid in my grade, Richie Something-with-Ski-on-the-End-of-His-Name.

He was shorter than me, pretty stocky. I remember that later, when we all got old enough to get our driver's licenses, Richie Something-Ski drove a black Ford El Camino. But on that day, he made the mistake of saying something snide to me. I told him to go fuck himself. Then, when he said something back, don't ask me what, I hauled off and hit him.

The bus driver hurried right over. I remember him yelling while he pulled us apart. I remember shouting at Richie Something-Ski that he'd better not say shit about shit to me ever again. And guess what? It worked.

Richie never called me a spic again, nor did anyone. In fact, from that point forward, every time I got on the bus, I heard not a peep. Which was fine by me.

My territory had been marked. It was a small victory, which I soon forgot. Not that I had any choice. I had no idea my life was about to get much more complicated.

CHAPTER FOUR

The Algebra Teacher's Prophecy

My lack of attention to school began taking a toll on my grades. The worst part of watching my marks slip was the effect it had on my mother. She was no dummy. She could read the hands on the clock when I came home late every night, or early morning, more precisely.

Mom spent many a sleepless evening waiting up for me, only to have me waltz in drunk and high, not caring one bit about school the next day. We argued a lot. There were plenty of tears and accusations, lots of slammed doors and long walks into the night, all alone. By my sophomore year of high school, Mom thought I'd end up working at Woolworth's the rest of my life, or land in jail, or someplace worse.

My saving grace through all this was my math teacher, a man named Malcolm McBain. Picture a nerdy little man with short gray hair, a pocket protector, and the deep resignation of someone who's been there once and done everything twice. St. Mary's was such a small school that McBain taught algebra, geometry, and calculus. An iconoclast, he despised doing things by the book just to say they'd been done by the book. McBain possessed vision. He took one look at me and saw the fuckup that I was, but it turns out he had a soft spot for fuckups. Perhaps he had also been one, back in his youth. For whatever reason, I think he saw potential in me, and so, like any good teacher, he set his sights on developing that and ignored all the rest.

McBain taught me everything: postulates, theorems, congruence. How to calculate rates of change. Integration, or how to accumulate quantities. "There are properties at work in math," he said, "that are also at work in life, if you just care to look for them."

So true. For example, take the commutative property: how the ordering of numbers during the processes of addition and multiplication may change, but this cannot change results. Or the distributive property, which says that when multiplying sums by a number, all sums get multiplied the same. The more I thought about such things, the more I saw this was powerful stuff.

I was getting straight A's in McBain's class and failing pretty much everything else except for history, which I loved, and still do. Noting how well I did in McBain's class, my poor mom approached him for counsel. They were colleagues, fellow teachers. She begged him to tell her what she should do to get me back on track.

McBain, unruffled, pushed his glasses up his long nose. "The first thing you should do," he said, "is relax."

My mother was aghast. "Relax?!"

McBain turned a page in the book he was reading. "George has a very unique and organized mind that, right now, is engaged in a particularly complex set of operations which are important to him. There's nothing wrong with his logic. The program he's running is sound. It's just years ahead of its time, which makes people who long for immediate gratification nervous. But I predict that his efforts will bear fruit in the long run. Very possibly lots of fruit."

Mom tried to believe him. However, to my discredit, I kept making everything hard. My grades continued to slip until I was literally failing high school. Meanwhile, my focus was utterly set on working as hard as I could to make money so I could buy beer and drugs and date girls.

***

Soon I was barely attending class. Most of my grades were C's and D's. I couldn't care less. When it came time to take my SATs, I declined to prepare for them. *Why bother?* I thought. Nobody asks for your SAT scores when you work at Woolworth's or bus tables each summer.

My mother saw things differently. She was a teacher. She understood that the SAT was an important ticket used by serious students to travel wherever they wished in academic circles. Three months before the test, she splurged on one of those big doorstop test prep books put out by companies like Kaplan and the Princeton Review.

"Georgie, mira aquí. This book will teach you how to do well on the test. All you have to do is read it and follow the exercises!"

I never opened that book. Not once.

Mom kept imploring me to give it a try. I ignored her until finally I had enough. I told her I wasn't going to take the test. She burst into tears. It was one of the only times I ever saw her lose her composure. Crying, she told me how scared she was for my life, my future, my Catholic soul.

"Fine!" I said. "I'll take the damn test!"

"¡No puedes simplemente tomar el examen!" she said. (You can't just take the test. You have to prepare for it!)

I told her she was being dramatic, blowing things totally out of proportion. But she had every right to be skeptical. The exam was being administered on a Saturday morning. Given my habits back then, this didn't bode well.

I always went out on Friday nights. Mostly, I hung out with friends and got regally shit-faced, after which I'd crash with some girl, usually in the basement of her parents' house. I wouldn't roll home until ten or eleven Saturday morning, at which point I'd shower, get ready for work, kiss Mom, and pretend that we didn't have things to say to each other before heading to Woolworth's to start my shift after lunch.

"Don't go out the night before!" Mom begged me.

I just stared at her. Don't go out? That was like asking a cow not to moo or a dog not to bark. Of course I would go out!

The night before my exam, I went to a party and I'm pretty sure I hung out with some girls, though I can't really say for sure. All I know is that the next morning, Saturday, I rolled into the testing center at eight, still drunk and still high. It was a miserable place, like the setting of some Charles Dickens novel. Students from several schools were congregating. Everyone was nervous about putting themselves through academic hell.

I remember meeting some classmates, a few of whom looked as hungover as I did. One of the exam proctors was a teacher, a nun from my school. I can't remember her name, though I clearly recall the disgust she aimed my way. Then we all took our seats and armed ourselves with semi-sharp No. 2 pencils. For the next three hours or so, I bubbled in letters on a grid sheet I could barely see because my vision was still so blurry. A couple of times I had to swallow hard and take deep breaths to keep myself from throwing up.

I was the first student to finish. I took my answer sheet up to the front and went outside to get air. I'm pretty sure I threw up in some bushes. Then I waited around for my friends to come out. It took a while.

Once they arrived, they all started talking. They were still nervous. They told all these stories, most of which were about how they hadn't been able to figure out the correct answers on certain questions, so they'd just guessed and guessed and guessed.

Someone asked, "How'd you do, George?"

I told everyone it had been rough, then I got the hell out of there, went back home, avoided Mom's questions, and threw on my work clothes. My shift was beginning at Woolworth's and I didn't want to be late.

Weeks later, an envelope arrived in the mail. Turns out I got a combined score of 1570. Nearly perfect. Even weirder, my verbal score was 800 (flawless) while my math score was 770. Let this be a lesson to anyone interested. No matter how confident you are in your ability to back-solve algebra problems, always check your work.

Everyone makes mistakes.

***

Getting my scores back didn't change my life much, though it made for an interesting meeting with my high school guidance counselor.

His name was Mike McDermott. St. Mary's was such a small place that McDermott was also my religious studies teacher. He was profoundly unimpressed by how little I paid attention in class. In fairness, I was disruptive, telling jokes, making quips, talking tough, flexing all sorts of muscles except for the ones that crack open books.

During our meeting, McDermott read through my academic file while I sat across from him, yawning. I could hear him grinding his teeth as he struggled to keep his comments professional.

"So, I'm looking at your SAT scores here. Excellent math scores, excellent verbal. Let's focus on math since those are the skills that can snag you a really high-paying job. Have you thought about becoming an actuary?"

I think I blinked at him. "A what?"

He told me that an actuary is someone who uses math a lot and gets paid very well. "What an actuary does," McDermott explained, "is calculate outcome probabilities, usually for insurance companies. For instance, how many houses are likely to catch fire in zip code X in the month of October? How many people ages Y through Z are likely to die a premature death, which is defined as value A minus a range between fifty and twenty? You see what I'm driving at? Actuaries use all sorts of tables to calculate these things."

"Tables," I said. Just to be sure that I'd heard him correctly.

Now it was his turn to yawn. "It's a good job with a great salary starting out. In fact, the only downside is that you don't interact much with people. It's basically you just sitting there, working your tables."

This sounded awful to me, the absolute last thing I would want to spend my life doing. "Why would you think I'd want to do a job like that?" I asked.

McDermott shrugged. The look he gave me said, *I'm speaking to a complete moron.* "We need to find something for you to do. And let's be honest, George. You've got a gift. If you go and pass all the actuarial tests . . . but you don't seem all that interested in doing much, right?"

He had me there.

***

I still didn't see myself going to college though Mom kept hounding me about it.

"¿Georgie, qué vas a hacer?" (What are you going to do, George?)

"Punt," I said.

"¿Qué es eso?"

"It's a football expression. It means, right now I'm not gonna think about it."

"¡Si quieres ir a la universidad. . .!"

"Yeah, well, maybe I don't want to go to college. Did you ever think about that?"

Right then, I wasn't so sure I would graduate high school, let alone anything after that. To be blunt, the only reason I graduated high school was because my mom was a teacher on staff at St. Mary's and her colleagues couldn't countenance failing her son in their courses. They told her everyone knew I was smart, so they weren't doing anyone a disservice, just sort of helping me get by. At the same time, we were moving again. St. Mary's was shutting down. The place was so small, it couldn't stay open. I ended up graduating, but Mom was losing her job.

She put out some feelers and cobbled together work teaching adjunct courses at Iona College and St. John's University. She made enough money to make ends meet, but only if she seized both ends in her hands and pulled really hard to bring them together. It cushioned the blow somewhat that she talked to her sisters about moving back to Flushing. This would end up being good for her. She'd be back with family again.

As for me, I kept playing my punt card, thinking how smart I was to be getting my way. Ha ha! No college for me! Then, one day, I came home and found a letter addressed to me lying on the kitchen table.

"Congratulations! On behalf of the faculty and community at the University of Connecticut, I welcome you to the incoming class of 1987."

Holy shit, I was angry. No. I take that back. I was fucking livid. I turned to my mom, who just stood there and smiled as I held up the letter. "What's this?"

"¡Felicidades!" she said with her trademark smirk.

"How'd I get accepted? I didn't apply!"

Well, I did and I didn't. Turns out, Mom applied for me. She did it in secret. And UConn accepted me. Probably because even though my grades were shit, my SATs were stellar.

"You did what?!" I shouted.

That got her dander up. "I won't let you sit around throwing your life and your talents away!"

"That's not your choice to make!" I tore up the letter. "It's my choice. See? Not going."

"But—"

"I don't care if I got accepted. Okay? Do you hear me? I'm not going."

Mom just shrugged. "Fine. But you can't stay here. I'm moving back to Queens."

"Great," I said. "I love Queens. Let's go home."

She shook her head. "I could only afford a studio. There won't be room for you."

I think I said, "What?"

She showed me a floor plan of the place she was getting. It was a shoebox with a kitchenette and a bathroom barely big enough to stand in. There was no bedroom. I asked where her bed would go and she showed me the spot where she said she would tuck it away, in a corner behind some bookshelves.

I felt gutted. Abandoned. "But . . . what about me?" I said. "Where will I sleep?"

"I already told you, there's no room. Which means you should probably go to school."

I railed and I argued until my tongue turned blue, but my mother stuck to her guns. She said she would help me go to school no matter the cost. In the end, I gave in. I had no choice.

We went over the math. UConn was a state school, and at that point I was still a Connecticut resident, so tuition was something like $5,000 a year. But Mom had only been making about $20,000 a year. No matter how we sliced the pie, we would walk away hungry.

Nowadays, I thank God that Mom took the initiative and made me go to college. Turned out to be one of the luckiest turns of my life.

***

The summer before I started my freshman year, Abuelo passed away. He was in his nineties by that point and he died in his sleep while a bunch of us were visiting him in Flushing.

To pass away peacefully, surrounded by everyone close to you? All in all, that sounds like a great way to go.

The fact that we were all present paid additional dividends. It ensured that we could all support one another through that very difficult time.

I remember thinking, *Dad's gone. My uncles are gone. Now Abuelo's gone, too. If that's not a sign of something, I don't know what is.*

At that point, the lingering question was: *What's the message I'm supposed to be getting? And how come I don't seem to be getting it?*

I understood in a vague sort of way that something had to give. I just wasn't sure what, and I wasn't sure how or when. But I felt that, whatever that change might be, I would end up finding it at UConn.

***

The University of Connecticut is one of those sprawling public land-grant schools commissioned toward the end of the nineteenth century. Picture a 4,400-acre spread near the village of Storrs-Mansfield, some thirty miles east of Hartford. It was founded as the Storrs Agricultural School, which should give you a clue as to what things looked like. Back then, the place was as rural as central Nebraska. The culture shock was jarring for me.

I'd only lived in urban environments, never ventured upstate. Together with my cousin, Jorge, Mom and I packed up a few of my choice belongings and drove away from the coast, up Route 95, toward Storrs. Once we passed New Haven, the landscape cleared out fast. I remember staring out the open car window, completely befuddled.

Why are there so many trees here? I wondered. *Where did all the buildings and people go?*

We found ourselves driving down two-lane roads whose primary traffic was pickups and tractors. I'd never seen fields and silos and cows before, let alone herds of cows. I wasn't a fish out of water; I was a fish on another planet.

My sense of alienation grew worse as we entered the campus. The first thing I saw was a dairy barn, huge, monolithic. Why would a barn be so big? I had no idea whatsoever. More fields, more cows, more emptiness.

I distinctly remember catching a glimpse of myself in the sideview mirror of Mom's car. I had short-cropped, spiky hair back then with a little braided tail that ran down back, big style in the eighties, very urban, very Latino. I wore a thick gold chain that had my name stamped on a heavy medallion in front. But then I tore my eyes off the mirror, looked out and saw . . . people who looked nothing like me. At all. And they were everywhere.

What the fuck have I gotten myself into?

We got to my dorm room, a triple in McConaughy Hall, third floor, on UConn's North Campus. Back then, folks called North Campus "the jungle." According to legend, it got that name when soldiers returning from Vietnam studied at UConn on the GI Bill. They were a rowdy bunch, to hear tell, and many of them lived right there, where I was setting up shop.

My roommates were two suburban kids who kept looking at me like I'd crawled out of the molding. Joe Antonelli was about my height, a good-looking kid who'd been a pole vaulter in high school; he was massively strong. Rich Richter was shorter and stockier, also an athlete, a baseball player. They were good guys and we eventually became friends, but at that moment I think we were all a little uncomfortable.

I claimed the centermost bunk of the three, then turned to say goodbye to Jorge and Mom. Much harder to do than I thought it would be. When they left, I felt more than alone; I felt bereaved.

I didn't unpack. I lay on my new bed, feeling awful. I was the loneliest I've ever felt in my life. Until I heard a familiar bright coining sound and looked out the window at a basketball court, where a bunch of guys were shooting hoops.

Bingo, I thought. *Just like home!*

Where I grew up, basketball was the great urban equalizer. Playing ball kept city kids from fighting each other by venting our aggression on the court. I rolled off my bed and hustled right out there and asked for a pickup game. That's how I met a new friend, Darryl Aiken.

He was a Black kid from New Jersey, not terribly urban. Darryl's father was a doctor and his mom was a lawyer, or maybe vice versa. Still, we hit it off. He was my first and, for a while, my only friend at UConn. Mostly because, as far as profiles went, Darryl was someone I felt more comfortable with back then. I was a city kid. Playing basketball with Black kids was like being back home.

My two roommates and I ended up finding common ground in sports, music, partying, and girls. Though we had to do it fast because Rich ended up flunking out of school by the end of our sophomore year.

Looking back, that set a tone.

***

I remember the first meeting I had with my freshman academic advisor. I was sitting in her office, watching her read my file, connecting the dots. The expression on her face said, *Hmm. What's this? Great SAT scores, terrible high school grades.*

At one point she looked up. It was clear she was having a tough time processing the extreme disparity between my grades and test scores. But she was kind. We talked very frankly. I told her my mom had filled out my application to UConn. That was the only reason I was sitting before her.

"Okay." She took a deep breath. "We'll figure this out. It's clear that you're bright. But I think it's also clear that you need to be challenged. Why don't we put you in a bunch of honors courses and see how you do?"

She enrolled me in honors history, honors chemistry, honors calculus, and honors English. And who knows? I might have done well in those courses if I'd ever gone to class. Which I didn't.

For a while there, I was so lonely, I'd figure out ways to get home every weekend. I would tell Mom I was coming to check on her but end up partying hard with friends and crashing on their couches before heading back to school. But little by little, this changed.

I kept playing basketball with Darryl, kept meeting his friends, who then became my friends. At one point, one of them asked me, "Hey, man, you want to join our club?"

I sank a foul shot. "What club?"

"The African American Club."

Somebody tossed me the ball. I bounced it three times. Shot again. Missed. "Yeah, case you haven't noticed? I'm not Black."

The kid scoffed at me. "Asshole. You don't have to be Black."

I still wasn't sold and I told him so.

He shrugged. "Okay, lotsa girls there. But hey, man. You do whatever you—"

"Wait," I said. "How many girls?"

I joined the club later that night. And that kid had been right. There were women all over the place and the dances were out of this world. Just like that, I started going home less and less on the weekends. And then, in a very real way, my identity changed. I got a new name.

It happened like this.

While still a fish out of water, I went to one of those parties that everyone goes to freshman year. The kind where you let yourself loose in ways that you never have before, and somebody notices. In my case, that somebody was an upperclassman whose name has long since faded away in the annals of memory. All I remember is that he had beer in his fridge and a shit ton of weed in his room that we set about smoking. And smoking. And smoking. All night long.

Somewhere during our work with the bong, this older guy shot me a look through a haze of blue smoke. "Your name is George?"

I coughed and nodded.

"The hell, man. You don't look like a George. That's, like . . . the name of the King of England or something. You're Hispanic? Why aren't you Jorge?"

I explained how my parents had wanted to assimilate. They gave me the name George because they felt it was more suitable for America than Jorge.

This dude shook his head. "Still not buying it. George you are not. What's your middle name?"

"Aldo," I said. "My dad's name."

This guy nearly jumped off the couch. He was pointing at me, wide-eyed and stoned. "That's it!" he said. "That's your name, dude! That's your true name! Like, that suits you. You're, like, an Aldo!"

From that point forward everyone I met at UConn called me Aldo. Al for short. In fact, throughout this book, you'll hear me called that from time to time. Aldo or Al. Now you know where that comes from.

If this all sounds very pleasant, let me correct you. At this point, I was still trying hard to derail my life. For instance, my first semester grades came in at a whopping 0.6 GPA. I can still see Mom reading the transcript and bursting into tears.

"¿Prueba académica?" she moaned. (Academic probation.)

I hung my head and said nothing.

"¡Si no mejoras tus calificaciones, reprobarás!" (If you don't get your grades up, they'll kick you out!)

I remember feeling such shame, I couldn't take it anymore. I got up and left the apartment and went for another one of those long, introspective walks that were becoming the norm for me by then. Long story short, I got my grades up enough to avoid expulsion. Barely.

Look, if I'm being totally honest, my life could have sailed off the rails at this point. But then something magical happened, something I've never stopped thanking God for.

I met Carol.

***

Back to school at the start of my sophomore year. September 1984. The school administration had announced it was converting McConaughy's third story to an all-women's floor. My roommates and I were given a choice: Relocate to the fourth floor or try a new dorm. We chose the fourth floor.

I mean, duh. One floor away from twenty-odd rooms with two girls in every room? Talk about a target-rich environment.

Once we unpacked, we headed down to the third floor and went from room to room, introducing ourselves. One of my roommates, Rich, and I became especially animated, riffing off each other like a comedy duo. Rich was the shit-talker, I played the straight man, setting him up for all the good punch lines.

In one of those third-floor rooms, I met Carol Marques. The first time I saw her, two thoughts occurred to me. First, that Carol was Spanish. This turned out not to be true. In fact, she's Irish, English, and German on her mother's side while her father was half-Indian, half-Portuguese. The result was Carol's glossy black hair, freckles, and that incredible spirit that shines in her eyes. She reminded me right off the bat of my biggest rock-n-roll crush, Linda Ronstadt. The dark hair. That dazzling energy. Which leads me to thought number two: I was smitten. At once.

Carol was rooming with her high school friend, Michele Rutsky. We were all hitting it off that first time we met. Michele happened to mention her birthday was coming up in a few days; she was turning eighteen. So Rich and I scraped a few bucks together and went out and bought her a cake, which we presented with suitable flourish.

I remember Carol turning to me with her gorgeous hazel eyes alight. "This is so sweet," she told me. "That's the sweetest thing ever."

And with that, we started dating.

We weren't alone. In total, eight guys from fourth-floor McConaughy began dating eight girls from the third floor. Long story short, we all became fast friends. After college, we all got married and went to each other's weddings. Our kids have grown up knowing each other. My friends and I are like surrogate aunts and uncles to them.

Think about that for a minute. Sixteen people living in the same dorm, dating through college. We all marry each other and we're all still friends after almost forty years. Those are pretty long odds.

It was all an abrupt about-face for me. Suddenly, my cup was running over. Not only had I found Carol, who became the love of my life (and for damn good reason), I'd found a new family, this group of people who support each other through ups and downs and everything in between.

If you're still keeping notes, small wonder my life turned around. And yes, I'd say that it happened right there. I'm forever grateful for that.

***

One final memory from this period. It's important because it's when I finally realized that I'd turned a corner.

It was the fall semester of 1986, my senior year of undergrad. The New York Mets were hot that season. Their roster was loaded with talent like Darryl Strawberry, Dwight Gooden, Gary Carter, Lenny Dykstra, and my personal favorite, Keith Hernandez. In 1985, this team had been knocking it out of the ballpark, sometimes literally. By early October '86, the Mets had become one of just three National League teams in baseball history to have won twice as many games as they'd lost in a regular season. (The other two were the LA Dodgers and the Cincinnati Reds.) Because of this stellar performance, the Mets were scheduled to face the Boston Red Sox in the 83rd World Series.

Everyone at UConn was excited. In my little college community, about 80 percent of my peers were die-hard Boston fans. The other 20 percent skewed hard toward New York. I remember how involved everyone was. If you walked all the floors of McConaughy Hall, you'd find most doors were open. Everyone's TV set had the game on and people were gathered in groups. They were yelling and screaming. It was a blast!

Game Six took place on Saturday night, October 25. For whatever reason, I was alone that night, meaning Carol and many of my usual friends were out. I ended up watching the game at a party hosted in the dorm room of some other close friends who were Red Sox fans. I was the only Mets fan; everyone else was pulling for the Sox. This was a potentially volatile situation because the Sox were leading 3–2. If they won Game Six, that was it. The Series would end and the Mets would go home in defeat.

That game was a real nail-biter. It went into extra innings. At the top of the tenth, the Sox hit a homer and, along with a single, drove in two runs in the inning, putting them ahead of the Mets, 5–3. In the bottom of the tenth, the Mets put a man on second, but were down to their last out with two strikes. Their situation looked bleak. One more strike, that was it—they were finished.

The Sox fans were out of their minds. They started to celebrate. Everyone was singing that song you hear when a team is about to bow out. You know which one I'm talking about.

"Na na na na! Hey hey hey! Goodbye!"

I remember somebody screaming, "It's over, dude! The Mets are goin' home in a body bag!"

I looked up in time to take a jet of champagne in my face. A guy who lived down the hall was a Sox fan. Let's call him Scotty Olsen. He'd entered the room, full of piss and vinegar, shaken a bottle of bubbly, and popped the cork. Champagne went everywhere. Everyone was laughing and covered in foam.

I just sat there and seethed. And that's when a miracle happened.

The Mets strung several hits together, the Sox made a critical fielding error, and just like that the Mets won the game, 6–5. That tied the Series! The Mets would advance to the final game to be held two days later, on Monday night.

From my perspective, this was beyond sufficient cause for joy. But I couldn't let it rest, not after taking a bubble bath in brut. I remember running out into the hallway, screaming, "Hey, Scotty!! Where are you now, motherfucker?!? Huh?!? WHERE THE FUCK ARE YOU NOOOOWWWWWWW!!!"

To put things mildly, I made a scene and I felt justified in doing so. I had been hazed. That's how I saw things. I had been taunted. Pushed over my limit. Payback was justified and I was going to get some.

But then another miracle happened. A smaller miracle but one worth noting.

It was like the wheels of time suddenly shifted and I was a spic on the bus once more. Only this time it was like I was standing apart from myself and watching my own behavior, which I could only describe as volatile. Suddenly it was clear to me I was losing my composure. And for what? Because some douchebag like Scotty Olsen had prematurely ejaculated French carbonated wine all over me? Was that sufficient reason to lose my shit? I decided it wasn't.

In a nanosecond, I went from being "George who wants to kill Scotty by seizing his goddamn bottle of brut and beating him over the head with it" to "George who breathes deeply." George who saw his classmates as a bunch of wild animals. Ignorant and undisciplined. That's when something clicked in my brain. Because, yeah, I'd dished out shit before—done that dozens, probably hundreds of times. But now (I saw this clearly) it was time to behave a bit differently. To try something new. To master myself. And so that's what I did.

And I felt it. A curious internal shift.

Holy shit, I thought. *I'm evolving.*

Now listen. I have to be clear on this point. This wasn't the end of my fighting. God no. For better or worse, I would wade into many more brawls as the years continued to pass. Some fights I got into for the right reasons, many for the wrong reasons. And before you go raising your hackles against me, yes, there are right reasons for fighting. Friends do it. Families do it. Nations do it. Fighting is a part of life.

I'm not saying that every fight should be fought, nor am I advocating for solving problems with physical violence. I'm just saying that when push comes to shove, either literally or metaphorically, it's best to be in a position where you can defend yourself.

It wasn't until I was in my late forties that I fully appreciated the balance of when fighting is necessary and when it isn't. As it happens, I've been clean and sober from physical altercations for years now. But I say this again: The option to fight should always stay on the table at least as a deterrent. At least to set boundaries.

Back in the autumn of 1986, my choice *not* to fight seemed divinely inspired. Because two evenings later, on Monday night, October 27, the Mets beat the Boston Red Sox, 8–5, and won the World Series.

Sweet rewards.

CHAPTER FIVE

Romancing the Stonecutter

Thanks to Carol's influence and that of my friends, I went from nearly flunking out of college to doing well, from tolerating school to loving it so much I never wanted to leave.

There was a problem with that, of course. Time stops for no one. Suddenly, it was late autumn 1986 and I found myself staring down the barrel of impending graduation. How had four years flown by that quickly? Two years earlier, I had applied to UConn's business school, but my application was rejected because my grades hadn't met the minimum threshold. I was therefore graduating with a Bachelor of Arts in economics.

Now what?

I had two choices: get a job with my economics degree or continue my studies in graduate school. I chose the latter. My next decision was which subject to pursue. I found legal studies intriguing until I researched the LSAT and discovered that it's heavily weighted in content-specific questions, which meant a lot of studying and preparation. Enter the notion of getting an MBA.

Applicants for MBA programs take the GMAT, a test that measures intellect rather than content knowledge and has two primary components, verbal and quantitative. The GMAT felt very similar to the SAT, whose ass I'd kicked despite taking it while deeply hungover.

Play to your strengths and ignore your weaknesses, I thought. Lean into what you're good at, disregard what you're bad at. That's the logic I used to go for a graduate degree in business. And wouldn't you know it? With no preparation at all, I got a perfect score on the GMAT.

Now for the next step. Where would I study?

My Tía Ela was very supportive. "Mira, George!" she told me. "Your grades in college were good. Not great. Just good. But you've got this perfect GMAT score! That's Ivy League material! So I'll tell you what. If you get into an Ivy League business school, I'll pay for it."

Clearly, this was an incredible offer. And it may sound ridiculous, but I never applied anywhere but UConn. I was asking myself, where else could I hang out with my friends, go to great parties, and have fun while getting an education? How could I stay close to Carol, who still had a year of college left? UConn had become my home, and home is a concept that's always been very important to me.

This time, UConn's business school accepted me! I got a full-time job as the night manager of a convenience store on campus. The money I made went toward tuition, but it wasn't enough to cover housing or living expenses.

Here again, Aunt Ela stepped up to the plate. Over the next two years, while I studied, she loaned me approximately $5,000. I could never have made it without her.

***

Graduate school was a much different experience from my undergraduate studies. I discovered I liked the work I was doing in my MBA program, and I loved the people. The curriculum was built around core business disciplines like finance, accounting, economics, operations, management, leadership, and marketing. From there, you could chart your own trajectory by taking electives and specializing in learning methods, adding interdisciplinary approaches that delved into sociology, psychology, decision-making frameworks, whatever got you fired up.

Of all these topics, I liked accounting the least. It was drudgery. Endless discussions about debits and credits and where they belonged on the balance sheet or income statement. I was like, *Who the fuck cares? What does this have to do with making a product and selling it to people?*

To be fair, there was one subject in accounting that perked me up: break-even analysis. That's the calculation you use to determine the point at which a business's revenue can cover its fixed costs, at which point every additional dollar of revenue increases your profits.

I remember sitting up straight during that class, thinking, *Now this is important. I like this!*

Understanding break-even, also called unit economics, is one of the most important parts of any business. I didn't understand that back then, but my instincts, which I have always trusted, were screaming at me to pay attention.

Warren Buffett once called accounting the language of business. Over time, I learned he was right and came to appreciate the practice. But it would take me many more years to knuckle down and do the work in this field. More on that later.

From the first days of my graduate studies, marketing and leadership courses held me spellbound. I loved digging into case studies that examined business problems holistically and demonstrated various approaches to fixing them—some that worked and some that didn't. I found it interesting to view a business from the top down, to imagine its various moving parts and attempt to integrate them with an eye toward creating the best outcomes. I loved developing plans that would help companies flourish. Analyzing new and existing markets. Exploring different opportunities to grow revenues and profit. Architecting the overall workings of a business and leading people to accomplish great things. That sounded like fun.

I thought, *This is what I want to do with my life.*

In some ways, it was like being back in the stockroom or manning the registers at Woolworth's. When I sat down to work on my projects, I felt like I was a kid again, sitting at the dinner table in our first Flushing apartment. And Dad was sitting right next to me, quizzing me on how to calculate on-base or slugging percentages.

. . . 1B + 2B(2) + 3B(3) + HR(4)/AB, where 1B equals the batter's number of singles, 2B equals his number of doubles, 3B equals his number of triples . . .

It was fun to do mock business analysis reports, to figure out where an enterprise was weak and how it could improve by taking different, even unusual vectors outside of what other firms did.

I learned a lot as an MBA student. But really, if I'm being honest, I learned more sitting on the couch in the off-campus apartment I shared with three friends, reading a very interesting book about baseball. That book changed the course of my life.

***

This was during my first year of grad school. My roommates were two guys from the McConaughy 16, and one of their younger brothers. Tom Russo was there, my bar-fight wingman, a chemical engineer, gifted wrestler, and one of the best friends a guy could ask for. Ken Young, the most principled, conscientious person I've ever met; he's the guy who keeps his cars running for fifteen years because it's the right thing to do and spends Sunday mornings cleaning up after a tailgate when everyone else is sleeping it off. And Ken's younger brother Tim, our very own voice of reason. When one of our parties got too loud, Tim jumped on the couch, started flicking the lights, and shouting that everyone had to go home. "Right now!" And wouldn't you know it? They did.

I was in a nice groove with my studies, getting A's and B's without working too hard. The parties we threw were outstanding, the camaraderie of my roommates even more so. Carol and I were going great guns. I was comfortable, I felt loved, and I guess you could say I was ripe for epiphany.

Enter a fat coffee table–sized book titled *Historical Baseball Abstract* by Bill James. Imagine over seven hundred pages of musings on our beloved national pastime. Once I started reading, I couldn't put it down.

James was a consummate baseball fan who wrote articles about the sport while working as the night watchman in a pork and beans cannery. But in addition to telling captivating stories about the game, James posed hitherto uncomfortable questions such as "How do you measure the precise value of every player on the field?" And he had the temerity to back up his assertions with data and mathematical calculations never used before in baseball.

Why was this important? Because for a hundred years up to that point, everyone in baseball had looked at the sport through overly simple statistics like batting average and earned run average. But here was James proposing a totally new way of looking at the game. His *Abstract*, originally published in 1985, was essentially a regression model of baseball that tore the sport down and built it back up by applying statistical analysis rather than personalities, emotional anecdotes, and mysticism.

James proposed brand-new metrics. His Pythagorean Winning Percentage explains the relationship of wins and losses to runs scored and runs allowed. His Range Factor measures a player's defensive contributions. His Power/Speed Number sheds light on the various and exalted "clubs" of elite batters and base stealers.

James coined a new term for his approach. He called it sabermetrics, a reference to SABR, the Society for American Baseball Research. This term has since become a blanket name for studying baseball through advanced mathematical models. You can probably see how, as far back as 1988, this approach appealed to me.

Sure, the math hearkened straight back to everything Dad taught me sitting at the kitchen table in our apartment at the Glen-Ora in Flushing. But there was something else that charmed me. Something far more important. No one had done this work before. I mean no one. To me, Bill James is the Nicolaus Copernicus of baseball.

You'll recall that in the sixteenth century, scientists believed that our Earth was the center of the universe. They based all their math on this assumption and, lo and behold, their math proved them right. When it didn't, they scratched their heads and began exploring the contradictions, which of course never worked. How could it? The foundation of their argument, their most fundamental assumption—that every heavenly body in the universe revolves around the Earth—was patently wrong.

Then along came Copernicus. In 1543, he dared to propose a different assumption. What if the Earth wasn't the center of the universe? What would the math show then?

He dug into this question and guess what happened? The math that was previously inconclusive, riddled with errors, began to line up. Copernicus showed how powerful assumptions can be. How they can dictate the plastic stage that most people call reality.

About four centuries years later, Albert Einstein put it like this: "Reality is merely an illusion, albeit a persistent one." I like this quote because, if you read carefully, it offers the key to creating massive change in life. Be more persistent in your examination and understanding of reality and you might find that what you thought was real was actually someone else's well-sold illusion.

In short order, James's model revolutionized baseball. Under his new vision, the general manager of a ball club was no longer effective in his time-honored role of backslapping used car salesman leading his troops into battle out on the diamond. He made far a greater impact by recasting himself as a data-driven master of statistics, preferably with a graduate degree in mathematics from MIT. Or UConn.

These days, most people know the story of Billy Beane, general manager for the Oakland Athletics. Beane applied sabermetrics to startling effect while leading his low-budget team through a storied upswing in the early 2000s. His story was the subject of Michael Lewis's excellent book, *Moneyball*, plus the subsequent film starring Brad Pitt and Jonah Hill.

I remember sitting on our apartment's communal couch, reading James's book while drinking a beer, thinking, *Holy shit!* Bill James just called out how millions of fans and thousands of so-called baseball experts look at the game. He's saying they're viewing the sport tautologically. "Why is baseball this way? Because it is. QED. End of story." Not so!

James's new analytics offered insight into creating economies and efficiencies that maximize productivity and win games. And how did he do it? Simple. By insisting on looking at things differently.

Here I want to point something out. *Historical Baseball Abstract* wasn't part of my assigned reading for courses. It was bigger than that. It created more impact. It fascinated me. I have since learned that fascination is what you follow. Every. Single. Fucking. Time. This was the moment my professional world turned around.

When it came to analyzing a business, I should listen to experts, sure, but I should also realize that experts are frequently wrong. Experts are the people you consult to understand how things currently work, but they're the last people you talk to if you want to make things better.

I resolved then and there to test their theories, to do my own work. To reach my own conclusions regardless of what all the so-called smartest people in the room think.

If my calculations ended up agreeing with the experts, fine. But if I could find a place where the experts were wrong, that could change everything. It could flip whole industries upside down. By which I specifically mean, I might make a business ten times better.

Keep this in mind as you continue to read.

***

I graduated with my MBA in late spring 1989. At that point, I wasn't sure what I'd end up doing with my degree. I didn't understand that degrees aren't a guarantee of success. They only mark a person's potential. Even that, I was soon to discover, isn't always an accurate reading.

In those days, the economy was slowing but still strong. To save money, I moved back to Flushing and bunked with my mom in the little studio apartment she was renting two blocks from the Glen-Ora. The two of us were packed in there like sardines. I think we both hoped it wouldn't be long before I found work and rented a place of my own.

It was a very exciting time. I remember being hopeful about finding a job that I loved, that paid really well, and that I could grow in. I had my sights set on the future, which is, of course, when the present comes around, smacks you in the face, and reminds you about where you're at.

Before I got my first real job, Carol graduated from UConn and broke up with me.

***

By that point, we had been dating for something like six years. Looking back, I think Carol was questioning whether this was her path. After dating me for so long, she was probably asking herself, *Is this it? This is the guy I'm going to marry, warts and all?*

It's a natural reaction, I guess. If I were in her shoes, I probably would have done the same thing. Still, I was devastated.

Mom saw me moping and gave me some decent advice. "You never had problems finding a girl before. Stop whining and get back out there."

So that's what I did. But it didn't feel right. In fact, it felt awful.

Over about three months, Carol would call me every so often. We'd talk as friends. Part of me liked this and part of me didn't. I remember feeling confused.

Mom would listen to me talking on the phone with her. Once I hung up, she would shake her head. "No! Georgie, you cannot do this anymore. It isn't good for you. Whenever you talk to Carol, you get upset all over again!"

I figured she was right, so I stopped answering the phone. *If Carol and I are through*, I thought, *we need distance. It's time to move on.*

Carol wasn't thrilled about that. When she couldn't track me down, she would call my mother.

One time, I heard Mom take the call on the kitchen phone in her studio. "Well, hi Carol. Hmm? What's that? Oh no, he's not here." She ducked her head through the arch to make sure I heard her saying this. "No, sorry, I really don't know where he is. He must be out. With who? Oh. Well, I'm sure I don't know."

Carol had gone back to living at her parents' place in Simsbury, Connecticut. But one day, for whatever reason, she got in her car and drove out to Queens and showed up at Mom's apartment. She rang the bell, but Mom and I weren't there; we had gone to hang out in Ela's apartment. Just like old times.

Carol knew how close my family was, so she buzzed Ela's place next. Jorge answered the intercom and spoke to Carol. I remember hearing Carol's voice. "Is George there?" She only called me George when I was with my family. At all other times, I was Aldo or Al to her.

What a pleasant surprise. The feeling that came over me then, knowing that she was downstairs; she'd come so far. She wanted to see me. It was amazing.

Jorge turned to me, cocking one eyebrow. "¿Qué le digo?" he asked me. (What do I tell her?)

I got up from my chair. "Tell her I'll be right down."

I took the elevator down to the lobby and let her in. We went up to my mom's place and talked for a while. Long story short, we got back together and we've been together ever since.

Remember that scheme I had of trolling the new all-women's floor on the third story of McConaughy Hall? That may be the best damn idea I've ever had.

***

We had no internet back then. To search for a job, you pored over the classified ads in your local newspaper. After circling various options, you mailed out your résumé or dropped it off in person.

I know. Stone Age, right?

I interviewed with lots of places and got a few offers, none of which I accepted. For instance, I interviewed with tobacco giant Philip Morris International. The position paid enormously well—there's a lot of money in cigarettes. But there was a downside.

That interview was awful. I remember sitting in this little cubicle with a guy who smoked. The. Whole. Time.

"So," he said. Puff. Puff. "You're bilingual? Spanish? We're expanding into Latin American markets."

"Is that right?" I was dying for oxygen. *Dear God,* I thought. *This must be what pets feel like when they're trapped in a burning building.*

"Oh, yeah," the guy said. "Tons of opportunity." He gestured to a map pinned to the wall of his cubicle. That's when I noticed his hand was shaking and had yellowed fingernails. "We need people like you." Puff puff puff!

I didn't leave so much as flee.

Eventually, I landed an interview for a business analyst position with a Manhattan-based media holding company, Capital Cities, run by Dan Burke and Tom Murphy. In 1986, they acquired the ABC television network for $3.5 billion. The interview I got was actually with a Cap Cities subsidiary, Fairchild Publications, which did beautiful fashion trade and direct-to-consumer magazines. This was back when magazine pages were laid out, photo by photo and column by column, on a designer's literal desktop.

The guy I interviewed with was very warm, very talented, about thirty years old to my twenty-four, with a pleasant round face. His demeanor was gentle and he was always smiling. Mario Ianetta. I'll never forget him.

"So." Mario looked up from my résumé. "Do you know how to use Excel?"

This was back before Excel was on everyone's desktop. I lied and said, "Sure."

"How would you rate your proficiency?"

"Excellent," I said.

"And you can use macros?"

What was he talking about? "Yeah," I said. "Macros? Of course."

Lying about my Excel skills got me that job. However, that backfired. Because I quickly discovered that knowing Excel was the job.

Being a business analyst at Fairchild meant creating performance reports for the twenty or so magazines under the company umbrella. Which meant that I had to produce approximately six gajillion spreadsheets, cross-checking their values, referring one to another. Insane.

Funny story. My first couple of weeks on the job, I kept moving around the office to make it look like I was doing stuff. I kept running into Excel files with titles like "Whitey 9," "Castle 32," or "Castle 17." And I panicked. I wracked my brain and cursed my state-school MBA education.

I remember thinking, *Dear God, nobody taught me the Castle Technique!*

We didn't have Google or AI back then to help us figure things out. Finally, I worked up the courage to ask someone, "What do these terms mean? Whitey? Castle?"

"Oh, that's the guy who used to run this department," I was told. "Whitey Castle. Those are his spreadsheets."

I nearly swooned with relief, and I laughed. I began titling my spreadsheets in a similar vein, like Barrios 3 and Barrios 4. But I wasn't out of the woods. Not yet.

Each day, our office began filling up at 9:00 a.m. It emptied out promptly at 5:30 p.m. I, however, was on a different schedule. Each day, I'd arrive at seven in the morning and stay until eleven at night. Alone in the office, I'd break out the Excel manuals and teach myself the software. There was no other way. We had no laptops back then, so I needed access to the company computers. Day after day and week after week, I did this.

A couple of months later, I was an Excel wizard. Five months into that job, I was better than anyone else in the place. And I proved it.

For instance, the routine was that on the fifth or sixth day of each month, our senior VP got a spreadsheet reporting each magazine's performance over the previous month. One day, Mario came to my office looking panicked. "Uh . . . George? You sent the wrong monthly report to the VP."

I looked up from my keyboard. "It's not wrong. I gave him the right report."

Mario shook his head with an even more panicked look. "Can't be right. It's five days too early. The books just closed today!"

So I explained how I'd rewritten all our files to automatically pull data off the mainframe and populate the fields, making calculations automatically. In other words, I'd reworked an operation that used to take five or six days so it took ten minutes.

He wanted macros? I was like, *Oh, yeah. I got macros!*

Mario couldn't believe it. Neither could the VP who started to grill me on what I had done. I had to explain the techniques that I'd used a few times before he got it and nodded quietly. Looking back, I should have told Mario what I was doing; he was my boss and I should have included him. Very soon, however, this became a familiar dynamic in my career. If I wanted to get something done, I would do it. In fact, I'd go out of my way to overdeliver on what I'd promised you. Still do.

I got a promotion for my adventures with Excel. I still reported to Mario, but I got a better title. Also, if memory serves, I jumped from about $25,000 a year to $30,000.

After less than half a year? *Not bad*, I thought. *Not bad!*

***

The Fairchild offices were on West Twenty-Seventh Street, near the Empire State Building. I'd moved back in with my mom at her studio apartment in Flushing. Each night, I set up my cot on the other side of her bookcase. Each morning, I folded the cot and put it away before taking the 7 train into Manhattan.

Once my income was stable, Mom and I moved back to the Glen-Ora and upgraded to a two-bedroom place for which, if memory serves, the rent was $375 a month, of which I paid half. Things were going well, but I wanted them to be better. Especially since, according to the classified ads, most business analysts were making more money than I was.

One day, I read that Time Warner was hiring. I sent them my résumé. A week or so later, I got a call from their HR department. Lo and behold, the woman on the other end of the line was someone I'd gone to high school with. Let's call her Mary Cappelli.

Mary had been sorting résumés for the job I'd submitted myself for and she'd recognized my name. I'll always be thankful she called me. We spent a few minutes catching up, at which point, I laid everything out for her. "Mary, I'd really love to work for Time Warner."

"Great! They're hiring in Accounting."

I winced. Like I said, I've always been good with math but the thought of drudging through debits and credits, day in and day out—that didn't appeal to me.

"Actually," I said, "I saw this ad for an opening in your strategy group. That's really more my speed."

"Oh." Mary drew in a breath. "Listen, George. I'm not supposed to say this, but Strategy only hires from the Ivies." Pause. "But I can get you an interview with Accounting easy."

To hell with it. I broke down and begged. "Please, Mary. Whatever you can do, just get me an interview with Strategy. If they don't hire me, fine. I get it. But let me take a swing here. Please!"

A week or so later, I found myself sitting across from a guy who is now a media legend. For the sake of this book I'll call him Steve Katz. At that point, he was a young VP at HBO, a division of Time Warner. I found him to be a nerdy guy, quiet and super intense. He didn't look up as he sorted through résumés. "So," he said. "Barrios . . . Barrios . . . I think I remember yours here. . . . Chicago, right?"

"Nope. I live in Queens."

He shook his head. "No. . . . University of Chicago? That's you?"

"University of Connecticut."

That was the first time he looked up at me. I'll never forget the shame I felt. In less than a second, I was diminished.

To his credit, Steve hemmed and hawed. "Look," he said. "Sorry. Not sure how you ended up here, but . . . we tend to recruit from the Ivies."

There was something about how he said that. I went from embarrassed to determined in less than a second. "I just took a bunch of tests for you," I said.

"Yeah, hey, sorry about that. If we'd known—"

"Tell you what," I said. "Pick up the phone and call HR. Check my results. I'll wait. If I'm not the highest score you've ever had, I'll leave right now. But if I'm the highest, you and I keep talking. Okay?"

Our eyes locked. Steve was dubious, but he picked up the phone and called HR. I watched him ask about my scores, saw him listen. Then I watched this little smirk twist up his lips as he hung up the phone and looked at me again. "Alright," he said. "Let's continue."

Long story short, Steve became my new boss and I jumped from making $30,000 a year to $40,000.

Don't get me wrong, there were still a bunch of hurdles in front of me, but that felt like a pretty big win. In fact, if anything, this is sort of where my career really began.

***

Early on, I felt very outclassed. I'd gotten my MBA from a state school but I was working in a sea of Harvard and Wharton graduates. As hard as I tried, I couldn't escape the feeling that I was inadequate. I got in my head about this until, one day, something happened.

I'd become friendly with a colleague who was a couple of years older than me. Let's call him John Cassidy. John had gotten his MBA at Wharton, a very intimidating pedigree. But one day, one of our bosses asked us to run an analysis and include a P&L. John and I reviewed the request and John said, "Let's divvy the workload. Which do you want to do? The P&L or the income statement?"

I had this moment of profound hesitation. Had I heard that right? Finally, I said, "John? The P&L is the income statement."

That look on his face. I'll never forget it. So blank.

Wait, I thought. *He went to Wharton? He's not smarter than me. And he doesn't seem to know anything I don't know, maybe even less.*

All those feelings of inadequacy disappeared in an instant. That's when I figured out that a person's pedigree doesn't mean shit. So what if I'd gone to a state school and other folks went to the Ivies? We all had the same textbooks, right?

I told this once to a friend who responded, "Yeah, but see, George. . . . Ivy Leaguers had professors who *wrote* the textbooks." He grinned.

"Maybe," I said. "But as far as I can tell, that doesn't prove they really *understand* their textbooks. Can you supply a metric for that?"

His face fell flat.

Just so I'm clear, I'm not knocking any school here. As my father taught me so well, education is all about what you want to learn and how willing you are to learn it. He was one of the smartest men I knew, and he taught himself practically everything. Imagine that.

These days, when I hire people myself, I take the quality of a person's character and the depth of their intellect over their pedigree any day of the week.

***

Working for Steve Katz was one of the best learning experiences of my life. He was deeply diligent, heavy on details. He possessed skills I needed to learn back then, and he taught me incredibly well. I watched Steve closely, picking up tricks from him, even imitating his mannerisms. Everything I could steal from Steve I stole and tried making my own.

Here's an example. Whenever our group gave presentations about a new strategic plan, Steve insisted that we generate a thousand different ways of looking at the same problem. I'm not kidding. A thousand different ways. He'd build a compendium of alternative universes. What if this happened? Turn to page 396. What if that happened? We have it on 482.

If our presentation was thirty pages long, Steve required us to build a 300-page backup book.

His approach was to dig deep into material and wallow in data to find hidden insights. Looking back, he was doing what Dad did, crunching the numbers again and again until they rolled over and yielded their secrets.

I took this approach and made it my own. In fact, years later, I became known on Wall Street for being the kind of leader who could delve deeply into any detail of a business. If you asked me for a P&L statement, I'd give it to you . . . plus page after page detailing our margins on the thirty most profitable products our business offered. And I was only able to do this because of what Steve Katz taught me.

However, in some ways, I imitated him too much. For instance, one of the first projects that I worked on at HBO was the launch of HBO Latin America. It certainly helped that I spoke Spanish. We did our work well. That project was a huge success, and I got promoted to manager with a staff of three people within a year. Problem was, I'd never managed anyone before and had no idea how to do it.

No problem, I figured. *I'll just copy what Steve does.* Why not? He was my mentor, a couple of levels ahead of me, and wicked smart.

What I didn't factor in was the fact that Steve was also stoic, super introverted, and laconic. There wasn't a lot of laughter there and I think it's fair to say that many people found Steve hard to approach.

Then one day, Jeff Bewkes came swaggering into my office. Nowadays, Jeff is a legendary media CEO. Back then, he was COO and a rising star at HBO. Picture a tall guy, mid-to-late thirties, sort of a twin to Warren Beatty, very polished, very charming, warm and expressive. Small wonder he later became CEO for all of Time Warner.

I remember Jeff filling my office. He was so tall and my office, at that point, was probably eight by eight feet, at the outside. "So, George." He closed the door. "How do you like your new management role?"

I remember looking past Jeff at the Nerf hoop I'd hung off the back of my door. *Please God*, I *thought, don't let him notice that. I have to make sure that I open the door for him before he leaves. . . .*

"I think it's going well," I said. "I'm laying down the law."

Jeff nodded. "Interesting that you say that. You did great work on the Latin America launch. Even people who didn't report to you took cues from you. You were so excited about that project, you organized work for everyone, gave them jobs. You were having fun and it was contagious. Everyone got excited just being around you. That's when we saw your potential as a leader."

He paused. "What I'm saying, you did really well when you weren't so serious. Where's that energy now? Where's your smile? Your sense of humor? Don't lose that, George. It's what makes you you. And it works."

To be clear, my management style could never be categorized as warm and pleasant. I can be self-deprecating, sure, and I have an irreverent sense of humor. But if we were speaking in basketball terms, I'd say I'm stylistically less like Magic Johnson or Isiah Thomas—smiling, happy, everything's great—more like Kobe Bryant. On the court, I'll kill anyone who gets in my way. I'm very demanding. I often tell my teammates, "Look, if it doesn't obviate the laws of physics, it can be done. So let's roll up our sleeves and just fucking do it."

Still, this thing that Jeff told me cued a dawning realization. "Oh," I said. "Okay. But see . . . I've been watching how Steve does things and—"

"George, you're not Steve," Jeff said gently. "Steve is great at some things and listen, you're right to keep the parts of his style that work for you. But we promoted you because we like who *you* are. You and Steve have different styles. And frankly? I think your style will take you farther than Steve's will. The fact that people want to follow you? That matters. You don't have to beat people up to do it. Yes, you can always demand more from people. But isn't it better to get them excited about the challenge? Use your charisma. That's your most powerful tool."

His point came through loud and clear, though it would be years before I'd mastered it.

Later, I heard someone else say it like this:

Management is about getting people to cut a lot of stone. How do you do that? By measuring the amount of stone that needs to be cut. Making sure that the best stonecutting tools are available. Incentivizing the best stonecutters. That's what management is.

Leadership is different. Leadership is about being able to paint a picture of the temple that's being built, making sure everyone always has that picture in their mind, and knows why the temple must be built.

Jeff Bewkes was basically telling me you can kick a stonecutter's ass if you feel like his productivity's dropping. But you'll probably get better performance if you sit down with him and imagine the temple you're building together.

That's a lesson I still use today.

***

Carol and I got married on July 20, 1991. The most important day of my life was also one of the hottest. The temperature hit 103 and our wedding party, which featured many of our friends from McConaughy Hall, was melting.

Still, it was a joyous time. The ceremony took place upstate in Simsbury, where Carol grew up, north of Hartford, at another St. Mary's Catholic Church.

I'll never forget standing at the altar waiting for Carol to appear. I had what I guess are the typical wedding-day jitters. I kept thinking, *Holy smokes, I'm getting married! This is a lifelong commitment! It's only natural to be nervous.*

But you know that moment when the bride appears in the church and everyone turns around to see her? I remember seeing Carol standing there with her father, whom I adored. I watched him take Carol's hand. And something inside me broke. I don't mean in a bad way. More like when a dam breaks and a river long restrained is released once more to find its own path. Or when an egg breaks as the bird inside it struggles to be born. Something old fractures so something new and wonderful can begin.

I was standing there at the altar with Jorge beside me. He was my best man. And I started to weep for only the second time in my life that I can recall. It all hit me so suddenly. The way we'd lost Dad and how, soon after that, my mom lost her job. How she and I hopped from town to town, school to school, and job to job after that, always struggling, always finding our feet only to have the rug pulled out from under us. Without realizing it, I'd grown up feeling like I had no home. An empty feeling.

But here was this beautiful, smart, capable woman—my Carol—walking toward me. She knew every part of me, even the difficult parts, the ones I'd struggled to hide from the world. She not only accepted these parts, she wanted to be with me in spite of them.

I wept because, there, in that moment, I felt overwhelming stability and love. It was there from Carol and from her family, who've always been amazing to me. It was there from my family and friends, whom I would do anything for—all of whom had come to the church to participate in our ceremony. I had a sudden vision of what it means to be part of something bigger than the sum of two parts. It was such an amazing feeling, you would have cried too, if you were there.

To Carol, I now say this:

We've been married thirty-four years now and our love for each other, impossibly, continues to grow. At this point, when I look back on my life, I see only two periods, Before You and After You.

Before You, I was a talented fuckup struggling to find my direction in life. After You, I began to invest in myself. I paid more attention to school, work, my planning, my future. All because I wanted to be the man you've always believed I can be.

Our years together have been filled with joy. Have we had some tough times? Sure, who hasn't? But we worked through those and always supported each other. We both knew that relationships take nurturing, but I doubt that either one of us ever envisioned what a wonderful life we would build together. And so I say this freely and publicly: Our marriage is the best, most meaningful thing I've ever been lucky enough to be a part of.

You are my everything, Carol, and always will be.

I love you.

***

For our honeymoon, Carol and I took two weeks in Nassau. I was initially uncomfortable with this. I'd never taken so much time for myself. Remember, this was back before laptops and cell phones. So the whole time I was away, I'd pretty much be incommunicado.

Oh, for crying out loud, I thought. *Stop overthinking this. You crushed the launch of HBO Latin America. You got promoted. Things are finally going great. You and Carol deserve some time for yourselves. Go relax for a change!*

With this in mind, I filed my vacation request. My managers approved it, whereupon Carol and I took off for the Bahamas and had a great time.

While I was gone, everything blew up in my face.

CHAPTER SIX

Down for the Count

While Carol and I were away, a project I was supporting blew up.

Multiplexing was HBO's initiative to proliferate content over seven distinct channels, each targeted at a specific market. HBO Latin America was a prime example, aimed at the Spanish-speaking world. We assessed each market's elasticity with an eye toward setting prices, which in turn would drive profits. We were asking questions like: Would our subscribers stick with a single version of HBO, or would they want to multiplex their subscription? If so, at what price points? How many subscribers would we lose by changing our prices? How many would we gain? I had built models to track all this and compare our assumptions to our results.

All well and good. But my boss at the time wasn't what I'd call the sharpest tool in the shed. Knowing I'd be gone for two weeks—and since this was before we had cell phones, laptops, or the internet as we know them today—I left my boss what I called a playbook. A descriptive and detailed action list that road-mapped everything that needed to be done and when to make up for my absence. My playbook listed where key information could be found in mission-critical Excel, Word, and PowerPoint files. It also listed which employees owed us deliverables by what dates and what should be done with the information they were submitting.

Mind you, none of this was required. No one sat me down and said, "Hey, George, you'd better write everything down so your boss won't screw everything up while you're gone." To me, it just felt like the right thing to do, the kind of thing I'd want someone else to do for me if our roles were reversed.

At the risk of sounding self-congratulatory, my playbook was excellent. Anyone could have followed it and succeeded. And yet.

Somehow, my boss fucked things up. It was as if he hadn't read my playbook—or worse, like he willfully disregarded what I was telling him had to be done.

The moment I got back, he called me into his office. He was a soft-spoken guy who'd been born to not rock the boat. Calmly, he told me that things had gone "awry" while I had been gone (that was the word he used to cover for his own ineptitude). I was upset but I figured that would be the end of it. His problem, not mine. That is, until Steve called me into his office.

Steve was congenial about what happened but less laissez-faire. "George, this is unacceptable," he said.

I agreed then politely hinted that the reason things blew up was because my boss hadn't followed my instructions. Twenty fucking pages of instructions.

Steve caught my drift but refused to concede. "I see it this way," he said. "Something went wrong here because you were in charge but you didn't check in."

"Check in? Eric, I left him instructions."

"But you were in charge of the project, yes or no?"

He had me there. That's when I learned a valuable lesson, one which I've always kept front of mind from that point forward. No matter how collaborative you are, no matter how well you understand something or how deft you are at delegating responsibility, when you take ownership of a project, you surrender the luxury of blaming anyone else for anything. Put differently, you can never trust that anyone will do your job as well as you would do it. Nor should you. Because if you're in charge and shit hits the fan, that shit will spatter on you.

I left Steve's office more embarrassed than angry. He was right. If I'd possessed even an inkling of doubt that my boss might screw things up—and I have to be honest, I did—then I should have picked up the phone and checked in to see how things were progressing. The fact that I hadn't meant that I wasn't holding myself accountable.

About six months later, my boss got let go from his job. Guess I wasn't the only one who'd noticed his work ethic was a bit—shall we say—lackadaisical. And sure, I can admit to a little schadenfreude when Steve asked me to fill my boss's position. Which I did. Happily, in fact. But ever since then, when I've taken vacation, I've made sure to stay on top of any open items.

One final way I can put this. If your finger should slip off the pulse, don't be surprised if you wind up dead.

***

Up until this point, Carol and I had rented apartments in Stamford, which wasn't a bad arrangement. But buying a home was important to us. Carol is a roots person. She wanted a place we could call our own.

"Fair enough," I said. "But a place of our own will cost money."

We sat down and did our first budget together. The numbers were painfully clear. And so, for a year and a half after that, I stopped eating lunch out and began making tuna or ham sandwiches at home and brown-bagging them into work. And I began looking for more lucrative employment. Lo and behold, a new opportunity popped up. I went to Steve and told him I was going to resign.

He got angry with me. "What do you mean, resign? We just promoted you!"

This was true. Things were going great at HBO. I had been promoted twice, in fact. Jeff Bewkes, who had given me such great advice, had become CEO of HBO, and a very talented guy named Bill Nelson had taken on the role of CFO. I worked under Bill.

"Come on, Steve," I said. "Look at the market for guys like me. I can make ten or fifteen grand more per year if I move." These days, ten or fifteen grand doesn't sound like much. Back then, it was the equivalent of fifty thousand a year. A bump like that would allow Carol and me to finally buy our own home and build equity in it. Start a family. I couldn't see how my idea to move up in the world wasn't anything but normal and understandable. But Steve got super cold with me.

Soon after that, Bill Nelson called me into his office. He said, "I heard you're thinking of leaving."

I told him I was and I told him why.

Bill said, "George, you've done an amazing job here. We owe you so much. And I want you to know if you ever need my help, you've got it. Also, if you ever want to come back, you'll have a place on my team."

This was a major lesson for me. Where Steve tried to make me feel guilty for leaving, Bill Nelson said, "I support you." The feeling that gave me? I'll never forget it.

Ever since then, I've tried to do what Bill did. Although he wasn't happy that I was leaving, he respected my decision and supported me in that moment. He taught me that it's hard to leave a team where you value your teammates and know they value you. He taught me also that jobs might end and people move on, but relationships and reputations stand the test of time. From Bill Nelson I learned that relationships can pay dividends if you let them. Assuming you put in good work, that work will always come back to reward you, and likely in ways you cannot foresee.

***

Soon after that, I went to work at ConHydro, a business run by a Swedish entrepreneur out of Greenwich, Connecticut. ConHydro used private equity to buy mom-and-pop hydroelectric businesses throughout the US and Canada and roll them up under its umbrella. It then profited from this ownership by maximizing federal tax credits for alternative energy facilities.

To be clear, I didn't take the job because I'm an environmentalist. I took it because my salary jumped from $50,000 to about $80,000 a year. Suddenly I had enough disposable income that I wrote my Aunt Ela a check reimbursing her for all the money she'd lent me through graduate school. ConHydro was based in Greenwich, which meant that when I wasn't traveling, I wouldn't have to commute to the city anymore. And Carol and I could finally buy our first house.

Looking back, this was a classic case of my impetuousness in chasing a few more dollars taking me down the wrong path. But money is money, and at that stage of my career, the financial bump mattered more than strategic career planning.

Despite my new salary, we discovered the only house we could swing was out in the sticks, a place called Newtown in Fairfield County, due east of Danbury. As a city kid, I was ambivalent about living out in the country. All I cared about was that (a) Carol was happy and (b) we purchased a place with a nice flat driveway so I could install a basketball hoop outside the garage.

Our house was out in the woods, situated on two acres. Compared to my boyhood apartment in Queens, it felt like Siberia. Way too quiet. I didn't sleep the whole first month we were there. I kept hearing this awful, high-pitched droning.

"What the hell is that?" I said.

Carol gave me a look. "Al, those are crickets."

Crickets? Huh. I'd heard about them.

Over time, I grew to love our house in Newtown. Mostly I loved it because Carol was there. And she was right. It became a place of our own.

Our home.

I stayed with ConHydro eighteen months before jumping again, this time to a completely different sector.

***

Praxair was a multinational industrial gas company that created and distributed products like oxygen, nitrogen, and liquid carbon to hospitals and factories. In 1995, I got hired to do strategic planning for them. The pay bump was nice, about 15 or 20 percent over what I made at ConHydro. Call it $100,000 a year. I worked for the company's deputy CFO, a competitive, charismatic guy in his mid-forties, J. Robert Vipond. Bob to his friends.

Maybe the most exciting part about working for Praxair was the culture. The company was entirely process-driven, rigorous to the point of stringent. Today, I tell people I got my MBA at UConn, but I really learned about business working for Praxair. We leaped from classroom theoreticals straight into work that got your hands dirty. The unofficial Praxair motto was "Learn by doing." This was a different approach than we'd practiced back at Time Warner.

Why did the two companies have different business models? From what I could see, the differentiating factors were money, sector, and status. Back then Time Warner was part of the existing media sector oligopoly, one of very few companies that dominated a sector and became practically unassailable because they could limit consumer choice, dissuade upstarts, set prices, and lean on their fellow members to uphold each other. When I worked there, Time Warner enjoyed monopoly-style margins, 40 percent if memory serves. They were basically a swashbuckling entertainment company with high growth potential.

Now look at Praxair. They were a big player in industrial gases, but I can't call them part of an oligopoly. For one thing, their sector was too highly regulated. Their profit margins weren't as huge as Time Warner's but they were still healthy, say 15 or 20 percent. The key difference, as I saw it, was that industrial gas, as a sector, wasn't a growth market. It was more stable. More staid. So management hired those kinds of people. If Time Warner was run by swashbucklers, Praxair was run by buttoned-up chemical engineers who wore glasses and pocket protectors and went to bed at reasonable hours.

Don't get me wrong. Under proper conditions, any business culture can work. And hybrids are possible. For instance, I've ended up bringing a little Praxair and a little Time Warner to every job I've taken since leaving both companies, much to my advantage. That's been one of the major edges I've acquired from switching sectors as often as I have. Where most executives develop expertise in one industry, I've benefited from cross-pollination. I've been able to pick and choose from tactics and models that seem to work best and experiment with them in different circumstances.

Show me any successful businessperson and I'll show you someone who, deep down, has a touch of the mad scientist about them.

***

I loved this time of my life. Carol and I were still newlyweds; we were enjoying our house in Newtown. My corporate office was in Danbury, five miles west of us, an easy commute. Carol had just finished her MBA and had gotten a job she loved. This was the first time I felt like everything was coming together.

If I was working round the clock, and I was, I did so by choice. I also spent plenty of time in countries like Mexico and Brazil. I was having a blast and enjoying immense success. Once again, I discovered that my deep-dive approach to analysis and strategy gave me the edge when it came to highlighting business opportunities and process improvements.

About eight months after I joined Praxair, I helped them acquire a company called Liquid Carbonics. Carbonics was located in Chicago, so suddenly I was spending a lot of time there. I focused on integrating Carbonic's $500 million overhead with our own $1 billion overhead to come up with a net post-acquisition overhead of $1 billion. Wall Street wasn't so sure we could generate savings like that. But we did.

When the deal was finally inked, Bob called me into his office. "George, you totally killed it. We want to promote you."

Well, well, well. Suddenly, I had direct contact with Bob *and* his boss, who was CEO of the company. They offered to make me CFO of one of their business units. The next question, however, was crucial. Which one?

The executive staff told me I had a choice between two opportunities. I could either go out to San Francisco and run a business that was more or less aligned with Praxair's core product offering, industrial gases. Or I could go to Dallas, whose business division was far less staid, focused on serving customers in the semiconductor industry with a more varied product portfolio.

Carol and I talked it over. The more research we did, we realized we couldn't decide. Between regional cultures, housing prices, costs of living, climate, and plenty of other factors, there were advantages and disadvantages to living and working in either city.

Then one day Bob called me into his office. "George, the way I see it," he said, "you'll do well no matter where we put you. And don't get me wrong. You still get to choose. But if I were you, I'd go to Dallas. I think you'll enjoy the work there more. Let me tell you why.

"Some businesses are what I call long-cycle, some are short-cycle. Long-cycle businesses are elephants, big and ponderous. They don't change much over time. A lot of them are practically monopolies. In that kind of job, you ensure your product's quality and raise prices at regular intervals. It's all pretty boring.

"By contrast, short-cycle businesses move faster. Customers are more demanding, and product life cycles are shorter. You've got to have the right temperament for all of this, which means you've got to be nimble. You're not an elephant. More like a mongoose. A short-cycle business requires a ton of innovation because your competition is always inventing new products and services to outclass you." He paused and looked at me. "You like baseball, right?"

I affirmed that I did.

"Then think of it this way. In San Francisco, you're guaranteed a single but you'll never be able to hit a home run. Whereas in Dallas, you might strike out, but, if you do a great job, you could hit a grand slam."

That was all I needed to hear. I chose Dallas. Here's why.

When describing each position, Bob had deployed the word "temperament." Jeff Bewkes, if you remember, had alluded to this very same concept when we spoke that day in my office at Time Warner. It's since become a touchstone concept I use when slotting people into roles where I think they'll be successful.

What is temperament? I've come to define the term as one of two factors that get people energized and enthusiastic about their work. The other factor is skill.

If I were to express this as an equation, I might do it like this: $T + Sk = E \rightarrow Suc$, where T equals Temperament, Sk equals Skill, and E equals Enthusiasm, which, in turn, produces Success.

As I see things, it's crucial that temperament and skill both be present to create enthusiasm. Why? Someone who has the right temperament for a job but lacks any skills to get it done will find themselves downcast, frustrated, stymied. By the same token, someone who is skilled at performing a job's technical aspects but doesn't *really* enjoy the work will never progress in it. You have to have both, or it's tantamount to having neither.

Whether or not a person has skills is typically easy to gauge. Temperament, however, is far more mysterious. Less understood. Including, perhaps most importantly, by the person themself.

Another way of thinking about temperament is that it refers to someone or something's basic nature. Consider examples from the animal kingdom. You don't put a Thoroughbred horse out to pasture and expect it to spend all day chewing cud. Thoroughbred horses love to run, whereas chewing on cud is something that cows like to do. Some animals simply aren't built for some things. And people, I've learned, are no different.

Everyone has a basic temperament which, once we allow it to work in suitable situations, produces our best, most aligned, least resistant, and most unique and effective job performance. Two crucial phrases here. First one: "in suitable situations." Meaning you don't assign a hothead to talk jumpers down off a rooftop or a pessimist to work at a start-up. That's just asking for trouble.

Second crucial phrase: "once we allow it to work." A lot of people I've met seem preconditioned to rein in their natural temperament. Which, in essence, is saying they go through life attempting to be someone else, someone who perhaps their parents, spouse, or society approve of. The way I see it, no good can come from this sort of acquiescence. Go back to my animal analogy. A frog who convinces itself it's a cat will nonetheless never catch mice, just like a dog who believes it's an albatross cannot hope to fly over the ocean.

Bob understood what my temperament was. He was an excellent judge of character with a discerning eye for talent. To extend his baseball analogy, Bob knew there was no way I'd be comfortable getting up to bat with a mission to hit singles or doubles. When I work, I swing for the fences. Go big or go home. That's the kind of animal I am. And that's why both Bob and I thought it would be better—for both me and the company—if I took the Dallas assignment.

Learning all this—having everything I've just stated laid out for me the way Bob and Jeff did—was one of the greatest educations I could have ever received as a manager. I'll always be grateful to them for imparting their wisdom to me.

Remember, at this point I was still in my late twenties. I was irreverent and liked to laugh with my team, tell jokes, and have fun. And I could be arrogant. Because underneath all that, the truth was that I still had a chip on my shoulder. In my defense, I kept trying to channel that rage through my work, charging hard, kicking ass, always looking to win.

Plenty of people have asked me how I succeeded in corporate America. Sure, a large part of it had to do with this hard-charging attitude. Working your ass off tends to pay dividends, but only a fool works harder, not smarter. My way of working smarter has always been to indulge my curiosities. To read widely, across different disciplines, and to cross-match ideas. I'm also a huge fan of finding and exploiting asymmetry between risk and return. Basically, I look for opportunities with limited downside but practically limitless upside.

It helped that I liked the money I was earning, the promotions, external validations. But let's be clear here. Everyone loves that. What's unusual, at least as far as I can see, is the commitment I bring to my work and the lifestyle that comes with that over time. Lots of people can knuckle down and push through a couple of tough years. Very few are willing to spend a big part of their lives in the swamp of despair (more on this later). However, from my point of view, that's required if you want to become truly great at anything. And I did. I do.

I recall that I thought of my dad a lot during this interval. An uneducated man who'd risen so high in a union? You'd better believe he worked his ass off too. Sure, he might not have been rich as we know the term now. But he'd done very well for himself.

With all this in mind, I accepted the position as CFO of Praxair Semiconductor.

Carol and I moved to Dallas in 1997.

***

This was another huge jump, bigger than any I'd made before, and in more ways than one. The title. The salary! My yearly income jumped to about $150,000. Holy shit!

Another huge jump was the learning curve. My customers were big American companies like Intel, Motorola, and Texas Instruments. Suddenly, I was tasked with selling them products I knew nothing about. I bought myself four thick textbooks that broke down the process of manufacturing semiconductors. It took me weeks, but I read each book cover to cover.

Then there was the geographic relocation. Talk about culture shock. I'd never been to Dallas. I still remember the first time I got there.

I landed at Dallas Fort Worth International Airport, picked up my rental car, and drove out onto a highway. Before leaving the airport, I stopped at a toll booth. The collector was a young woman (this was long before EZ Pass and RFID technology). I passed her some bills, she gave me some change, and said, "Thanks, honey. Y'all have a nice day."

I think I just blinked at her. Have a nice day?

I thought back to all the times I paid the toll crossing the Whitestone Bridge linking Queens to the Bronx, a bridge famous for people honking their horns, jamming their middle fingers out open windows, and shouting, "Fuck you!" for no good reason at all.

Have a nice day?

But as I was saying: culture shock.

Turns out that in no time flat, I began to enjoy the Southern politeness and manners I heard all around me.

***

It wasn't all unicorns and rainbows. The relocation to Dallas caused some initial angst for Carol and me. We grew up in the Northeast. Our families still lived there. So did most of our friends. Neither one of us wanted to pick up and go halfway across the country where we had no roots, no support network, the wrong accent, and a lack of cowboy boots. But my new job required it.

I remember at one point before we moved, we took a trip out to Dallas to look for a house. God, what a heartbreaking experience. The real estate agent was driving us through different neighborhoods. I can still hear Carol crying in the back seat. And it didn't end there.

There were tears when we packed up the Newtown house, the first home we'd purchased together. Tears when the movers came to ship everything south. Tears on our last day alone in that place. We pulled out of the driveway, bound for the airport. Both of us weeping.

I kept thinking, *What have I done? This woman. My wife. I adore her. She's been my rock. Is this how you treat her? Look at her crying. God, George. Is this worth it?*

But Carol wanted to support me, and we both knew this was a major opportunity. So the answer, it turned out, was yes.

Carol and I ended up having a blast in Dallas. It was a great place for people our age. The house we ended up buying was huge because housing was so much cheaper down south.

Carol found work fast, first for GTE, then for a consulting company. She got a great job and we ended up genuinely enjoying our stay in Dallas. With two salaries, we weren't quite rich, but I remember thinking at one point that this was the first time in my life where I could basically get anything I wanted.

Fly first class? Sure. The company paid for it. Lease a car? No problem at all. Buy expensive wine? Yawn.

On weekends, we'd drive down to concerts in Austin or San Antonio. We took trips to San Francisco, Napa Valley, and Hawaii. And we got our first dog, a Kerry Blue terrier whom we named Bailey.

Meanwhile, I was killing it at work and discovering I'm good at leading. In fact, I was so good that within a year of our moving to Dallas, the CEO of Praxair Semiconductor proposed that I take on a dual role.

"What if you stayed on as CFO of the global business but also served as general manager of North America?"

I accepted.

This made me the youngest GM at Praxair and kicked off a phase where whenever I walked in a room, I was the youngest person there by fifteen years. It was now my duty to interface with and sell directly to some of the biggest tech companies in the US.

Professionally, I was on top of the world. I thought things couldn't get better. Then my first daughter, Alayna, was born.

***

It was 1999, eight o'clock in the evening. I was in the delivery room, taking part in what was happening, thinking, *My God, my God, my God! Look at this!* The beautiful miracle of it. But also, I have to be honest, the overwhelming fear of having this tiny human life as a new responsibility. For the first time, I finally understood what my mom must have felt about me. The protectiveness. That undying love.

It's true what they say. You don't really understand how much your parents love you until you have kids of your own. And it came to me in a flash. Jesus Christ, what the hell was I doing, making Mom's life so miserable all those years? Nearly flunking out of high school. The attitude. The arguments. I owed her an apology.

At that point, Mom was in her late seventies and semiretired; she taught Spanish and Spanish literature classes as an adjunct professor at Iona and St. John's. When Alayna was born and her class schedule freed up, Mom flew down to help us. What a gift to have someone you love so close and to watch them enjoy their time with their only granddaughter. But there was a downside. The moment Mom flew back, the geographic distance between Carol and me and our family and friends back home began to feel crushing.

Carol had planned to go back to work once the baby was born, but once she met Alayna, she changed her mind. She had an overwhelming feeling that she could contribute more to our family by being a full-time mother. This made sense to me. Carol's great at nurturing people. It's endemic to her, like a superpower. I wanted our little girl raised around Carol's energy, though of course it presented new problems.

At that point, Carol was earning about $100,000 a year. Once she became a full-time mother, we wouldn't have that income anymore and we'd still be left with the problem of feeling cut off from our loved ones.

After talking it through, we decided we'd try to move back to the Northeast. I began putting out feelers in Praxair, seeing what was available, even if it meant making a lateral move.

And then something happened that would become one of the most valuable learning experiences of my career.

***

Like I said, I was the CFO for the business. Which meant that every day I was looking for ways to grow our revenues, make operations more efficient, and find new markets to enter. That was my job, and I noticed something in our accounting practices that I believed could be improved.

Our P&L averaged the costs on what we'd paid for items while logging revenue for items sold. Fair enough. But none of our calculations tracked our inventory in transit. These were products sitting in the purgatory between getting made and being delivered and sold. In my view, this created timing discrepancies that underrepresented the performance of our unit. I believed we should be calculating the cost of every 100 units made, including inventory, rather than waiting for delivery cycles that could take one or more quarters. To me, this was about accuracy and transparency—giving a clearer real-time picture of our performance.

I had people working under me who kept feeding me reports and I told them, "No, these numbers need to be more accurate. I want you to average the cost of every 100 units made, including the stuff we have in inventory. That'll give us the clearest picture of what we're spending versus what revenue is."

"That's not how we've always done it," one guy on my team said. "We've only calculated items after delivery."

"I don't care how we've always done it," I shot back. "We paid for those items, they're sold, they're just not distributed yet. Our numbers shouldn't wait for the transit cycle to complete itself."

Again and again this went on, and I was relentless. I kept sending back the numbers I got, saying, "You're not getting it. Look. You have to work harder. For instance, how much specialty product do we have in inventory?"

One of my people just looked at me. Then he said those three little words I've always hated. "I don't know."

"You don't know? Then fly out to the plant."

Looking back, I was trying to implement what I believed was a more accurate accounting methodology. But I hadn't yet learned the lesson Jeff Bewkes tried to teach me. My persona at work was still Hard-Charging George. I was goading my crew with a stick rather than guiding them with a carrot. I didn't like questions. I certainly brooked no dissent.

This didn't go over so well.

Someone from my finance group filed a complaint. They said I was pressuring them to manipulate reporting practices. I had no idea this was happening until one day when I walked into the office and our receptionist stopped me.

"Hey George. There's a guy here from corporate to see you. Ray Ruger?"

That wasn't his real name. I've changed it here for privacy.

"Ray's here?" I said. "Really? Why?"

I knew Ray. I liked him. He worked for corporate internal security. He was ex-FBI with the steel-colored crewcut to prove it. Picture a well-built guy in a gray suit, medium height, creased face, late fifties. I hadn't seen him for months, since the last time I'd been back in Danbury. We'd grabbed a few beers and talked shit at a bar.

I found Ray sitting in one of our conference rooms and went in to shake hands. "Hey, man. Good to see you. Didn't know you're in town."

Ray's face stayed federal-agent serious. "George, close the door. Take a seat."

For the next two hours or so, he described the complaint that the company got. How there was going to be an investigation and I should leave the office while it was going on. As in immediately. I was stunned.

The moment I got home, I called up Bob Vipond, who'd hired me six or seven years back. Then I called John Clerico who, at that time, was CFO of the entire company. Both of them basically said the same thing.

"George, we get it. What you're saying makes sense from an analytical standpoint. But this is the way things are done, see? Please just let the process play out."

A couple of days later, I had dinner with one of the senior corporate leaders for my division. I was there with all his direct reports and we all spoke normally, talking business and planning for the future. I remember going home after that dinner and thinking, *Well, that was awesome. Maybe I'm blowing this whole thing out of proportion.*

They let me go a week later.

***

This experience taught me one of the most valuable lessons of my career. In hindsight, if I were in Praxair's shoes, I would have done the same thing. They were a big, publicly traded company with established processes and little tolerance for ripples, even those that skewed toward innovation.

In the end, I was told that I'd done nothing legally wrong. The issue wasn't the methodology I was proposing—it was how I'd pushed for changes without building consensus or following proper change management protocols. It was suggested—emphasized, might be a better word—that I transition.

Don't you love corporate-speak?

Telling Carol was maybe the worst part, probably because we didn't fight about it. She was incredibly supportive about everything. Obviously, she wanted to unpack what had happened. Though it sometimes seems impossible, she's even more detail-oriented than I am.

We did a postmortem. But finally, I had to beg off.

"Honey, please," I said. "Enough with the twenty questions. It can't change anything now. It's done."

I remember the way she looked at me. "No," she said. "It's not done. It's just gonna change."

"What do you mean?"

"Al, you're a rock star. Sorry to break it to you. This whole thing . . . it'll blow through. We'll figure it out and we're gonna be fine."

I didn't believe that. In that moment, I was devastated.

By that point, my whole identity was constructed on the premise that I was a successful business executive. If I'm being brutally honest, I'd built my sense of myself around that a lot more than being a husband or a father. But suddenly, that identity was gone. Blown to smithereens. Why? Because I'd made a crucial error in judgment about how to drive change in a large organization.

I'd never faced a setback like that. Or its consequences.

***

The day that Praxair let me go, I stayed up all night, unable to sleep. How was it that all our financial plans had been thrown in the river and drowned?

By that point, we had surrendered Carol's income. I was our little family's sole breadwinner, and I'd lost my job. But we still had a mortgage on our great big house. We had car leases. We had expenses for our bright-eyed baby girl.

From dream job to uncertainty. From financial security to questions.

But this wasn't about to break me.

What would Dad have done? I wondered. What did he, in fact, do when his very life was threatened? The life of his family?

The very next morning I got up, had coffee, and started rebuilding.

PART TWO

The Journeyman

CHAPTER SEVEN

Back Up and Punching

For the first time in my life, I found myself jobless, with no income and not much in savings. Looking back, that was a saving grace, because when your back's to the wall, you have no choice but to act.

Carefully, I began to disclose what had happened to people who knew me well. Who knew how my style might be misperceived. Calls began trickling in. One of them came from a friend who had a friend who ran a relatively small tech company.

"This guy . . . he's thinking of hiring a CFO. Want to meet him, see if it fits?"

It fit, indeed—at least for that moment. I cut a deal for about thirty bucks an hour in 1099 income. It was a pittance compared to my Praxair salary, but enough to pay our mortgage and lighten the load while we figured out what to do next.

***

A couple of months into this limbo, I had some interesting talks with Cornelius "Pete" Peterson, the founder and CEO of NetSilicon. They were a small NASDAQ-listed company that provided integrated hardware and software for networked devices. Pete and I had met at a semiconductor conference while I was still at Praxair. I took the stage and spoke for about forty minutes to an audience of two thousand people. Pete liked what he saw so much, he reached out to me afterward and we stayed in touch.

He was probably in his mid-sixties at that point. Not a tech guy, more of the entrepreneur–mad scientist type. His tremendous depth of vision had led him to found a number of start-ups and carve out a life for himself in the tonier suburbs of Boston.

Long story short, Pete hired me. Six months after Praxair let me go, I signed on as president and chief operating officer of NetSilicon. I was working directly with Pete at a salary of about $250,000 a year. And if all that wasn't good enough, NetSilicon was based in Boston.

Carol smiled when she heard this. "We wanted to head back north. And Boston's a lot closer to Connecticut than Dallas. So I guess we got what we wanted after all."

But talk about a culture shift. Praxair, as I mentioned, competed in an established value chain using a rigorous MBA-style approach to strategy, operations, and leadership. In that sort of ecosystem Praxair Semiconductor was considered on the bleeding edge. But they were snug in their beds with lights out by 9:00 p.m. compared to what Pete was doing.

When I climbed aboard NetSilicon, it was a publicly traded company that operated more like a start-up. Not uncommon for a NASDAQ-listed company. Still, it presented challenges, notably that we relied a lot on outside funding to finance operations. Back then, the company's annual revenue might have been $40 million. But we had negative cash flow. So day-to-day, we were a small fish fending off sharks in a very big pond while bootstrapping ourselves among burgeoning technologies in a rapidly evolving sector.

Call it a case of building the plane while we flew it. The business space we operated in was less like New York City during the Industrial Revolution and more like the Wild West. Lots of big characters with big egos, no rules to speak of, and guns a-blazing.

In this precarious situation, I discovered something wonderful. Most of the tools I'd acquired in my career up to that point could be useful in Pete's environment, albeit with tweaks. For instance, a traditional SWOT analysis works best in fairly static settings. I figured that SWOTs would be toilet paper in a situation where circumstances changed daily, sometimes hourly. Until I learned to improvise. SWOTs became my jumping-off point, working with old and new models, stitching theories together, creating novel associations. All to deliver what Pete and the board had asked for: a scaled organization that could bring tailored hardware, software, and services to major industry players.

My analysis showed that NetSilicon had a pretty good semiconductor business. At a high level, we designed low-tech microchips that powered simple devices like household printers. Once we designed them, we took orders to have the chips made at a foundry, or semiconductor fabrication plant—also known as a "fab." Most of our company's revenue came from these low-tech chips and our best customers were some of the biggest names in printer manufacturing—Toshiba, Minolta, and so on.

This was right around Y2K in the midst of the dot-com bubble. The internet was still young, still mysterious. Some people were hyping it up like mythology. Under such circumstances, it was considered sexy that NetSilicon had a NASDAQ listing—never mind the state of our finances. Our company story boiled down to three sentences: "The Internet of Things is real. Soon, every device will connect to the World Wide Web through a chip. If you want to be part of this brave new world, work with us."

It sounded good, it played well to certain audiences, *and* it was true. Behind the scenes, however, we weren't quite as stable as I would have liked.

For instance, there was our situation with design wins. A design win is when, say, SiriusXM radio makes a deal with General Motors to install their product in every Buick that GM manufactures. That's big news for SiriusXM. With their product embedded in Buicks, SiriusXM can legitimately advertise that they're going to sell as many radios as GM sells Buicks. In other words, a design win equals a guaranteed volume of products presold. All well and good, right?

We had a guy on our staff who shall remain nameless, but he was pretty high up the food chain. Let's call him Nick. Nick kept trumpeting, "Look at this! We've got hundreds of design wins in our portfolio!"

A few days after he said this, I pulled him aside. "Nick, this sounds great," I said. "These design wins you're talking about. Can you share them with me?"

"Yeah, sure!"

He sent me a Word doc containing a long list of names. That was it. Nothing more. Just a list.

Unacceptable, I thought.

I called my sales team together and asked them questions. I made an example of the first name on Nick's list. Let's call it Company A. "Which of our chips is Company A ordering?" I asked. "And how many units of each variety? At what price point are we selling them? What volume? What are our profit margins per unit type? What's the length of our contract with each company?"

I was just getting started. "What kind of devices are the chips we're making being embedded in? Computers? Printers? Automated drip coffee makers? What's the end-user demographic for each product? Home use? Commercial? Industrial? How many units of each chip variety is Company A forecasting to contract for per month, per quarter, per year? Does Company A have budget approval to back up these volume forecasts?"

My sales team looked at me, silent, blinking like owls.

"Call your customers," I told them. "Get answers. Nail this stuff down."

One guy had been scribbling notes. "Can you repeat all that?"

"I'll write up a questionnaire. Twenty data points I want you to populate for every customer." I waggled the list of design wins. "We're gonna turn this doc into a database packed with answers to pivotal questions."

Nick seemed a little upset by this. "Uhm, George? Twenty questions times hundreds of customers . . . that's a lot of data points. What do we need all that for?"

I remember electing not to get angry. "How can you sell chips if you don't know what they're used for, where they're going, who they're serving?" I said. "How can we scale our own business if we don't understand which chips have the most use cases and why? Which customers need them the most and at what volumes? The best way to run any business is to know every facet of it from every angle."

Right after that meeting, I went to Pete and told him I was going out on the road for the next three months.

"Where are you going?" he said.

"To meet our customers." I opened my calendar. "Not all of them. Say, about fifty. In San Francisco, Germany, Ireland. I want to put faces to names, see their businesses running. Ask questions. Start conversations."

It soon became clear that most of the deals we'd been calling "design wins" were anything but. Sure, a lot of them panned out fine. We'd cut excellent deals with some pretty large companies. But a few of our "wins" were cases where small to midsize companies had bought our development kit for $10,000. Beyond that, they'd committed to nothing.

To say I revised our list of "design wins" would be an understatement.

I don't want this to sound like I'm kvetching. Mostly, I loved the people I worked with, loved my job. I was flying all over the world, checking in with our customers, paving the road for new deals. Here again, I discovered my talent for leading.

For instance, the Friday of Labor Day weekend in early September 2000, I was in a meeting with Pete, our CFO, and a few of our top operations people. An admin interrupted and said that a call had just come through from our largest customer, a printer manufacturer based in Tokyo. We put the call on speaker and recoiled when the guy on the other end started lambasting us. Lots of colorful expletives in broken English. Something was dreadfully wrong.

Apparently, there'd been an issue with a production run of their chips. We took down the basics and said we'd look into it fast and get back to them. Then we signed off and the room erupted. Everyone was talking over each other, then shouting. Not good.

"Stop this. Stop!" I grabbed my phone and called my assistant. "Book me a flight to Tokyo."

"For when?" she said.

"Right now. Put me on the next flight out."

The other guys in the room stopped talking and looked at me.

"What are you doing?" one of them said.

I got up from my chair. "This company's our biggest customer. We lose them, we're fucked. So I'll go there, address the issue, and show that we care. That's important to them."

"But how do we fix the production run issue?"

"That's your job. Figure it out."

Pete shook his head. "We need you here, George."

"No, you don't. There's twenty people at this company who can figure out who fucked the production line and how to unfuck it. The customer doesn't care about that. They want one person's head on a platter, and they deserve that. I'll be that person."

I got in my car and drove straight to the airport, calling Carol from my car phone. "Hey," I said. "Sorry. Change of plans for this weekend. I'm leaving for Tokyo."

She was befuddled. "When?" she said.

"Now."

"Right now?! Al, who flies to Tokyo on the Friday of Labor Day weekend?!"

I explained what had happened. And this became one more reason why I love my wife. She wasn't happy but she got it. Carol knows who I am and she knows what I do. She respects both.

God, this woman.

The next morning, I arrived at our client's Tokyo headquarters. During the overnight flight I had sketched out a preliminary root cause analysis and cobbled together a rudimentary remediation plan. A plan that unfucked that which was fucked. While far from perfect, it included enough substance to show them that we were on top of the issue. We even offered a 10 percent credit for missing our contractual deadline. Was it perfect? No. But it saved the account. In fact, from there, it started to grow.

At the next board meeting, I remember one of our members saying, "Christ, that took balls. See, that's actual leadership." It made me proud.

I would have loved to have stayed at NetSilicon longer. But then September 11, 2001, changed everything.

***

I won't waste time attempting to tell you what 9/11 meant for New York City, our country, or the world. Suffice it to say that everything everywhere flipped upside down. Economies went into freefall with everyone flailing, screaming, and crying.

Warren Buffett once famously said, "Only when the tide goes out do you discover who's been swimming naked." Fair point.

NetSilicon, as I mentioned, relied on funding to keep us afloat. Which meant we were swimming without any trunks when commerce everywhere ground to a halt. The markets stopped buying our products and our lenders stopped taking our calls. The result was massive liquidity issues that we tried to fix through all of the usual channels. Calls to VCs. Mezzanine financing to bridge the gap. Nothing worked. Financial markets had gone risk averse. All bets were suddenly off.

The writing was on the wall. Our business was fucked. There was one way out.

I stayed on for the next few months helping Pete sell the company to our competitor, Digi International. Pete got pennies on the dollar for years of backbreaking work. It was heartbreaking to watch. Meanwhile I was wondering what came next for my own life and career.

Carol and I had bought a nice house on two acres of manicured lawn in Marlborough, a suburb due west of Boston. We were close enough to neighboring Sudbury that our place was bucolic, enjoyable, stately. "Like living in Sudbury at Marlborough prices," I used to tell people.

I think we paid $480,000 for that house. We loved it. Alayna was two years old and that felt awesome, being her dad. But again, that question: Now what?

I tried taking the long view. Before running NetSilicon, I'd been general manager of a large business. I was on track to do what I'd promised my dad, become CEO of a company. But I figured that no one was going to give me that chance until I'd established more credentials.

I talked to some mentors. Everyone agreed that becoming CFO of a large publicly traded company was the best route to the CEO role. I was already on the CFO track, so I decided it was best to focus there first. "Once you've bagged that," one of them said, "you can transition wherever you want."

Right around here, serendipity struck. Not long after that, my phone rang, and I found myself talking to a guy named Len Foreman.

Len was the corporate CFO of the New York Times Company. He and I had been introduced through a mutual contact at Praxair. Len told me the *Times* was looking for a CFO to lead its second-largest business unit, New England Media Group. NEMG encompassed *The Boston Globe*, the Worcester *Telegram & Gazette*, and their nascent digital properties. The unit had been formed when the Times Company had purchased *The Boston Globe* in 1993.

But this was in 2002. The internet, though still in its infancy, was becoming a thing. And while nobody knew how it would affect the media space, plenty of people were nervous. I got hired to ride the wave of approaching disruption. Also to position *The Globe*'s print media holdings to profit from the changing times.

If memory serves, NEMG was pulling down $1 billion in revenue with about $400 million in profit back then. A nice healthy business. But it was another new sector for me, another new challenge. Once again, I would hit the ground running, learning everything soup to nuts.

Len made it clear I was being hired to add a fresh perspective. The *Times* had fielded a million candidates for the job, all interesting in their own ways. "We like you because you're an outsider," Len said. "A young change agent with a hard-charging temperament. That's you?"

It certainly was. But this caused friction right from the start.

For instance, days after I started my role, I was in the company cafeteria. After finishing lunch, I picked up my tray and brought it to the trash intent on dumping its contents and putting the tray on a stack to be cleaned. But somebody stopped me and said, "Don't pick up your tray. That's a union job."

"Are you kidding me?"

I voiced my opinion about this. It didn't go well. And that was just the beginning.

***

Digging into *The Boston Globe*'s business allowed me to rub elbows with the likes of Marty Baron, a newspaper legend who was then *The Globe*'s executive editor. Marty came up through the ranks as a journalist at the *Miami Herald*, the *Los Angeles Times*, and *The New York Times*. He was also an MBA, a very unusual thing for a journalist. And he spoke fluent Spanish with a wonderful grasp of Cuban dialect, having written extensively about Elián González. While I worked for *The Globe*, the paper won a Pulitzer for its coverage of the Boston Catholic sex abuse scandal in 2003. Marty went on to become executive editor of *The Washington*

Post. He later went on to write a book, *Collision of Power: Trump, Bezos, and The Washington Post.* So I'll say it again: This man was a legend.

I'm not mentioning Marty here to drop names. More to give credit where credit is due. If I ended up being successful in my role at New England Media Group, and I did, it was because people like Marty indulged my requests to learn how our business ran, inside and out. Since I had no idea how *The Globe* got its ideas for stories, I asked Marty if I could sit in on an editorial meeting. He graciously obliged and I became a fly on the wall listening to top reporters kick around ideas while serving the press and its sacred mission.

But let me be clear. Throughout our exchanges, Marty knew who I was and what I represented. It often falls to the executive editor of a newspaper to protect their journalists and the rights of free speech from publishers, boards of directors, and other executives tasked with the calculus of corporate profit. Which is why, one time, he came back from a trip and entered my office proffering a bottle of tawny brown liquid. Genuine Cuban rum. I was pleased.

"¿Por qué?" I said. (What's this for?)

Marty's look turned impish. "Reciprocidad," he said. (Cooperation. Quid pro quo.)

I thought, and still think, this was a wonderful, smart, pragmatic gesture. Marty and I had a great time getting to know one another, particularly while chatting in Spanish. We had many critical debates during my time at *The Globe.* Our conversations were always candid, fact-based, and respectful.

During the deep dive I did on *The Globe*, one of the stranger things I discovered was that their printing presses only ran about 20 percent of the time. When I asked why, I was told, "That's the industry standard." Which struck me as an absurd answer.

"Why," I asked, "are we losing out on revenue and incurring costs when 80 percent of our production capacity is going unused?" Again, this was just the beginning.

I'll never forget one of my first presentations. I gave my analysis of *The Globe*'s operations to a senior strategist at the Times Company. He was one of the best and the brightest, an Ivy Leaguer with all the right names behind him.

"George, George, George," he said, in this condescending tone. "What you're pointing out might be true of other businesses. But we're in the newspaper business."

"Respectfully?" I said. "No, you're not. You're in the *news* business. And how news gets delivered is changing fast. If we don't figure out how to meet this new future, even hundred-year monopolies like *The New York Times* could fall."

I'd seen this happen at Time Warner and Praxair. Successful companies get complacent. They adopt a worldview that makes little sense to someone who doesn't share their same level of complacency. In this view, the primary feature is that economies and technologies must shift to accommodate the successful companies' status. Dead wrong.

Within months, I was seen as a rabble-rouser in the *Times* family of companies. My recommendations were too off the wall. My attitude grated on nerves—I was always laughing, joking around. If memory serves, I was also the only Latino in senior leadership. Everyone else was . . . not.

In my mind, this cemented the crime of homogenous thinking that nearly killed that business dead in its tracks.

***

I was still in my early days at NEMG when Carol and I took another Caribbean vacation. I took a book with me, *The World Is Flat* by Thomas L. Friedman, the Pulitzer Prize–winning commentator on politics, foreign affairs, and global trade. Friedman wrote about how digitization was creating opportunities to connect people and businesses all over the world. One of the offshoots of this was the notion of exporting work to intellectually rich but economically disadvantaged regions. Like India.

I dug into this big-time and found myself shocked. American companies were suddenly free to hire hundreds of talented Indian accountants and analysts who would work nonstop on every angle of company finance for pennies on the dollar compared to the cost of US labor. Take Alcoa, for instance. A global leader in the manufacture of bauxite and aluminum, it was one of several giant Fortune 500 companies that had exported its entire finance group abroad.

My interest was so piqued, I came back from the Caribbean and requested a meeting with my CEO. During that meeting, I passed him a one-pager I'd drawn up.

"What's this?" he said.

"Read it," I said. "It's a précis of *The World Is Flat*."

He put the page down and smiled. "And?"

"The salient point," I said, "is that we're entrenched in a highly unionized labor environment that we can't undo. Unless. If I'm reading our contracts right . . ." Here I broke out my copy of our union contracts. "Process changes can be made so long as said process changes result in reduction of workforce."

My CEO blinked at me. "What are you saying?"

"I want to go to India."

"What? Why?"

I told him why. And he approved the trip.

I flew to India alone and spent a week there touring many different companies. Couldn't believe what I was seeing.

We can do this, I thought.

And we did. Though it took a lot of hair-pulling.

My CEO was against what I had planned. So was most of our senior leadership. I kept showing them my analyses, charts, projections. I held my ground and refused to give up.

In the end, we exported enough operations to India that our business units combined saved over $100 million over the next four to five years. In case it's not clear, this was not a popular decision.

The worst part was when we announced the changes internally during an all-hands meeting at *The Globe*. It felt like a thousand people were packed in that room. And every person there, including most of the executive staff, felt certain that exporting all this work meant they were going to lose their jobs. They were scared, and they eyed me with a hatred I still find difficult to describe.

I went through everything I'd prepared and I kept things simple. Not because I didn't think the crowd wouldn't appreciate nuance. These were some of the brightest people in the news business. No, it was more about a bit of wisdom I once heard attributed to Albert Einstein. To paraphrase: If you really understand something, you can explain it to a six-year-old. If you can't explain something to a six-year-old, then you don't really understand it.

That meeting got pretty damn tense. I was accused of being everything from a union buster and a racist to a heartless corporate profiteer and the bastard spawn of Satan. Once it was finished, a colleague approached me and took me aside.

"You know," he said. "You got one good thing from this meeting. If anyone there didn't know who you are, they do now. And they sure as hell know what you stand for."

I think I just grunted. I felt pretty lousy. It was also another reminder that real leadership is often about doing things that can be very painful. The easy thing to do? Nothing. Let the company fail. Have *everyone* lose their jobs. Meanwhile the "leader" moves on and finds something else. The hard thing to do? Fix the business so it can grow and prosper in the future. Yeah, that might mean cutting 20 percent of the jobs. Or is it *saving* 80 percent of the jobs? You tell me.

This guy was persistent. "George, you told the truth," he said. "And whether or not they like it, people respect that. They might hate what you said, but on some level, they know what's at stake here: the long-term survival of news as a mission. If we lose that battle, it's not just our jobs, it's the culture, the country, and maybe the world."

Okay, I thought. *Maybe.*

Not long after, the economy slowed again and we found ourselves sorely tested.

***

This was a couple of years before the subprime mortgage crisis. I was keeping an eye on all sorts of factors, from the Fed's target interest rate to the pace of hiring both generally and in our industry. I'd concluded that something was afoot, something big, and we had to be ready to meet it because it would complicate the problem we already faced: digitization.

It was clear to me that newspapers were a dying medium. Again, not the news. Just newspapers. I set out to prove this with all sorts of charts and graphs showing ways we could leverage the new trends. But everything I said fell on deaf ears.

For months, I watched some of the smartest people at Times Company twist themselves into knots to deny what I was telling them. My analysis showed that our basement was flooding. The water was up to our necks down there, rising faster and faster each day. Our leadership responded by asking me to get an eyedropper and grab a few drops of water for analysis. It was insane.

Our fights continued. Another tense meeting came about over the classified ads, which, since newspapers began, have served as a publisher's revenue pipeline.

"They're going away. The classified ads," I said.

Once again I was presenting to the CEO and management team of the entire *Times* organization.

"George, George, George . . ." The CEO rolled his eyes.

"Why should anyone place their job ads with us for . . . I'll make up a number here . . . $500? When they can practically place it for free on Monster.com and get wider reach plus instantaneous results?"

"Is this about the recession again?" The guy who said this was one of their strategy geeks, a Harvard MBA who'd been with the company twenty-plus years. This guy was brilliant, I'd be the first to admit it. He knew I was deeply concerned. But he considered it one of his pet projects to talk me down whenever I said the sky was going to fall. "This is a hiccup," he said. "We've weathered recessions before."

"Not like this one, we haven't."

"George." This guy glanced at his colleagues and grinned. His subtext was clear. *George is like Chicken Little, always crying, "The sky is falling!"* "George, I just think you don't really get what's going on here."

I broke out my laptop. It was bigger than laptops are now. By a lot. I also reached into my bag, brought out a copy of *The Sunday Times*, and gave it to Mr. Harvard MBA. "Let's try an experiment," I said. "You and I will both look for CFO jobs, okay? I'll probably need one after today. I'll check websites. You check the paper. Ready?"

The guy held up the paper I'd given him. "I—"

"Go."

You can probably guess how this ended. In a matter of minutes, I found thirty advertisements for CFO jobs before Harvard MBA found even one in the tried-and-true Classifieds section. I closed my laptop and looked around the room. "Who here sees what I mean? It's not just speed. It's the reach, the convenience, and the cost. Listing a job on the internet can be done for a tenth of the price we're charging right now. Plus, when they work via websites, employers and job seekers both can file postings from anywhere in the world, whenever they want."

I paused and made it a point to look everyone there in the eye. "You might not like what I'm saying, but this is the future. We have to face it. Because if we don't prepare ourselves, right now, we're finished."

The thing about being the canary in the coal mine? Everyone hates you once you start singing.

And sometimes you end up hating yourself.

This can lead you to make bad choices.

***

I was still in my mid-thirties, and by any assessment, things were going well. I had a beautiful wife and daughter. We lived in a gorgeous home and could afford things I'd never dared dream of when I was a kid growing up in Flushing.

Yeah, sure. I was working my ass off. So what? I've always been great at hard work. Long hours meant nothing to me. Bottom line, I'd become the CFO of a billion-dollar business. I was setting my sights on the ladder's next rung, my dream of becoming CEO of a company.

But then.

One night, a work colleague threw a party at his place and invited people from work. I drove out there. It was a barbecue. Hamburgers. Hot dogs. Beer. I was among friends. I really enjoyed myself.

Back then, it was pretty common for me to go out after work—say, once or twice a week—with my colleague, Yasmin. We were cut from the same cloth. She's a hard-charger too, a change agent who'd been with the Times Company over twenty years before a new role had sent her to Boston. We would grab dinner, have a drink or two, and talk shop about 80 percent of the time. The remaining 20 percent we split between politics and family stuff.

Yasmin sometimes checked in with me as I headed back home for the night. "George, you okay?"

"Sure," I said. "Why?"

"We had a couple of drinks."

I caught her drift but I assured her. "I'm good."

"George." Yasmin would give me this look. "Think it through. You don't want a DUI. Imagine the field day the *Post* and *The Herald* would have with that."

The *New York Post* is *The New York Times*' ancient nemesis. The *Boston Herald* has the same relationship with *The Boston Globe*. Yasmin was right. If an executive from the Times Company showed up on somebody's police blotter, the other papers would make hay of it. Big-time.

"I'm fine," I always told Yasmin. When, truth be told, sometimes I probably wasn't.

Case in point, I was most certainly not fine after that barbecue. While I was driving home, a police officer pulled me over and I was over the line. I got arrested. They put me in jail and I went to court where—yup, you guessed it—I got slapped with a DUI. Which meant that I lost my license, but I also lost something bigger and much more important: my dignity. Not to mention this constant battle I'd been fighting all my life with perhaps my most powerful personal demon.

There are obvious lessons here. Don't drink and drive? Yeah, sure. Okay. But let's go deeper.

A couple of years later, the guy who threw that barbecue party took his own life. A few days before he killed himself, he reached out to me. Said he wanted to have dinner. It worked in my schedule, so we did.

He seemed pretty normal. I had no idea he was suffering. He left his family behind. Young kids. It's a tragedy. Why do I mention this?

Before this book was published, I asked my cousin GGQ to read it. He was shocked and dismayed by my DUI confession. "Wow, George," he said. "Are you sure you want everyone to know about this?"

Absolutely. I told you before, I won't bullshit you. Talking about myself—the good and the bad . . . how else can I move forward unless I admit to where I have been? What good will it do you, the reader, to hear the sweetness without any sour?

In Japan, there's an artform called kintsugi where broken pottery is mended using special gold lacquers. In kintsugi, fractures aren't hidden but glorified. No one says, "See? This vase or this cup is brand-new!"

Instead, they say, "Look at this weld. This is where the vase was broken once. But look how much stronger it is because it was broken. And isn't it more beautiful this way, because of its imperfections?"

I believe in this approach to work and to living. So many people struggle to hide the wounds left behind when painful things befall us. The cracks in our self-images. All our fissures and imperfections. Why bother? Remember what Leonard Cohen once said: "There is a crack in everything. That's how the light gets in."

Let's go back to this man who died by suicide. I can only imagine that he was fighting a terrible battle inside himself, a battle that nobody else could see. Perhaps in his mind—that theater where all of our private worlds play out—titanic forces were pushing against one another. And whatever pressures were crushing this man from within, they must have been unbearable for him to do such a terrible thing to himself, not to mention his friends, his family, the world.

Back then I had something similar going on inside me. Something that needed to be addressed before it caused irreparable damage. And not just to me, but to everything and everyone I cared about.

I won't lie and say I never took another drink after my DUI. But I will say this to anyone reading this: Take care of yourself. Do the work. By which I mean, take stock of what's going on inside you. Do not run away from what you find. Go into your issues and try to make sense of them. And always remember: You're not alone.

Here again, if I hadn't had Carol, my kids, and the rest of my family, I wouldn't have a life worth saving in the first place.

CHAPTER EIGHT

The 10-K Revelation

Getting a DUI became a royal pain in the ass. Up to that point, I had driven myself to work. Not anymore—it was public transportation for me, the headache of buses and trains, on top of which I waged a campaign to hide what had happened from everyone in my office.

Mercifully, Yasmin had been wrong. The *Post* and the *Herald* never ran stories about me. Even so, I was deeply embarrassed. If anything good came out of my mishap, it was my renewed focus on someday becoming the CEO of a company. Being CFO of a business unit was no longer good enough. Now, more than ever, it was a stepping stone, not a destination.

All this happened at a strange moment in the economy. This was around 2004. The Enron collapse was still rippling through the economy. For those who don't remember, Enron was an energy and commodities company based in Houston. Between 1985 and 2000, its founder, Kenneth Lay, built Enron from a start-up to a juggernaut boasting over $100 billion in revenue.

The key word there is "boasting." Enron built its fabled success on what later turned out to be widespread, intentional accounting fraud. In fact, the conduct of Enron's officers was so egregious that today, the name "Enron" is synonymous with corporate corruption.

The blowback was massive. Exposure to Enron stock was endemic throughout world markets, which were already straining under the weight of a recession plus ominous rumblings that something was terribly wrong in the subprime mortgage market. Every corporation on the planet feared what happened to Enron happening to them. Many became so risk-averse, they started demanding that CFOs of public companies be not just MBAs but certified public accountants.

Lovely, I thought. I'm so fucked.

I was thirty-nine when this happened, and by that point in my career, I'd realized that business was my passion. Certainly not accounting. Accounting was a backward-looking art, whereas I preferred forward-looking strategies. Don't get me wrong, I knew how to do the work—it was part of my role and I had become *very* good at it. But I'd always let someone more skilled in that domain run those processes. Not anymore. The job market had spoken. If I was to keep climbing toward a CEO position, I'd have to earn my CPA.

The situation looked bleak. By tradition, you became a CPA by working first as a public accountant for some large firm that audited companies. But I already had a job. I was a CFO. I wasn't about to switch careers at that point. Mercifully, I discovered there were exceptions. The Commonwealth of Massachusetts would grant CPAs to people who had sufficient financial background, provided they had taken at least eight accounting courses. My transcripts showed I only had two. I needed six more.

Enter the University of Phoenix online. I applied and got in. Then I knuckled down, doing the work.

Alayna was four when all this was going on. She's always had an amazing memory, and during this period she recalls me coming home from work and spending a few hours with our family before rushing off to sit with my desktop computer in our tiny office. One whole year of this, then another six months boning up for the CPA exam.

This wasn't like how, back in high school, I'd aced my exams on a wing and a prayer. If the SAT is a glorified IQ test, and it is, the CPA exam is driven purely by content. Different animal. There's no way around it. You have to prepare. To help me with that, I bought a pack of audio CDs and listened to them over and over. The narrator had this curious Southern American accent. Hard to forget.

"This next question will test your knowledge of auditing and attestation," the narrator drawled. "Suppose that a former audit client requests a CPA to reissue the auditor's report for a prior accounting period. Before reissuing such a report, the CPA should . . . (a) Review the former client's records to see whether or not the client has been compliant with its loan and debt—"

Alayna walked into the office. "What are you listening to, Daddy?" she said.

I kept things simple. "I'm learning how to be an accountant."

The Southern-fried narrator's voice continued. "(b) Make inquiries into pending litigations by sending a message to the client's attorneys of record—"

"What's an accountant?" asked Alayna.

"They're the people who track all the money in a business and make sure the business is healthy," I said. "You want to listen with me?"

She nodded. I pulled her into my lap and we sat there together as Chicken Fried Narrator said, "(c) Consider the client's ability to exist as an ongoing business . . ."

"Daddy?"

"Yeah, honey?"

"I want to go play."

"Okay," I said.

Once, during this period, my mother came to visit us. She saw how hard I was working and joked, "Espera. ¿Cuántos trabajos tienes ahora?" (Wait, how many jobs do you have now?)

She said that despite how long and hard I was working, I was probably earning less per hour than fry cooks made at McDonald's. Who knows? She might have been right. And I didn't care. The potential returns were worth it.

I was carrying incredible pressure during this time—juggling a demanding CFO role, CPA studies, and family responsibilities while keeping my struggles to myself. I never shared the weight of it with anyone, not even Carol. This tension continued for years. Unfortunately, it sometimes manifested itself in getting frustrated with my family. This is one of my biggest regrets. Today we might call that a mental health issue.

I ended up earning my CPA just as Enron melted out of economic consciousness. No matter. I'm still glad I put in the effort. In some way, I felt as if I had atoned. I'd shown myself that when something is really important to me, even if I don't like it, I'm still willing to go to the mats for it. I *could* study accounting!

I also got over my previous distaste for accounting arcana. While I'll never proclaim myself a gifted accountant, I can say—with no small pride—that I know what I'm talking about.

Then Carol got pregnant again and our world flipped upside down once more.

***

This is one of my life's most vivid memories. We were in the doctor's office to get an ultrasound. I was sitting in the waiting room thinking, *No problem, we've already been through this once with Alayna.* At precisely that moment, the nurse poked her head out. "Mr. Barrios? Could you please come into the room?"

The human imagination is perhaps the most powerful force on earth. Give it the tiniest seedling, it can grow gardens, forests, and jungles of thought and emotion in less than a second.

Wait. What? I thought. *They didn't ask me to do this the last time. Is everything okay?*

I almost threw up while walking the hundred feet or so back to meet Carol. Imagine my surprise when she looked up from the bed with tears in her eyes and this huge smile on her face.

"We're having twins!"

I remember we held one another and, God, what a powerful moment that was. But then my imagination kicked in again. The voices of fear and doubt started murmuring inside my skull:

I hope it's not boys. You know how hardheaded you can be, George. You'll probably get in a fight with your own sons. Please please let it be girls. . . .

For the record, I've since learned how wrong I was. Raising girls can be . . . ahem . . . challenging.

Still, God must have been listening. Carol gave birth to two beautiful girls, Katrina and Celia.

God, we were so happy.

***

There were new challenges. Alayna was five by then, self-sufficient for her age and thrilled to have two baby sisters. But she still needed lots of attention. And one infant alone takes an army. But two?

How are we gonna manage this? I wondered. I work late and travel a lot. Even with family to help us, Carol can't do this alone.

I logged onto the internet—that growing stream of constant possibility—and did some research. There were professional services that provided in-home nurses and caregivers, particularly in the evenings and overnight, and helped out with newborns. My concern was the expense. I couldn't believe how much these services cost. Carol had different concerns. She didn't want strangers coming into our home. She was adamant about this.

But a couple of weeks after we brought the girls home, I woke up one morning and stumbled into our living room, wiping sleep from my eyes. Carol was on the couch, holding Celia in one arm, Katrina in the other. Somehow she'd managed to give them both bottles.

We were both in that zombified stupor that parents of newborns plunge into for a year or so. I was trying to recall if I'd been the one who got up at midnight to feed the girls.

Yes, I thought. *Remember? Carol took over the next two shifts so you could get four hours sleep and be fresh as a spoiled daisy for your big meeting today at the office.*

I'd been promoted again to a dual role, CFO and COO of New England Media Group.

"How did it go last night?" I mumbled.

"Call the nurses," Carol said. "We need help."

So I did.

That turned out to be one of the best moves we ever made.

To hell with what it cost. Money's worthless if you don't spend it on what's important.

***

Our corporate CFO, the financial head of the entire New York Times Company, was about to retire. The company announced it would launch the requisite search to find his replacement.

This is what I've been waiting for! I thought.

Being CFO of a blue-chip name-brand company would be the perfect springboard to becoming CEO someplace else. As I saw it, I was perfect for the role. I'd been with the Times Company a few years and had plenty of institutional knowledge. I was both CFO and COO of their second-largest business unit, kicking ass and taking names. I was young but not too young. And, because of my cost-saving initiatives, I was respected at the company if not exactly beloved.

I was thrilled when the company's CEO told me I was one of two internal candidates for the job. Excited, I went through the interview process, but the job went to somebody else and I didn't take kindly to that. In fact, I took it so poorly, I began looking for CFO jobs outside the company.

In short order, I got an offer from a reputable private company in Boston.

Well, that's that, I thought. *Time to move on.*

I accepted the offer and went back to work, preparing for my transition. Then one weekend Carol and I took the girls to a family amusement park called Story Land up in New Hampshire. It's a great little place where kids can go on all sorts of age-appropriate rides and take part in interactive nursery rhymes like "Humpty Dumpty" or "Goldilocks and the Three Bears." The girls were in love with the place, which made Carol and me feel great.

I remember us angling toward the part of the park where Little Miss Muffet would sit on her tuffet to eat her curds and whey when a booming announcement came over the loudspeaker.

"George Barrios . . . George Barrios . . . if you are in the park . . . you have a phone call. . . . Please come to the customer service kiosk. . . . George Barrios . . ."

Cue terror. Had something happened to Mom? To someone in Carol's family? Remember, this was before cell phones became ubiquitous in our lives, so a random phone call in the middle of the day was *not* normal. I left the girls with Carol and took off running.

Turns out the call was from Janet Robinson, CEO of the Times Company. "Sorry to interrupt your vacation," she said. "I heard you're moving on, is that right?"

I told her it was.

"Listen," she said. "Before you do that, come in and talk to me. I think I can offer you something."

Long story short, Janet offered to make me treasurer of the New York Times Company. I wasn't charmed by the offer.

Technically, being treasurer of a large publicly traded company was outside my skill set. Corporate finance has three main branches. First, accounting, auditing, and tax—making sure the numbers are right. Second, capital markets—how do you fund operations and invest profits? Third, strategy and operations—how do you grow the business? Being company treasurer falls into the second branch, while my experience fell more in the third. I was all about growing businesses. That was my passion. I was about the future.

I explained how I saw things to Janet, but she dismissed my doubts. "You're a fast learner, you'll figure it out," she said. "We'll support you in the role and help you grow into it."

But there was also a staffing issue. The then-treasurer at NYTCo. was a guy named Anthony Benten. Like me, Tony had offered himself for the CFO position. Like me, he hadn't gotten the job.

"How can I be company treasurer if that's Tony's role?" I asked Janet.

"Tony's moving over to the controller position."

Again, I had my doubts. Tony and I knew one another; we got along well enough. He'd been a passionate treasurer for the Times Company. It was my understanding that being treasurer was his dream job. Would he take kindly to such a move?

"I don't know, Janet," I said. "To be honest, I wanted the CFO position so that I can segue into a CEO position at a publicly traded company. That's really the trajectory I'm angling for."

"George, think," Janet said. "As treasurer of a public company, you can later become CFO anywhere you want. It's actually a better stepping stone for you than being CFO of a private company." She shook her head. "This will look better for you. Also, you'll be working out of Manhattan. Which means you and your family can move back to Connecticut."

I think I blinked at her. Janet had certainly done her homework on me. She sold the job so well that in the end I accepted the role, albeit with some trepidation.

Turns out my doubts were justified.

***

First, I had to untangle myself from the CFO role I'd already accepted in Boston. For anyone reading this book for career advice, I don't recommend reneging on commitments. That's a great way to burn bridges in the comparatively small universe of senior executives where reputations mean everything. And as you'll see in a forthcoming chapter, I ended up making this mistake again anyway. Sometimes you have to learn the hard lessons twice.

Then there was Tony Benten, who I think is a really great person and deeply talented. I had heard that Tony resented me for pushing him out of the treasurer role. That he didn't want to be the controller, and he aimed his ire over being displaced at the guy I suppose he saw as the architect of his downfall: me.

I felt like I got zero support from Tony in my new role. And boy, did I need it.

For instance, as company treasurer, one of my responsibilities was to run the board's finance committee, which focused on the ins and outs of debt, dividends, cash flow, and so on. I'd never been to a board meeting for the Times Company, let alone run a committee meeting. I couldn't make heads or tails of Tony's notes from the previous meetings. When I approached him for clarification, my calls were never returned. At that point, I got the impression that he hated my guts.

I'd only been treasurer a few weeks and I had no idea what I was doing when I led my first finance committee meeting. I walked in armed with a one-page agenda. I was nervous, out of my element. The room was filled with titans from the pages of *Bulfinch's Business Mythology*. And who was I? Just some mortal, an annoying gnat who buzzed around their ears.

For instance, Jim Kilts was our committee chair. Jim was big-time, the real deal. Physically, he was central casting's idea of what CEOs should look like, well over six feet tall with a full head of gray hair, handsome, smiling, and commanding. If you'd told me he'd served in the US Marines as a battalion commander, I would have believed it. He had that kind of grit and it served him well in 2005 when he orchestrated the sale of Gillette to Procter & Gamble for $57 billion. I was also a huge fan of his book, which was new on the market at that point, *Doing What Matters*. Highly recommended.

Doreen Tobin was there, too, a legend in the telecom sector. She was one of those success stories you love to read about. Fresh out of college, in 1972, she took an entry-level position in the treasury department of AT&T. Then she moved to Bell Atlantic, where she managed crews of channel switchers and ditch diggers. She was literally in the trenches. Verizon bought Bell Atlantic, and years later she was the company's CFO. When I worked with her at the *Times*, Doreen was smack in the middle of leading an $8.5 billion acquisition of Verizon's rival, MCI. She'd helped her company reduce debt and pour funding into the developing sectors of fiber optics and broadband. As a corporate strategist, she was at the top of the game.

Tony also attended my first meeting. Someone had asked him to be there, I guess, to ensure continuity. I recall getting nothing from him but this constant schadenfreude grin as I introduced myself and began my presentation. Which, if memory serves, took approximately two minutes.

This can't be right, I thought. *I'm fucking this up.*

I was still wet behind the ears in this role. I was not prepared to lead meetings like that. Not by a long shot. When I finished, I looked up knowing full well that this was the worst meeting I'd led in my career up to that point.

Dead silence. The board members glanced at each other. Uncomfortable stares.

Jim broke the impasse by chuckling. "Well," he said. "That was the shortest finance meeting I've ever been in."

Looking back, I can see he was trying to be kind. But everyone laughed and I felt humiliated. Like the spic on a bus all over again. So I did what I've always done when adversity happens. I stiffened my spine. I went back to work and I vowed to do better. To dig even deeper and come up with something that I could be proud of.

***

Things got better, little by little. Janet was right. I picked up the job pretty fast and began to enjoy being treasurer. It helped that Mom kept gushing to friends and family about how successful I was. Our clan had always been big newspaper readers. Now my name was listed on the masthead of maybe the greatest newspaper in the world.

“Mira a Georgie!” Mom would trumpet at gatherings, pointing at me from across the room. “Mira a mi hijo! Es un monstruo!” (He’s a beast! In Cuban Spanish, this means that a person is at the top of their game.)

Suddenly the years of suffering I’d put my mom through all seemed worth it.

Meanwhile Carol, the girls, and I were having a wonderful time. We’d moved back to Connecticut and bought a home in Fairfield, where we live to this day. I’d long since gotten my license back and I drove my car to the train station every day to make the 5:56 into the city. Eight minutes of alone time. Bliss. The meditation of working my turn signals, gliding from one lane into another, the burr of the wheels on the road.

Looking back, I believe it was this feeling of peace that allowed me to meet my next challenge.

I’d only been treasurer six months and spent most of that time poring over the company’s financial data. I was parsing everything I read eight ways from Sunday. Dad, Malcolm McBain, and Steve Katz would have been proud. And that’s when I saw it.

I presented my findings at the next finance committee meeting. “In absolute terms, the *Times* doesn’t have a large pension plan,” I said. “However, our plan makes up a significant percentage of our total assets. In fact, compared to other public companies, we have one of the largest pension to total asset ratios. Now look at this.”

I toggled a slide. Then another slide. And another. In fact, I spent the next ninety minutes toggling slides. I was deconstructing the company’s capital structure, focusing on the interaction of our debt, dividend policy, and pension strategy, and the effect all of these had on the company’s overall cash flow. Why was this important? Because every company’s cash flow is directly tied to its ability to execute its long-term strategy.

The finance committee had sat through the two-minute fiasco of my first meeting. Now they were witnessing my master class in pension plan management.

A robust discussion followed. People questioning assumptions. We kept flipping back twenty pages in the materials to review, once again, what we’d already discussed. I remember people hardening their thinking throughout the back-and-forth. The process was both exhausting and exhilarating.

When the meeting ended, Jim and Doreen approached me.

"George, I've been on several finance committees in my career." Jim looked at Doreen. "Together, we've been involved in issues like these for more years than either of us wants to admit."

Doreen nodded. "We've never seen anyone explain what you did this way. So clear, so simple. The issue looks so small. . . ."

"But it could be big," Jim agreed. "Too big for us to handle if something goes wrong. We're going to recommend your plan. How long do you think it will take to complete?"

"Give me six to nine months," I said.

I got to work. And just in time. At almost exactly the moment I finished, 2008's global financial crisis struck. Markets everywhere collapsed. It was the most severe financial downturn since the Great Depression and it ruined many businesses.

Years later, as I was segueing out of the treasurer role for my next opportunity, a senior leader at the *Times* thanked me for making two key contributions during my tenure there. First, I helped adapt the Times Company to a new global digitized media model. Second, I'd recognized the risk our company faced and taken the proper steps to avoid it.

Initiatives like these never get a ton of airplay outside a company. But they're two accomplishments that now, looking back, I'm most proud of.

Being treasurer at the Times Company confirmed my view that experts are invaluable when you are seeking to learn. However, very often experts are the last people to consult if you wish to make a significant leap forward. Most of the time, experts are just too invested in what *is* to see what *can be.*

***

Okay, back to my dream of becoming CEO of a publicly traded company. My closest advisors were still saying I should land a CFO role first. So I began making subtle inquiries to recruiters.

I'm treasurer at the Times Company, I thought. *That's gotta be worth a lot.*

Not really, as things turned out. Sure, my role was impressive. But I was still facing a catch-22. Recruiters told me that nobody wanted to hire someone as CFO of a public company who hadn't already been CFO of a public company. One recruiter suggested, "You could break into that loop by becoming CEO of a private company that goes public."

Right, I thought. *Or this weekend I could win the Powerball.*

It was a frustrating situation. But one day I got a call from a guy in his early thirties who'd been assigned my account at consulting firm Spencer Stuart. His name was Adam Kovac and he'd been working his tail off for me.

"George!" Adam said. "I've got a really interesting opportunity for you, CFO of a publicly traded company in the media business. Right now, they're pulling down $300 million in revenue, $40 to $50 million in profit annually."

That was smaller by far than the Times Company. But if Adam was right, it was a shot at what I wanted. "Okay, Adam, I'll bite," I said. "What's the opportunity?"

"It's WWE."

"Who?"

"World Wrestling Entertainment?"

"What's that?"

"You know, professional wrestling. Hulk Hogan? André the Giant?"

Ah. Of course. My mind flashed back to sitting on the floor of my Aunt Ela's living room with Jorge and Abuelo in Flushing, watching muscular men in spandex hurl each other around a ring. "You mean that fake wrestling shit you see on TV?" When Adam didn't answer, I said. "Dude, are you fucking kidding me? This is the shit you call me with?"

What Adam did next endeared him to me forever. "George," he said. "You're always telling me you've got to dig deep and get the data. To look at things differently. Right?"

"Come on, man . . ."

"What do you know about WWE as a business?"

"Adam, look . . ."

"No, you look, George. 'Just give me the data, I'll form my own opinion.' How many times have you told me that? Maybe you should learn something about these guys before you dismiss them outright."

This son of a bitch was quoting me back to myself. And it worked. He was right.

"Let me send you their latest 10-K," Adam said. "Look it over. Then, if you're interested, we'll keep talking. Alright?"

Funny, I'd said almost the same thing to Steve Katz years before.

"Fine," I said. "Send me the 10-K."

Then I hung up.

CHAPTER NINE

Into the Ring

A publicly traded company's 10-K filing is its mandatory annual financial report. The US Securities and Exchange Commission requires such documents for transparency. Without them, investors can't make smart decisions. I spent a great deal of time poring over WWE's 10-K. I liked what I saw, so I called Adam back and ate crow.

"Okay, you hooked me," I said. "Pretty interesting opportunity. There hasn't been a lot of growth over the past few years. But the business has a good size and it's been consistently profitable." I paused. "Can you get me an interview?"

"Consider it done."

Adam made good on his word. A couple of weeks later, I began meeting with WWE's senior leadership. My fifth and final session was with Vince McMahon.

Meeting Vince felt weird. Like I said, I'd grown up watching him parade around various wrestling rings on TV. And I'd followed his life a bit. It was hard not to. He was in the news. A lot.

For instance, I'd read how the US government went after Vince in the 1980s for steroid use. His lawyers told him to settle the case, but Vince refused to admit he'd done anything wrong. He ended up winning in court, which never happens. When the US government wants you for something, they normally end up prevailing.

There were also the handful of moments that Vince lost his shit on camera. Like the time in February 1985 when he interviewed Dr. D. David Schultz on an episode of *Tuesday Night Titans*. Schultz was in the middle of showing Vince his gun collection (yup, live and on camera) when one of the weapons went off and Vince . . . well, he didn't take kindly to that. I'll let you look that one up for yourself.

Or there was the time in 1998 when Vince kept telling an interviewer for *Inside Edition*, "Don't tell me what I'm saying!" He did this over and over again with this weird demonic grin on his face. Or that time in 2001 when he threw down with Bob Costas in a televised interview over the failure of Vince's business venture, the XFL. The list goes on.

Now imagine me sitting in the same room with this guy. I made the mistake of expecting him to be like that character I'd seen: a tough guy, the muscle-bound swaggering villain. I wasn't prepared for the fact that Vince is brutally introverted. In fact, I found him so shy, he seemed at pains to make eye contact with me.

Huh, I thought. *Guess it's true what they say. You can't judge a book by its cover.*

Vince largely kept quiet during that meeting. He asked a few questions, all insightful. Then he said, "You know, there's been a lot of stuff written about me. People talk about me in the media. Any of that make you uncomfortable?"

I looked him in the eye and said, "No."

Of course I had done my research. I knew there might be events in Vince's past that you or I might not have approved of. But I'd made my own mistakes and I'd learned that people can change. They can grow. I believed that then and I believe it even more now. I also considered how the media often portrays people unjustly. Bottom line, I felt comfortable with Vince's past. At that point, I was focused on the future. Working with him to help the business grow. That would be my focus.

By that point, I'd learned that only about 40 percent of WWE stock was publicly traded. The rest was owned by Vincent Kennedy McMahon. It didn't matter that Vince's wife, Linda, was CEO and Vince was chairman of the board. From our very first meeting, I got the impression that Vince ran the company. Full stop.

I remember being myself in that interview: outspoken and direct but with lots of data to back up my assertions. When it was over, I had no regrets. I left everything on the floor and walked out proud, but my expectations were low. I had to face facts. Technically, I was a weak candidate since I'd never been CFO of a publicly traded company.

I resolved to forget the interview took place. If I got the job, great. If I didn't, so what? I was still doing well at the *Times* and I figured some other opportunity would come along.

***

When I mentioned the WWE interview to my friend, Yasmin, she was appalled. "Are you kidding?" she said. "You're leaving the *Times* to go work with wrestlers?" Once she calmed down, she gave me two pieces of advice. One: I couldn't leave the *Times* unless the jump I was getting in salary was huge. I assured her it was. Two, she wanted my assurances that we would still get together for dinner once a month. I assured her we would.

Yasmin wasn't the only friend who thought I was crazy. Pretty much everyone had that reaction. Whenever I mentioned WWE, people said, "Wrestling? You mean those lunatics who run that TV show, *Monday Night Raw*?"

Lunatics? At that point, to my recollection, *Monday Night Raw* topped the list of most watched shows in America. Clearly, WWE was doing something right. Even my father-in-law, Erwin, whom I adored and whose advice I valued so highly, thought working for WWE was a bad idea. "Who's that guy who runs the company again?" he said. "McMahon? Is that his name? Al . . . isn't he a criminal?"

No, I thought. *Not a criminal.*

None of the allegations I'd seen or read about Vince bore any resemblance to the man I'd met. I thought it entirely possible that people were living in an echo chamber. They'd been fed fantastic stories and so had formed unsubstantiated judgments about Vince.

Here's where I get on my soapbox. I've never been the type of person who appreciates judgmentalism in the sphere of a person's private behavior. For instance, from my point of view, it's nobody's business what people do in their bedrooms—so long as it's consensual. Therefore—again, from my point of view—this leaping to judgment often indicates, at best, a lack of curiosity and, at worst, the kind of reverse discrimination that too many people celebrate as virtue. To me, it's also anti-American. It all boils down to four words: Live and let live. Now back to WWE.

My preliminary analysis showed me that the company had an immensely popular product with good revenue and profits but still retained massive room for growth. If the business itself looked cartoonish to people of a certain mindset . . . who cared? I've never let other people's biases distract from what my own impressions tell me. Also, I've always been willing to tolerate risk, so long as I see the possibility for asymmetric returns. For instance, if I see a 10 percent chance for making a 100x return, you can bet I'll pull on that string. From my point of view, the greatest risks in life don't come from pushing too far, they come from not pushing far enough. From playing things too safe, being too conservative. By not venturing into the unknown.

The contrarian in me was intrigued when so many smart people kept telling me to stay away from WWE. In situations like this, I use a simple decision-making framework.

everyone right	2 really bad	3 okay
everyone wrong	1 bad	4 awesome
	you're wrong	you're wrong

Pictured: A 2x2 grid with four quadrants. Let's go through each of the quadrants.

In Quadrant 1, YOU'RE WRONG and EVERYONE ELSE IS WRONG. You thought the stock market was going up, and so did everyone else. Then it crashed. That sucks.

In Quadrant 2, YOU'RE WRONG when EVERYONE ELSE IS RIGHT. You were scared to invest but everyone else did and the market spiked high! That *really* sucks.

In Quadrant 3, YOU'RE RIGHT and EVERYONE ELSE IS RIGHT too. You followed the herd and the herd was right. Everyone did the same. Otherwise called mediocrity. And that's okay. No harm, no foul.

Quadrant 4 is the sweet spot, the place where the real magic happens in business and in life. It's the place where YOU'RE RIGHT and EVERYONE ELSE IS WRONG. This is the type of situation that can turn relatively talented people into icons. Bezos. Zuckerberg. Gates. Musk. Page and Brin. The list goes on and on.

Consider our leading lights in various industries. How many of them started out tilting at windmills? How many nurtured a dream and followed their instincts and put in the work—the incredibly punishing work—all while staring into the fangs of sneering critics? The people who change the world are never right when everyone else is right. That's why we cherish them. That's why we need them.

Now let me point out something important about Quadrant 4. It's where contrarians live. It's where fortunes are made. It's where meaningful change can happen. But no one can be a contrarian all the time—or even most of the time. If you're a contrarian just for the sake of being a contrarian, there's a high probability that you'll lose. A lot.

Being a successful contrarian requires wisdom. It requires understanding the true *essence* of the situation. It requires first principles thinking. It requires a depth of knowledge about the situation that others don't possess, likely because they're too lazy to acquire it.

So how do you acquire this wisdom? Work. Tireless, endless work. Why is this level of work so rare? A lack of fascination. Fascination with a topic is the pixie dust you need to find success in business and in life. When you are so fascinated by something that you'll spend all your time pulling on that string, it's no longer work.

Now let me be clear, at this point I had no idea that WWE was in Quadrant 4. But my instincts were telling me that there was something there. A lot more on this later. For the moment, I'd set my goal to become CFO of a publicly traded company. I wanted that goal so badly I could taste it. Which is why, a couple of weeks later, when Vince called to offer me the job, I took it.

***

It was a strange time. Peculiar rumblings were percolating throughout the economy. For instance, in the summer of 2007, giant global investment bank Bear Stearns suddenly announced that two of its hedge funds had lost all their capital and would file for bankruptcy. It was later revealed that both funds had been deeply positioned in something called collateralized debt obligations, or CDOs.

A CDO is basically when some financial wizard bundles debt-backed assets, such as subprime mortgages, with other risky assets, turns them into securities, and sells them to investors. That's like having your dog shit in a box, wrapping the box with glitzy gold paper, putting a bow on it, and selling it to some rube—who doesn't understand what they're buying—for $6,000.

Don't laugh. This is how our economy works sometimes.

In hindsight, the failure of these funds was a canary in the coal mine, the first sign of global economic meltdown. Was I paying attention to that? Not at all. In retrospect, nobody was.

It was January 2008.

***

I told Vince I'd like to stay on at the *Times* until March or April so I could get my annual bonus. We agreed that I'd spend those two or three months digging deeper into WWE's fundamentals, learning the business inside and out.

Good, I remember thinking. *This will work perfectly. I'll spend two years as CFO of WWE, kick ass, and move on to a more reputable company.*

I began by creating a fifty-page report of the company as it existed at that point. My report showed the company's cultural, financial, and business model arcs. This wasn't a document for public or even internal consumption. It was more a book I wrote for myself. I was getting my thoughts in order about what kind of company I would be working with, how it worked, and how it became the business I was about to run.

WWE assigned me one of their internal finance people. Angela had been at her job for a while and she had plenty of institutional knowledge. I found her tremendously helpful. We spent long hours going over the company's particulars on the phone after work. And we argued a lot.

I would say, "Angela, that information you sent . . . it's too high-level. Can you tranche out the data, make it more granular?"

I'd explain how I wanted the data cut up. Angela would listen and say, "George. Why is all that relevant?"

"Angela . . . please? It would really help me and I'd appreciate it."

"But no one's ever asked for that information."

"I get it. But I've developed my own approach. Humor me, okay?"

"It's just . . . I'm not really sure what you're looking for, George."

"Me neither," I admitted. "Not yet. But if it's there, I'll know it when I see it."

Exchanges like this reminded me of something my controller at NEMG told me once. "George," he said. "For you to accomplish something, all you need is a compass and a machete. The compass tells you the direction you want to move in. The machete's for hacking through anything that gets in your way."

I thought this seemed fair and said so. But then this guy flipped the coin. "You know," he said. "Hacking through jungles is all well and good. But that's just the beginning. You still need to drain the marshes and level the land and put in the roads and build cities. You need sewers and streetlamps. When something catches fire—and something always catches fire—you need a system to put that fire out as quickly as possible." He looked at me closely. "What I'm saying . . . you need other people. Doesn't matter how good you are at what you do. Everyone needs other people."

"Fair point." I glanced at my watch. "But your job is to go build those sewers and streetlamps. My job? I'm going to sharpen my machete."

His point was well taken. Little by little, it was beginning to sink in my brain that I was indeed good at my job. But I could be even better if I partnered with people whose skills were different and complementary to mine.

If this seems like it should have been obvious, what can I tell you?

I'm human. I'm flawed.

***

Three major events occurred while I was preparing to work at WWE.

First, somebody apparently leaked the news that the Times Company's treasurer was leaving to become CFO of World Wrestling Entertainment. The *New York Post* ran a one-page article whose tone was less than flattering to both *The New York Times* and me. I can't recall the actual headline, but it went something like Wrestling Gives Gray Lady a Black Eye! I remember reading this and sighing. As I mentioned, since time immemorial, the *Post* has delighted in hurling jabs against its archnemesis, the *Times*. The *Times* never reciprocates, of course. It would never demean itself by punching down at the *Post*. Too easy.

The second major event was me going down to Orlando to attend WWE's big annual event, WrestleMania. This was about two weeks before I officially started with the company. I had been plowing through its numbers, formulating concepts. Imagine my shock when I found myself in a stadium packed with 50,000 screaming fans. Suddenly all my theories got tossed out the window.

Here it is, I thought. *Right here. This kind of event, this show, these fans . . . they're the heart and soul of this company.*

The energy at WrestleMania was off the charts. I remember flying home more stoked than ever. I thought, *I did the right thing by joining this company.*

The third major event was the subprime mortgage crisis. In one week, global investment bank and financial services giant Bear Stearns collapsed. On March 11, 2008, Moody's downgraded Bear's entire portfolio of mortgage-backed securities from B to C. This triggered a panic that set off a run on major financial companies like GE Capital. Two days later, on March 13, Bear Stearns announced it was broke.

The following day, the Federal Reserve arranged an emergency bridge loan for Bear. To anyone paying attention, it was clear that the US government plus all the leading lights of international finance were doing everything in their power to stanch the wound to the global economy. On March 16, Bear Stearns accepted an offer to merge with JP Morgan Chase. I guess people thought that would contain the damage. It didn't. The crisis had only begun.

The global exposure to toxic assets kept rippling out until October 24, 2008, when market indices worldwide dropped an average of 10 percent. Main Street America panicked, which only made things worse.

This was a hell of a way to start work as CFO of a publicly traded company. I remember thinking, *Thank God WWE's in solid financial condition.*

Sure, a small percentage of our cash was invested in assets later deemed risky. We took steps to address this without incurring any losses. Importantly, we had no debt to default on, so the economic downturn was never an existential issue for us like it could have been at the *Times*. My time as treasurer of the *Times* gave me the opportunity to help position the company for the rocky road ahead. I'm still very proud of making that happen.

But I'm getting ahead of myself. There's a funny story I want to tell you that happened about a month after I officially joined WWE. I decided to go out on the road and catch a few shows on what we called a loop. This turned out to be one of the most eye-opening experiences of my career.

***

When I started with WWE, it was basically a touring company that produced two core TV shows a week, *Monday Night Raw* and *Friday Night SmackDown*. Each show had its own weekly loop, or tour, which made stops in different American cities.

To give you an example, *Monday Night Raw*'s loop kicked off as the weekend began and featured live shows on Friday, Saturday, and Sunday. The shows on each loop were clustered so they were within driving distance of each other. This made it easier for production units to break down a set, truck it to the next location, and set it back up again, all in a matter of hours. Most *Raw* venues featured seating capacities of between five and ten thousand spectators. Once the Sunday performance was finished, production geared up for the loop's largest event on Monday evening, which was broadcast live over our network partners around the world as *Monday Night Raw*.

The loop for *Friday Night SmackDown* took place in the same basic region as *Raw* and followed the same protocol, but its shows were produced in different venues. The only real difference between the productions was that each *SmackDown* loop's final event took place on a Tuesday night. Since the *Raw* loop had closed out the previous night, and since the final *Raw* venue was usually close by, some *Raw* talent would appear in Tuesday night's *SmackDown* show. Crosspollinating our wrestlers on different programs helped build their popularity with different audiences. The Tuesday-night shows weren't shown live, they were taped. Three nights later, the footage got broadcast around the world as *Friday Night SmackDown*.

Each loop's Monday- or Tuesday-night culmination show was a well-catered event often attended by executives from our business partners. They were also more technologically sophisticated than the loop's previous shows, with jumbotron video screens and enough pyrotechnics to humble the Fourth of July.

By now, I hope you're getting the notion that planning these loops, and keeping them in motion fifty-two weeks every year, was a logistical triumph. We were only able to pull it off by having the best team to handle the constantly shifting venues, the moving of people and equipment, regional marketing, regional ticketing, insurance, stagehands, and so on. The WWE loop machine was so well-organized, so efficient, so consistent in delivering excellence that at one point we were asked to make a presentation to the US Army, which Vince supports whenever he can.

Doing the *Raw* and *SmackDown* events back-to-back cut down on production costs. Each week, WWE bore the cost of flying our performers to their first show and home from their final show. However, getting back and forth between venues on a loop was the performer's cost to bear as an independent contractor. To cut costs, a lot of our wrestlers rented the smallest two-door compacts they could find and drove them hundreds of miles between gigs. I did the same thing for my first loop. I wanted to get the same experience our athletes had.

For that particular loop, I flew into Mobile, Alabama, on a Thursday. The Friday and Saturday night shows were nearby, although I can't remember which cities. After the Saturday night show, I jumped into my car and drove some 200 miles west to Monroe, Louisiana. While out on the highway, I glanced to my left and stared at the positively absurd image of the Undertaker, Mark William Calaway, one of WWE's most iconic performers. All six feet ten and three hundred pounds of him had been shoehorned into this little rented Honda Accord. Since wrestlers often saved cash by carpooling, there was another performer whose name escapes me now in the car beside Mark. Suffice it to say that whoever he was, this guy wasn't small. Even our shortest performers were wide in the shoulders and built like brick shithouses. To me, this image of two huge men putt-putting along in a car so small as to be cartoonish perfectly encapsulates the traveling carnival atmosphere that WWE had in those days.

The *Raw* event in Monroe was held at a fairground. Picture a place where the local 4-H club holds its annual meetings, only minus the animals. I recall the space as being big enough to hold three or four thousand people. Not a high-tech state-of-the-art venue. Just a ring like you see in the footage of old-fashioned boxing bouts from the Great Depression with an announcer shouting into a big microphone they lowered from a wire in the middle.

Rudimentary or not, the place was packed and everyone in the audience was screaming their heads off. I remember looking around, marveling at the energy and wondering, How did I, a Latino kid from Queens, find himself in the deep South at such a venue? It felt weird, but I had to get over that fast because this was the business I'd chosen to run.

Another moment I'll never forget. The announcer grabbed the mic and said, "Laaaadiiiiiies and gennnnnntlemennnnnnn! In our audience tonight, we are pleased to welcome NBA Hall of Famer . . . power forward for the Utah Jazz . . . The Mailman himself . . . Karrrrrrl Malone!!!!"

That was the first time I understood the diversity of our fan base. Karl Malone, NBA star and future Hall of Famer . . . was a wrestling fan? Yes. And he wasn't alone. As I would soon come to see, there are die-hard wrestling fans all over the world. Many of them are people you wouldn't normally think of as being wrestling fans. Celebrities. Politicians. Professional athletes. The list goes on.

In fact, a couple of years later I was having my first colonoscopy. My doctor and I were chatting before he put me under. "So," he said. "What kind of work do you do?" When I told him I worked for WWE, he went nuts.

"WWE?! Are you kidding?! I love wrestling!" He started ticking off his favorite characters, the latest rivalries, his predictions for outcomes of upcoming bouts. All this about two minutes before he slid a camera scope up my ass.

I remember meeting Ricky "The Dragon" Steamboat and being shocked at his size. Whoever had billed him at five-feet-ten was lying. I'm five-feet-ten and all I can say is Ricky was notably shorter than me. All those years I'd watched him on TV, he'd looked so much bigger. Whatever. We hit it off famously.

After Sunday night in Monroe, I drove up to Nashville for the main event, *Monday Night Raw*, which would be broadcast live around the world. This gave me a firsthand, up-close look at how *Raw* transformed as it headed toward its Monday-evening live broadcast. Bigger venues. More fans. A lot more fans, in fact. The energy started to hockey stick.

Our last event for that week was in Bridgestone Arena where the NHL's Predators play ice hockey. In one night, we jumped from 4,000 people in a gymnasium to 17,000 screaming fans packed in a major venue tricked out with massive LED screens, fireworks, and a world-class sound system. The performers wore full makeup and outlandish costumes. We flew in guests from all over the country. I remember feeling like a VIP at an A-list rock show or Broadway opening. Everyone knew that whatever took place that night in the ring would be seen live on millions of TV screens around the world, and here at home on our partner, USA Network. The energy was off the charts. Believe me when I say that it was something to see.

From that point forward, I was hooked.

***

Funny thing. I hadn't told Vince I was going out on a loop. I figured I was CFO of the company. For the most part, I could do what I wanted.

The day I got back, Vince called me into his office. He'd been out on the road himself. Vince made it a point to personally produce every *Monday Night Raw* live broadcast and every Tuesday-night taping of *Friday Night SmackDown*. This meant he was right there, getting things done and running the big shows straight from the Gorilla Position, that area behind the curtains where performers gathered before they went on. Vince named it after Gorilla Monsoon, the legendary wrestler who was often seen in that very space psyching himself up before he went out and made history time and again.

It was a grueling schedule for Vince. He'd work his ass off out on a loop. Then, late Tuesday night or early Wednesday morning, he'd be on our private corporate jet flying back to Westchester County Airport. A car service shuttled him home and he'd be in the office by Wednesday at noon to tackle the rest of the week. How he did this, week after week and year after year, is still beyond me. The man had incredible energy. Still does.

"So, George. I hear you went out on a loop." When I nodded, Vince made a face and said, "Why?"

"I want to learn the business, and a business isn't just numbers. The three most important parts of any business are its people, its products, and its customers. Or in our case, fans. If there's a fourth part, it's how they all work together. The loop was perfect for seeing all of that."

Vince said nothing for a moment. Then he said, "That's never happened before."

"What's that?"

"I've never had one of my executives do that. I've had them go to the big arena shows on Monday or Tuesday, but not the little ones."

At that point, the company might have had three or four hundred employees. About twenty or thirty of those had been with Vince since the beginning. Three or four among that twenty were a powerful cabal who had Vince's ear. I was given to understand that they, too, were impressed by what I had done.

Oh yeah? I thought. *That impresses you? Just you wait.*

By the time I left WWE, no one was renting shitty little Honda Accords anymore. We were flying on chartered planes, shuttling talent back and forth on massive tour buses. Doing things right. But all that lay in the future.

In a matter of months, I made my first real contribution.

***

Throughout all this, Vince and I were getting to know one another. I learned that he doesn't have a traditional business background. On the other hand, he's deeply, intuitively bright and he knows how to go with his gut. For instance, a little bit later he told me, "George, do you know why I hired you? I remember hearing you speak during that first interview and I thought, 'We don't have anyone like him here.'" I took that to mean someone who was comfortable discussing a topic at both strategic and conceptual levels while still being willing to get into the nitty-gritty of how things actually work in the real world.

He was a man who was driven by hunches. I like to think they paid off in my case.

Like the first time I gave an interview talking about the company for one of the TV business channels. Vince gave me a couple of pointers before I went on air. He basically told me to treat the whole thing like it was theater, so I did.

The day after that shoot, he called me into his office again. "George," he said. "You're a natural at this." I got the impression that at that moment, he thought I was an actor that he, the director, had cast really well in a role.

I was still doing my deep-dive analysis into all facets of the business, asking my staff to generate different ways of looking at our fundamentals, reading earnings call transcripts, anything and everything I could get my hands on. My first earnings call was coming up.

One of our board members said, "It's not really fair to expect George to be up to speed so quickly." I was advised to let my staff handle most of the questions we got. In my defense, these people had no idea how determined I was. I knew that this wouldn't be another meeting like my first time with the New York Times Company finance committee. In both cases I'd prepped my ass off. But an earnings call? That was right in my sweet spot. I was made to do that. I went into that meeting excited, ready for a battle, like a basketball player heading into a playoff game. And I killed it. There wasn't a question that I couldn't answer. And some of the questions were very provocative.

For instance, usually it's the sell-side analysts asking questions and making comments on a call. But we had this one investor who kept piping up. "I'm concerned by how much money you're spending. I'd say you guys are burning through cash like drunken sailors on leave. Except that's an insult to drunken sailors on leave."

I remember I paused before saying, "So what's your question?"

The investor launched a few jabs that I countered with facts. I knew exactly how much we were spending and why, and I told him this, answering every concern and rebutting every objection.

A couple of weeks later, we had our annual company meeting, which was attended by a core group of about 120 investors, analysts, and fans. A wide-ranging crowd. Picture the Berkshire Hathaway annual meeting, only on a smaller scale and attended by people who like to wear tights and body-slam each other. We also broadcast the meeting over the web.

Usually, the company CEO runs that meeting. They're armed with an opening script that includes perfunctory statements about how the company's doing and talking points tailor-made to deflect the barrage of questions they know they'll get hit with. All pretty dry toast. In the days leading up to the meeting, Vince and I had prepped and he had told me he would handle the opening remarks. Made sense.

However, the day of the meeting things changed. Our management team was standing around backstage waiting for things to begin. Vince tapped me on the shoulder and said, "George, why don't you do this?"

I think I said, "Do what?!"

He waved at the podium. "It's your show."

"Vince! I thought you were doing the intro. I didn't prepare to speak!"

He shrugged. "You know the business better than anyone here. Go on."

He was right. By that point, I had a better, more holistic understanding of how WWE operated than anyone else on staff. I was so prepared that I flew through that meeting and answered all questions without a cheat sheet. Live and without a net. I totally wowed them.

For those of you paying attention, here's the lesson: Preparation is everything.

CHAPTER TEN

Pinned in the Early Rounds

A couple of months later, the subprime mortgage crisis struck full-on and crippled the global economy. By September 2008, most companies saw how exposed they were to the plague of CDOs. Companies around the world went into damage control. At WWE, we decided that conserving cash was our most prudent course of action. This meant reducing our cost base and dealing with our dividend.

This bears some explanation. Shortly before I signed on with the company, WWE had raised its dividend significantly—by about 50 percent. The new high payout raised eyebrows since high payouts are sometimes deemed to be unsustainable. From my point of view, I thought our dividend was unique for two additional reasons.

WWE had a dual-class share structure, which generally grants one class of shareholders more control than the other class. Our A-class public shareholders' payout dwarfed the payout Vince received as the sole B-class shareholder. Vince's B-class shares granted him super-voting rights that allowed him to control WWE with as little as 10 percent overall ownership (at that point, he probably owned about 60 percent of the company). My research showed that there were other dual-class companies with different dividend payouts per share class, but I couldn't find one where the controlling shareholder received *less*.

Second, when you added everything up, we were paying out more in dividends than the company's annual cash flow. We made up the difference with the cash on our balance sheet. My public statements about this strategy remain a matter of record. I said that we believed very strongly in rewarding our shareholders while growing over time into the high-yield dividend we'd set. But of course, all that changed when the financial crisis hit.

Suddenly, markets weren't in choppy economic waters, they'd been struck by a tsunami. Everyone was concerned, and rightly so. But there was good news. WWE had no debt. This put us in far better financial circumstances than most other companies, but we still had no idea what would happen next to the global economy or the impact the crisis would have on consumer spending, and therefore on our revenues and profits.

It was time to take the bull by the horns. I called a meeting of WWE's leadership and outlined the situation as I saw it. "We can view what's happening now as a crisis or as an opportunity," I said. "As opportunities go, this is a perfect interval to restructure. We can cut costs, bootstrap ourselves, and streamline the company. From a certain point of view, we have no choice. Economically, the world's in survival mode now."

I developed a plan that would take a ton of costs out of the company, then went before the board and officially asked them to reduce the dividend they'd so recently taken great pains to raise. I told them, "I don't have a crystal ball. But I believe the world is entering choppy financial waters. We have to think long-term."

One of the board members got feisty with me. "George, this dividend cut you're proposing is pretty significant. People will think we're desperate."

"I agree it's significant. Look, let's be clear. Nobody likes cutting a dividend. However, given what's happening, the current environment . . . shouldn't we be taking less risk?"

The board took my advice. We ended up compromising on how much to cut, but the cut got made. This episode placed my relationship with Vince in jeopardy. He had trusted me from the get-go. But I learned pretty quickly that Vince is a big shiny penny guy. He likes to bring new people on board and lets them wow him. Then, after six to nine months, the honeymoon's over. Just like in a marriage, this is when the rubber hits the road, and the tires can fall off the car if you let them.

I remember a few tense meetings where Vince shot me looks like he could have cheerfully tossed me out a window. Not one to keep my mouth shut, I addressed this head-on. "I know what I'm saying is hard to hear," I said. "But hard or not, I know for a fact this is best for the company. Not tomorrow, next month, or next year. I'm talking long-term."

Vince taught me a lot about fortitude then. He asked plenty of smart questions and stood his ground on cherished positions while yielding on others. Like any good parent, he did what he thought was best for his child. I don't offer that analogy glibly, by the way. Vince had raised WWE from its infancy. He loved it. Now it was starting to grow, and he would do nothing to jeopardize that. Not even if it injured his pride.

I remember thinking, *That's what a real visionary does. A real businessman. A real man.*

Here I'll mention a couple of phrases that Vince liked to use. I call them "Vince-isms," nuggets of business wisdom wrapped in pithy allegorical sentences. Once you heard them, you never forgot them. Once you employed them, they saved you time and mental processing power. Eventually Vince and I used them all the time.

For instance, he would say, "Don't lose the wrinkle in your stomach." As best I can tell, this phrase came from Vince's time growing up in North Carolina. At any rate, my ears hear it as vaguely Southern in its inception. Picture someone who hasn't been living too high on the hog. Their stomach is flat from a lack of caloric intake—so flat there's a lateral crease running across their abdominal muscles. Whenever Vince used this phrase, he meant it as, "Don't get fat. Good organizations tend to run lean. Stay wary. Stay hungry."

Another Vince-ism was "Don't blame the all-night gas station." This one also sounded Southern to me. The first time I asked Vince to explain it, he told me a story. Once upon a time, there was a manager who ran a highway convenience store. One day his boss, the store's owner, stopped in. The boss pointed out that revenues were sinking and he asked why.

The manager threw up his hands. "What can I do?" He pointed to a new building across the highway. "They just opened an all-night gas station. See? Now everyone shops over there."

The boss didn't like this answer. He told the manager, "Who cares? I want my revenues. Figure this thing out." Then he left.

In other words, "Don't blame the all-night gas station" is tantamount to saying, "No excuses. Get the job done."

Vince also liked to say, "We've got to do our job and everyone else's." Mostly he said this in the context of dealing with our business partners. He meant that it's never good enough to assume someone else is going to do what they said they would do. You've got to get in there and get your hands dirty, take the initiative and show everyone how it works. In times past, people would say, "If you want a job done right, you've got to do it yourself." The same idea applies here. In the balancing act between self-reliance and collaboration, self-reliance tends to win because self-reliant parties uphold their own standards and therefore their own vision. Vince also used this phrase to nod at the interwoven nature of WWE's revenue streams. We all understood that we made a great product. But we also understood that we needed our partners to hold up their end of the bargain. It therefore made sense to support them however we could. Or, if need be, do their jobs for them. We often did.

I've said this before and I'll say it again: Though his methods are unorthodox, Vince is a talented businessperson whose career bears further and serious study. I was deeply impressed by his wisdom, to say nothing of how he applied and communicated it.

***

Around this time another huge event occurred at WWE. We hired Michelle Wilson as our chief marketing officer.

Spoiler alert. As I write this Michelle is my business partner. In different capacities, we've worked together for fifteen years. She's a friend and one of the smartest people it's been my good fortune to learn from. I'll write more on this later. For now, I just want you to know that where Michelle is concerned, I'm totally, unrepentantly, blissfully biased.

Michelle had worked with Vince on the launch of the short-lived XFL. A joint venture between WWE and NBC, XFL was designed to provide an alternative to the more traditional National Football League. Chronologically, XFL offered football programming beyond NFL's eighteen-week season, which culminates each winter with the Super Bowl. Stylistically, it offered a different take on the sport.

Officially, the X in XFL has no meaning. But it was no stretch to call it the Extreme Football League. Vince saw NFL games as staid and stuffy. He imagined a type of football that was faster, simpler, and frankly more violent than what the NFL produced.

Michelle was a perfect choice for the job Vince hired her for. She'd worked in professional sports almost her entire career with organizations as big and complex as the NBA. From the beginning, I was amazed at how people mischaracterized her. A lot of people pigeonholed Michelle as a marketing rock star. Which she is. But she also trained as a chemical engineer before earning her MBA at Harvard. In other words, she's fucking brilliant.

People used to say that we complemented each other. "George and Michelle have different skill sets that dovetail nicely." I heard this time and again. But the truth is, Michelle and I are more alike than we are different. We're both super analytical, hard-charging, conceptually oriented, connect-the-dots kinds of people. Our careers have been different, of course, but that's merely the result of the jobs we've selected. Today it's my conviction that if at any point in our trajectories, you'd asked either of us to step into each other's roles, we'd have done spectacularly at them. We think that much alike.

WWE only weathered the financial crisis thanks to crucial help from Michelle. I'm grateful she was there because things were crazy for a long time. To understand how many ups and downs we got hit with, check out the company's stock chart during this period. Complicating matters, we tried a few plays that didn't work out as well as we'd have liked, like investing in movies. And while I still believe in a lot of those less-than-perfect strategies, the truth is we could have executed a lot of those initiatives better than we did.

As Michelle and I successfully navigated various challenges, I think it's fair to say that Vince's trust in us grew. He seemed more comfortable stepping back from certain processes and deferred to us more and more.

Before long, Michelle and I were effectively running the company alongside Vince.

***

During those early years, I was getting a lot of inbound calls from headhunters looking for people to fill bigger CFO roles. I always listened to what they proposed. Why not? I still had my dream of becoming CEO of a publicly traded company, and I understood all too well how a lot of my peers thought I'd ditched the traditional business community to run away with the circus. A lateral move to become CFO of another publicly traded company, using that as a stepping stone, was never off the table for me. But I couldn't shake my conviction that there was untapped gold in WWE.

The financial crisis blew itself out in mid-2010. Yes, there were still a few fires to put out, but Michelle and I used the relative calm to focus on WWE's future. Where were the big opportunities over the next five to ten years? Going back to first principles, we asked ourselves, What does WWE do? How is what we do different from what our competitors do?

To answer these questions, I had our strategy and finance teams parse shit tons of data and draw up reports that were read by Michelle and me alone. In many ways, this felt like I was back working for Steve Katz at Time Warner. If your presentation is supposed to run ten minutes, be ready to go for an hour. If your SWOT analysis is supposed to run thirty pages, expand it to over a hundred.

Go deeper, I thought. Go further. If you think you've hit gold, don't stop. Keep digging.

During this process, Michelle and I kept coming up against the fact that WWE video content was positioned as a loss leader for our company. We got paid less for *Raw* and *SmackDown* than what it cost us to produce it. Sure, we made money off our ticket sales, but that didn't change the fact that we were subsidizing what our fans loved most about WWE.

People later asked me why Vince was okay with this. The way he'd imagined the company, our televised broadcasts were infomercials designed to propel ticket and merchandise sales. "It's fine if our TV work breaks even," he once told me. "So long as everyone's buying a WWE hat or a video game. So long as one out of every five people walking the streets of America wears a *Monday Night Raw* T-shirt."

This strategy had merit. Back in the late 1970s, George Lucas famously kept the merchandising rights for his *Star Wars* films. Wise people laughed when he did this. They said he'd never make any money off lunch boxes, posters, and action figures, but I hear he did okay. Vince was employing a similar strategy. He'd built an empire on the American soap opera model. The dramas—what takes place in the ring—were to entertain the fans, and Vince was passionate about that. The actual money came from selling the soap.

Some people have asked me why Vince pursued this loss leader strategy. I think it's because he understood better than anyone that wrestling was considered a déclassé pastime. But rather than run from that, he'd embraced it. In fact, he kept pushing the envelope on it.

Some readers may recall how, back in the 1980s, a lot of viewers assumed that professional wrestling was an actual competitive sport. Vince allowed this to play out until the gambit no longer served the company, at which point he himself pulled back the curtain to show how the bouts had all been scripted. That they were, in essence, performance art, like Japanese kabuki or the kung fu films coming out of modern China. It was a brilliant maneuver on his part, and it paid dividends. Rather than tuning out when the truth was revealed to them, our fans grew more loyal than ever, and the company really took off.

This is all my way of saying that Vince's model was working. The company was profitable. But Michelle and I weren't looking for slow and steady returns. We imagined more value than that. We wanted to kick off a massive shift.

Again and again, we returned to the fact that our network partners were underpaying us for our broadcast rights. Why? Our TV ratings were killer, among the best in the industry. The National Basketball Association on TNT cable averaged 2.5 million viewers per broadcast hour. Major League Baseball on FOX averaged about 1.9 million viewers. WWE had as many viewers as the NBA and MLB combined, but we were only getting a nickel per viewer hour while the NBA and MLB got a dollar, only getting paid $80 million per year while those two sports each raked in about $6 or $7 billion.

"It makes no sense," I told Michelle once. "Our fans are just as passionate, just as sticky as basketball and baseball fans. They come from approximately the same socioeconomic base. And we're live TV. That's what really matters. *Live*."

We both felt that selling WWE's broadcast rights for a measly $80 million per year was a travesty. But it was a symptom of the real problem we faced.

"We're undervalued in the market because we're undervaluing ourselves," Michelle said.

I agreed. "Getting paid more for our broadcast rights will be great. But at core, it perpetuates an old idea that broadcast rights—that model of business—is sustainable. When it isn't. To really get ahead of this game, we have to reimagine who we are and what it means to be in sports entertainment." In my mind, I was seeing that square diagram I told you about. Specifically, the quadrant of the square where YOU'RE RIGHT when EVERYONE ELSE IS WRONG.

After more painstaking analysis, Michelle and I came to believe that the world was changing fast and that the rate of change was about to accelerate. Connectivity was becoming the key element in global trade and culture. In other words, Thomas Friedman had been right when he wrote *The World Is Flat*. Globalization—fueled in particular by internet access and communication technologies—had altered key economic models that most people and companies still took for granted.

Michelle and I agreed that most media businesses of the day were operating like mule-driven carts in the early 1900s. The cart drivers looked up from their whips and their reins and watched the newfangled contraptions called automobiles roll by. Shaking their fists after them, the drivers hollered, "Get a horse!" They were unwilling to relinquish the past and unable to accept the future, let alone embrace, enjoy, and profit from it.

This pattern plays out over and over in every industry, including the media sector. Remember back in the late 1990s when Netflix was still mailing DVDs to its customers? At one point, Netflix was literally begging Blockbuster Video to buy them. By that point, Blockbuster had dominated the home entertainment sector for more than a decade. At its peak, the company boasted 9,094 stores nationwide and 84,300 employees. They were the 800-pound gorilla. But Blockbuster turned Netflix down. Its executives believed their stores were their competitive moat. They didn't see the value in Netflix's niche mail-order DVD business.

Arguably, their rejection was the best thing that happened to Netflix. As broadband speeds increased, the company pivoted and disrupted the home entertainment market by introducing streaming services. Netflix changed with the times while Blockbuster didn't, which is why Blockbuster filed for bankruptcy in 2010. As I write this, the chain has only one remaining store in Bend, Oregon. Netflix, of course, is now an entertainment industry titan.

Michelle and I were aware that millions of new customers were connecting to the internet each day. Everyone knew that. But what I'll never forget was my feeling of awe when we saw the numbers coming out of India. Over the next five years, India was set to connect an additional 200 million people over broadband. Two hundred million new customers in five years!

Making this prospect even more attractive was WWE's popularity in India. As part of our deep dive, Michelle and I had done what no one at the time was doing: commissioned fan research in India. We had learned that WWE was the second-most watched sport in India behind cricket. And other developing markets showed similar promise. If we could somehow combine those two elements—expanded connectivity coupled with our repositioned WWE content—it seemed possible, even likely, that we could transform WWE into a leader in twenty-first-century global media and entertainment.

Michelle and I discussed all of this ad infinitum for months on end. "For years, people claimed that WWE is a niche industry," I said. "But 'niche' is meaningless now. There are giant global communities just waiting to be tapped. Suppose you live in Malaysia and want a peek into the secret lives of Florida crocodile handlers. No problem. Log onto the internet. Or let's say you live in Toronto and want to learn Sanskrit, sandcastle art, quantum physics. Same deal. The whole world has become one big audience."

Michelle nodded. "People can watch whatever they want whenever they want, and a huge degree of what's out there is UGC, user generated content."

"Right," I said. "And everyone's worried that all this content will fragment their audience and cannibalize their profits." I closed my eyes, thinking. "That's bullshit. It's lazy thinking. The research you and I did shows that audiences are already fragmented. Which means that content producers who stick with one platform are putting their eggs in one basket. How about this for a hypothesis: Having multiple platforms will expand our audience. We just have to figure out how."

Michelle was quiet. She was thinking too. "For now, let's put that aside," she said. "Assuming our take on the new landscape is correct—"

"It is," I said.

She nodded. "Then the question in my mind becomes, *Who wins in such an environment?*"

"Simple," I said. "Whoever wins the battle for time and attention. Right now, every other media company is talking about ratings, clicks, views, likes, shares, and so on. Everyone's missing the point. Those are all the same. They're abstractions of time. What if we reimagined our core value proposition? Center our strategy on what matters: time. How much time our fans are spending with us. And let's not just talk about it, let's get maniacal about measuring time. What if our new hot KPI is total viewer hours? Let everyone else in the industry talk about clicks. We'll focus on increasing the time and attention viewers give to our content. Because if we do that, we know that the dollars are sure to follow."

This was a pivotal shift in our thinking. We became obsessed with making it work. The course we imagined would expand WWE's content from one platform serving a primarily domestic audience to multiple platforms across every country on earth. And we could excel in this new global arena because wrestling, like other combat sports, is easy to understand. It crosses cultural boundaries almost effortlessly. Whereas the NFL—for years the unbeatable leader in US sports broadcasting with an average of 18 million viewers per hour—had struggled to find an audience outside the US.

"We'll never beat the NFL in the US, but we could blow right past them outside the country," I said. "But to do that, we need to set up the right kind of infrastructure worldwide."

Now that we had architected our strategy, we needed to draw up the blueprints. We felt we needed outside help to design the plan we envisioned. We engaged premier Manhattan-based strategy firm L.E.K. Consulting. We instructed them to size our fan base in our top twenty markets around the world and stratify them by levels of enthusiasm for

WWE content. Were they hardcore fans? Aspirational hardcore? Casual? Lapsed? And so on. At the same time, we purchased third-party viewership data from markets around the world. Today, I feel confident saying that we were the first sports and entertainment property that did this for markets outside their countries of origin.

The final report on all this was shocking. "Holy shit," I said to Michelle. "Am I reading this right?"

She nodded. "We have more than 150 million WWE fans around the world consuming over 3 billion hours of content per year. And our market rankings are better than we imagined. We're the number two sports entertainment provider in the US We're doing just as well in many developing markets. It's incredible."

"It's better than that. It's fucking incredible." I sat back in my chair and closed my eyes. "So the opportunity's there and it's huge. Now what?"

"Rephrase that. You mean: How do we fundamentally change the company to maximize existing, underperforming revenue streams while also building the infrastructure to profit off an untapped global audience?"

"Right," I said. "That."

It took us another few months but we finally hammered out a plan.

First, we would reposition WWE content as premium *live* sports entertainment. With the emphasis on *live*. So what if we were the only scripted sport? As the software makers like to say, "That's a feature, not a bug." The fact that our "sports-like" content was so entertaining was what made our fans love us.

Second, we would realign our operations to create thousands of hours' worth of content without any duplication across various platforms. Eliminating the duplication would be the hard part. By this point, other content creators were starting to at least dabble on multiple platforms. But they were putting out the same content across all platforms. WWE would do something different. We'd build a *content factory*.

"That's how we'll counteract the dangers of viewer fragmentation and platform cannibalization. Every platform will have its own unique content," I said. "Moreover, we'll be smart and let UGC work for us."

Our fans had been using snippets of WWE videos to create their own content. At first, we tried to stop them. Now we would help them.

Give them the tools. They'd help us grow our audience, and since they were using our intellectual property, WWE would keep the dollars.

At the same time, we'd start to have our wrestlers produce their own content. Here again, we'd help them. Hire teams of producers to create alternative content by trailing the athletes, traveling with them, documenting their lives, rivalries, backgrounds, training regimes, that sort of thing. Basically, we would unleash our wrestlers to boost their own brands and give them the tools to do it.

Third, and concurrent with all this, we would build out our data infrastructure to support the creation of content with real-time feedback on who was consuming our programs and how. This would grant us deeper insights into the trackable health and growth of our fan bases in specific strata such as geography, socioeconomic classifications, language bases, and so on. Which, in turn, would allow us to court more lucrative sponsorship deals from advertisers and sales partners for everything from T-shirts to ticket sales.

"Fourth point," I said to Michelle. "We'll do this all on a grand scale. Globally. And at once. We'll put people on the ground in key markets to oversee their expansion. In certain countries, we'll also recruit local talent to fuel regional fanbases. And we'll make use of third-party platforms to grow audiences in places such as the Middle East where TV is notably under-penetrated."

Michelle absorbed all this. "Okay. Next step. How do we monetize?"

"Got that here." I read from some notes I had made. "First, we'll self-disrupt our traditional pay-per-view business and replace it with a WWE direct-to-consumer service. We've been charging around $50 for pay-per-view events. But we split our fees with broadcasters and other partners. If we cut out the middlemen, we can charge less per event, which in turn should attract more customers, growing our customer base while we end up profiting more.

"At the same time, we deploy our new cache of digital content to generate advertising revenue off watch times across our new global viewer base. This should self-perpetuate. As our brand continues to build, it'll drive value across each of our content channels while cementing our status as a provider of premium live content for a worldwide audience. Also, we make certain content evergreen. Post it for asynchronous consumption on YouTube, Facebook, Instagram, and so on. That'll also generate revenue while growing our base and it won't cost us much. Ultimately, putting out content over social media channels will help us win the battle for time and attention while building a wider moat to facilitate further strategies."

Michelle leaned back in her chair and looked up at the ceiling tiles. She does this a lot when she's thinking. After a moment, she nodded. "I like it. What else?"

"*Monday Night Raw* and *SmackDown*," I said. "They're premium live content, right? Yes. And we need to get paid for what they're worth, right? Yes. Everything we've just talked about works on its own, but the magic is how it will all work together. If we do this right, time and attention will grow, the brand will grow, and the next time we're in the market with *Raw* and *SmackDown*? We get paid what we're worth."

Michelle nodded. "The communications piece of all this will be crucial. Our plan isn't worth anything unless we communicate it to stakeholders. I mean current partners like Walmart, USA, Sony India, and Take Two. But also potential new partners like Netflix and FOX. We need to tell our story at every industry conference we attend. Wherever flesh can be pressed, this story has got to be on our lips."

Now I nodded. "Meanwhile, we'll need to handle the business and sports media. The usual suspects. *Wall Street Journal*, *The New York Times*, *LA Times*, *Variety*, CNBC. We tell everyone everywhere what we're doing."

Michelle thought this through and she nodded. "We're gonna get pushback. You know that, right?"

"Oh yeah, I know it. Some of our friends in the media and even some of our partners will say we're crazy."

"It's a pretty big plan with a lot of moving parts." Michelle paused. "But I think it'll work." She looked at me. "The first step might be the toughest. We've got to get Vince to buy into this. The board after that."

I shrugged. "So let's make a case that's so compelling, they can't say no."

***

We thrashed out the details over the next nine months, into 2011. Wrote reams of documents, every detail mapped out, including fallback plans in case our initiatives failed. Call them emergency parachutes. Michelle and I were under no illusions about what we were doing. The good news was that the course we were charting would fundamentally change WWE. The bad news was that, in the short term, there would likely be pain. We just never imagined how much pain.

Somewhere in all this, I was privileged to read an article that told me we were on the right track. The author was legendary reporter and truth pirate David Carr, who used to write a column called Media Equation for *The New York Times*. Carr was talking about a subject I believe few business leaders understand: counter-positioning. The art of confronting incumbent enterprises by pursuing a strategy the incumbents know they should follow but find too painful to execute. Why? Because following the new strategy could damage their existing business.

Carr asked his readers to picture incumbent businesses as sitting in a room full of money. It's comfortable there. They're flush and they're smug. But there's a problem. More and more of their customers are leaving that room to go to another room. Try as they might, the incumbents can't stop them. Eventually, the incumbents realize that to survive, they must leave their own room and enter the room where their customers are going. However, to do that, the incumbents must walk down a long dark hallway where anything could happen and all bets are off.

Picture me gobsmacked after I read this. As fast as my thumbs could work my iPad, I sent the article to Michelle. "David Carr gets it!!!" I wrote. "Holy shit!!! Read this!!!"

I was just about to hit send when I got a message from Michelle. She'd sent me the same article. "Holy shit!!" she wrote. "This is us!! Read this!!"

That's how alike our minds work. We both knew we were walking down our own long, dark hallway. But we were determined to keep going. To face whatever happened next.

Remember in the beginning of this book, I shared that quote from *Inherit the Wind*? "It's the loneliest feeling in the world—to find yourself standing up when everybody else is sitting down." Michelle and I both understood that.

When our ducks were finally in order, we presented our plan to Vince in his office. He listened carefully. Again, I was struck by the notion that the character he played on TV—the swashbuckling crazy man in a suit—that was all just an act. The guy sitting before us was a businessman, best in class. He was the guy who'd once envisioned a Super Bowl for wrestling called WrestleMania. The guy who'd gone bankrupt twice while pursuing that dream but came out on top in the end. He kept his mind open. Asked thoughtful questions.

He was tentatively on board.

I probably could have predicted his biggest sticking point would be unwinding our pay-per-view business. No surprise there. Vince invented pay-per-view with WrestleMania. It was his baby and a significant revenue stream for the company.

We addressed his concern head-on. "We get that, Vince." I said. "Look, only a fool would cancel pay-per-view lightly. But there's no way around it. It has to be done if we want to keep growing. Like we said." I held up our 100-page plan document. "Nothing we've outlined here will be easy. There's gonna be pain along the way."

Vince chuckled and looked out the window. "Always is." Then he centered himself and shot me a look I'll never forget. He said, "If this is what needs to be done, why isn't everyone else doing it?"

"Because they're afraid they'll get fired." I looked at Michelle, who nodded. "I'll be blunt. Executives, boards, and investors like their jobs. They know that a lumpy 15 percent return per year is better than a stable 5 percent return per year. Ten years out, you end up with a *much* bigger number. Simple math. But following the lumpy path is tough. People who do it are going against the herd. You can bet there will be downturns. History shows that leaders who try to disrupt their own businesses to save them get the axe.

"If we were at nine out of ten other companies, we'd never be able to pull off a change like this. Sure, we might get it started but we'd never see the other side. Along the way, we'd get sacrificed, kicked to the curb. Somebody else would come in behind us to take all the laurels and reap the rewards."

This was the pivotal moment. I took a deep breath and jumped in. "Vince, for all practical purposes, WWE is your company. You control it. You get to do what's right as opposed to what's easy. That's what might make this possible. That and that alone."

Vince thought about that. Then he gave us permission to bring what we had to the board. Which didn't go well. Michelle and I underestimated how intransigent certain members could be.

For instance, one person who had been on the board forever said, "On the subject of us getting paid five cents per viewer hour when NFL and MLB get paid a dollar. . . ." Sighing, they folded their hands. "Maybe we get paid that much because that's what wrestling's worth."

"Says who?" I shot back.

The mood in the room changed at once. I'd thrown down the gauntlet and everyone felt it. Shifty looks around the table. People were checking each other's reactions, playing to herd mentality.

"Look," I said. "Bottom line, we've got to reframe who we are. The most obvious example of this is the loss leader model. Our content is not, or shouldn't be, a loss leader. It's not a soap opera. It's not—God forbid—an infomercial." I glanced at Vince. "No offense."

Vince shrugged. He was listening.

"Networks don't pay for infomercials, infomercials pay networks to get on the airwaves and sell their stuff. So let's get rid of that paradigm. Here's the truth. We've been conditioned to accept less than we're worth. That works for the networks, it doesn't work for us. Check your packets. Look at the charts. The data is clear. Our partner, USA, has been the most watched cable network in the country for the past thirteen years. We're proud of that, we want them to succeed. But the data also says that if we pulled *Monday Night Raw* off the network they'd drop like a stone. What they pay us doesn't reflect our value and that's not fair to us."

"I still don't buy it," said another board member. "George, the reason we get paid so little is because the networks can't sell our advertising."

I flipped to a page in the packet. "It's true that we sell less advertising than, say, the NBA does. But it's also a straw man argument. Networks can cry about lack of advertising all they want. Truth is they make 70 to 80 percent of their revenue off the affiliate fees they charge to cable companies. And affiliate fees are driven by . . . guess what? Viewership. Which I've already proven we have in spades.

"Bottom line, the more viewers we have, the more cable companies are willing to pay the networks to air our content. So we're back to the idea of us getting our fair share, and right now we're not. I'll be blunt. If USA doesn't appreciate that we're the anchor for their success, we should go be the anchor someplace else." I held up a chart. "Frankly? Given these numbers? We'd act as the anchor for any network that wants to do business with us. Michelle and I are saying we should exploit that as part of our opening shift in the company's profile. We've got some case studies here. . . ."

I began presenting our analysis of all the other networks—what they were worth, how they made money, what they were paying providers like us. This prompted another board member to disagree. "I think you're way off base here."

"We can disagree," I said. "But numbers don't lie." I motioned to another chart. "These are the numbers. They don't lie. So I guess what I'm asking is, what's your vision for this company? Because Michelle and I know what ours is."

I looked at Michelle, who nodded. She had my back. Then I chanced a look at Vince, who met my gaze. He was still listening.

"Our vision is that, from now on, WWE offers premium live sports entertainment content. And we do that over every platform, existing and emerging, traditional and digital. Our vision has this company growing by leaps and bounds by demanding what we're worth from our network partners and expanding globally, developing a truly international audience using streaming and social media services. Once we do that, we'll not only have disrupted the sports entertainment sector, we'll be primed to become whatever the hell we want. At which point, we should probably look to acquire another company to reach monster scale . . . or be acquired." Sitting in our boardroom in 2011, I had no idea how prophetic that last statement would be.

That was a tough meeting. Michelle had been right. There was a lot of pushback. But it didn't matter. We knew we were right. And we sensed that Vince was still in our corner.

"Intuitively, he knows the company's undervalued." Michelle and I were debriefing after that board meeting. "So how do we proceed?"

"We stick to the plan," I said, and grabbed my phone to make calls.

From that point forward, every conference I went to, every interview I gave, I upped the ante on what WWE was worth. With no great subtlety, I would say, "It's so interesting. We've analyzed fees being charged by other sports entertainment organizations to their network partners. These are organizations we beat in the ratings. But they're getting a lot more money than we are. Isn't that fascinating? It leads us to think that WWE's premium live content might be worth more than the rest of the sector suspects."

Concurrent with this, Michelle and I kicked off the other initiatives in our company-wide transformation. We leaned heavily into WWE's social and digital presence—more aggressively than any other sport at that time. Which is how we eventually acquired a billion social media followers and 40 billion video views across all our platforms. In fact, as I write this, I think WWE is still the number one sports brand on YouTube. Bigger than the NFL. Bigger than FIFA. And the company's gone international. Right now, over 70 percent of WWE's social audience is outside the United States. No surprise there since, commensurate with all this, Michelle and I worked our asses off to build audiences in India, the Middle East, Southeast Asia, and other regions—all on the backs of digital media.

These efforts dovetailed with our overhaul of the legacy pay-per-view business. We kicked off our new direct-to-consumer service by offering monthly events for which consumers paid less money than ever to access. I calculated that the new initiative would net us 3 million subscribers over time. We only hit just over 2 million, but it was still a very profitable business. Again, we were the first sports brand to do this, and yes, the risk was immense. We were actually cutting off the spigot to our current pay-per-view business to start a new subscriber-based model. No one had yet attempted such a maneuver, but it worked because of our new factory-driven take on content.

I made sure to tell business analysts, "We're winning the battle for time and attention. To quote Reed Hastings, cofounder of Netflix, 'Our biggest competitor is sleep.' When people sleep, they can't watch. As far as we can see, the way to win time and attention is to put our content on every available channel. But no, to answer your questions, we won't cannibalize ourselves because we'll put different types of content out over different platforms. Right now, WWE probably does 250 hours of live content a year with forty to fifty hours of shoulder programming. We want to reimagine that. We want to hit 300 hours of live content with about 2,000 hours of shoulder programming. This should help us build a very profitable direct-to-consumer business and continue to grow the company."

It all sounded good to Michelle and me. But was it convincing other people? That was the real question, and the only one that mattered.

When we announced our plans publicly, the reception was positive. The media heralded our strategy as fit for the new digital age. Business partners were excited to see us investing for the future. Investors and analysts, while cautious, saw the potential. But then reality hit. This would be difficult. It would take time and cost money.

As time went on, we began getting accosted by the same people who'd cheered us on. Fierce battles ensued in the first six to nine months. Reporters and analysts watched our profits decline as our pay-per-view business unwound more quickly than we were able to acquire new streaming subscribers. They started questioning our judgment, our assumptions, our strategy, our plan. They got brutal with me and Michelle.

"Guys!" they said. "Where's the growth? Where's the money? All this digital, social, subscriber stuff is a waste of time!" In essence, they did a complete 180.

I remember Michelle called me one time. "Did you see the article this asshole wrote?!"

Quick bit of trivia. Michelle and I might think alike but we have different temperaments. She sometimes gets bothered by things that don't faze me. Sure, I can get angry. I've already talked about the chip I've got on my shoulder. But I once heard Josh Wolf of Lux Capital say, "Chips on shoulders equal chips in pockets." So true!

Josh is a venture capitalist who goes out of his way to find people who'll fight for what they believe in. This reinforces my notion that anger is never a bad thing in and of itself. Yes, it's not healthy, especially when disproportionate or improperly aimed. But once it's channeled, I find that my anger becomes a rage to compete. Much more useful and very effective.

So where Michelle sometimes reacts to opinions from the peanut gallery, I normally pull what I call a Tina Fey. After winning some big award for being such a stupendous TV writer, Tina Fey once disclosed that she'd kept a Fuck You List all her life. Anyone who told her she had no talent or would never make it, that women can't work at the same level men can . . . she wrote their name on her Fuck You List. Then, when her circumstances changed and she was able to issue comeuppance, you'd better believe that she did.

"What does the article say?" I asked.

Michelle read it to me over the phone. I remember that one part basically said that WWE was in trouble and if Vince McMahon was smart he'd take these two people—Michelle and me—up to the top floor of our headquarters and throw us out a window.

"Michelle," I sighed. "Would you ask this guy his opinion on *any* part of our strategy?"

"No," Michelle admitted.

I shrugged. "Then why should we give a fuck what he thinks?"

Though I didn't reflect on it then, there's something called Gates's Law, attributed to Bill Gates. It proposes that most people overestimate what they can achieve in a year and underestimate what they can achieve in ten years. This held true for our efforts. As clear as the landscape was from my and Michelle's viewpoint, it took the rest of the world a long time to see things our way.

But Wall Street started to listen. Analysts did their own research into WWE and slowly came to believe in our strategy. Investors too. And wouldn't you know it? Our stock price started going up.

That's when the shit hit the fan.

PART THREE

The Master

CHAPTER ELEVEN

The Boss

Before I go any further, I want to describe one of the most important models that's guided my career. This is something I think anyone reading this book will profit from knowing, and it's actually very simple. The graphic I've included below neatly summarizes the concept. It tracks the journey almost everyone goes through when attempting to do something great. I've made it a habit to ponder this image often and I encourage you to do so as well.

Many people refer to this model as the Emotional Journey to Success. I prefer to call it the Swamp of Despair because, to me, that places the focus on what matters most. An emotional journey? That's a given—everyone goes through that. But for those who don't have the grit, the patience, or the sheer stamina to make it through the Swamp of Despair, there's really no reason to start such a journey in the first place.

The picture shows how we all start at the top of a hill where everything looks bright and shiny and awesome. *I've just had the best idea ever!* you think. I call this phase Inspiration. You get an idea and you know it's amazing—just like Michelle and I had the idea to transform WWE.

There's only one problem. To get from the Hill of Inspiration to the hill on the other side of the picture (I call it the Height of Success), you must first wade through a massive depression called the Swamp of Despair.

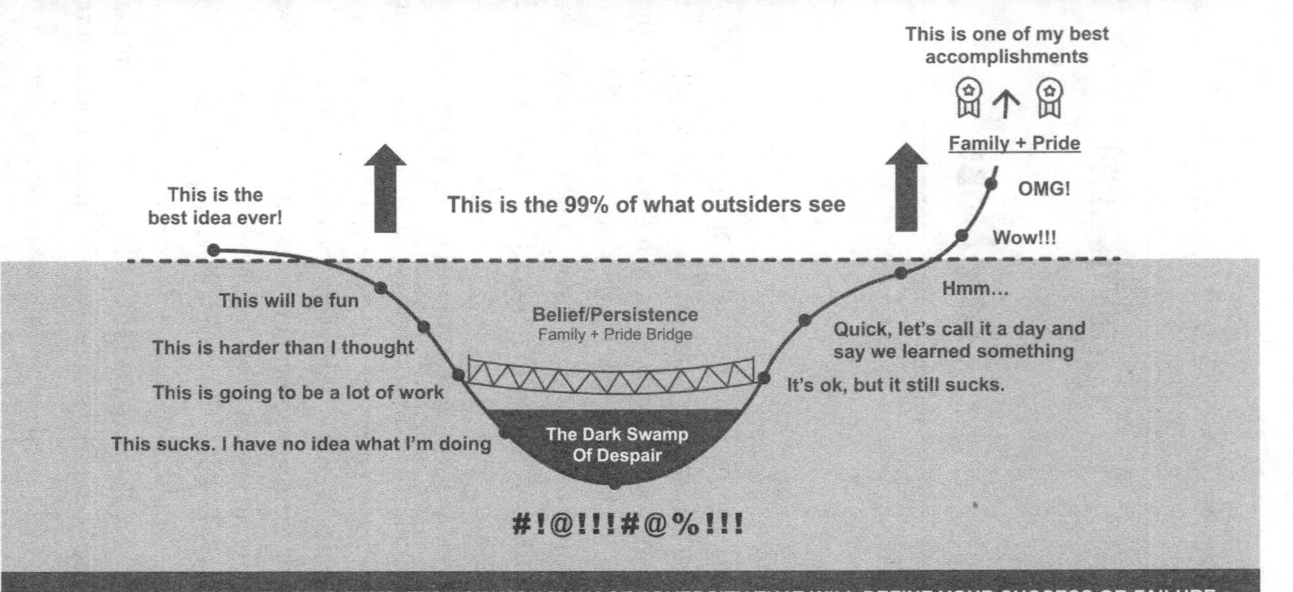

Emotional Journey

Let's pause here for a bit so I can reminisce. There's a children's movie that came out in 1984 called *The NeverEnding Story*. It demonstrates this principle in a dramatic way. The young hero, Atreyu, is sent on a mission to meet an ancient prophet named Morla who will give him priceless knowledge. Atreyu undertakes this journey on his white horse, who also happens to be his best friend, the steed named Artax. En route to their meeting with Morla, they must cross the Swamp of Sadness, a dark forest whose soft and shifting mud can, at any moment, suck anyone down into it.

This happens to Artax. While crossing the swamp, he starts to sink. Atreyu grabs hold of his reins and tries pulling him out of the mud. "Fight against the Sadness, Artax!" Atreyu says. "Please . . . you have to try. You have to care. For me. You're my friend! I love you!"

Spoiler alert: Artax dies in the Swamp of Sadness. After it records Atreyu's desperate pleading, the camera cuts to him sitting alone in the swamp, staring at the black mud that just swallowed his friend. It's one of the most heartbreaking moments I've ever seen in a movie, let alone in a movie for kids. But it contains a lesson I believe everyone has to learn.

The moment we leave our shiny Hill of Inspiration, we must enter the Swamp of Despair. There's no way of getting around it. The Swamp of Despair is tantamount to the dark, cold isolation that caterpillars enter en route to becoming a butterfly. It is the very notion of Hell in Christian theology, a place where, as depicted in Dante's *Inferno*, the sign hanging over the gate says Abandon All Hope, Ye Who Enter Here.

Now here's the thing. Once you understand this journey, you naturally prepare yourself for unforeseen obstacles. Intellectually, you get it. But emotionally? Not so much. When you encounter those obstacles, you begin to question everything, including yourself. *My God!* you think. *What the hell was I ever thinking, electing to come here? Nothing adds up anymore! Not a damn thing seems to make sense!*

Again, none of us is exempt from the Swamp. Even the most optimistic people languish there, cursing themselves for having ever conceived of their bright idea in the first place. Up to this point in my story, I'd been in the Swamp of Despair many times—and I've been there many times since. So I can assure you, traversing it never gets easier. Never. And yet, I've learned a few tricks, one of the most important of which is having a keen sense of humor.

Look up the term "gallows humor" in a dictionary. The one I consulted defines it as "humor that makes fun of life-threatening, disastrous, or terrifying situations." Amen to that. Small wonder I make use of gallows humor so often when dealing with colleagues. As you've probably inferred by now, I'm a smart-ass. Okay, "irreverent" might be a kindlier word. I'm trying to say that when things get rough, I don't play Pollyanna. I won't pretend that shit doesn't hurt when it does. But I also refuse to complain, since in my estimation, pointless griping betrays a lack of focus and faith, which in turn betrays a lack of character. Instead, I laugh. And I try to get others to laugh along with me.

Laughter is healthy. I mean that literally. There's an article from the world-famous Mayo Clinic that cites how laughing relieves pain by flooding the body with endorphins. It also improves immune system functions while stimulating key organs, easing stress, and decreasing both heart rate and blood pressure. In team settings, I use laughter as a force multiplier. When my teammates see me laughing at unforeseen complications and bad twists of fate, it galvanizes them. *Whoa*, they start thinking. *If George can laugh at this shit sandwich we've just been served, there might be hope.*

I've been known to apply a related model when summoning determination. It's called the Stockdale Paradox, a term that author and business consultant Jim Collins popularized in his fine book *Good to Great: Why Some Companies Make the Leap and Others Don't*. The Stockdale Paradox refers to the incredible journey made by Medal of Honor recipient Admiral James Stockdale. In 1965, while serving as a navy fighter pilot, his plane was shot down over North Vietnam. Stockdale spent the next eight years as a POW in the infamous Hanoi Hilton prison camp, where he was tortured almost daily.

Despite suffering atrocities, he fulfilled his duty as ranking officer among the prisoners, rallying them to stay alive and, whenever possible, to prosper. Though the odds seemed stacked dead against it, Stockdale believed that one day he would return home to the United States and be reunited with his wife, Sibyl. Collins therefore defined the Stockdale Paradox as maintaining unwavering faith that you can and will prevail in the task you set for yourself, regardless of the difficulties, while at the same time having "the discipline to confront the most brutal facts of your current reality, whatever they might be." These days, a similar—though not precisely identical—system can be found in the New Age concept of "manifestation." That is, concretizing events—or circumstances that seem unlikely or even impossible—into reality through the power of focused belief.

Personally, I believe there are nuances pertaining to the Stockdale Paradox that need to be explored before anyone embraces it as a principle. For instance, given the direness of the situation he found himself in, Stockdale was basically left with two choices: He could believe that he would prevail, or he could succumb to despair. Since succumbing to despair was a death sentence, I'm hardly surprised that he chose to have faith. After all, even a 10 percent chance of survival is better than a 0 percent chance. I'm not trying to undercut Stockdale's bravery here. Rather, I'm pointing out once again that math doesn't lie. Understanding this might clear up certain misconceptions about my behavior over the years.

For instance, I've heard people say that once George gets something into his head, he'll never let go of it, never change his viewpoint or admit that he's wrong. Bullshit.

Look at my life. You'll see plenty of times when I kicked off some new venture with gusto only to abort it when a critical belief was disproven. Like I've already said in this book, I'm willing to bear enormous pain when I feel there's a 20 percent chance to make a 200x return. But if new information comes up and that ratio alters to say, a 1 percent chance at a 2x return, I'll happily walk away and won't look back.

If you talk to professional poker players, many will tell you they win by applying the cards they've been dealt against a clear understanding of the amount they stand to win. This is called pot odds, and to calculate it accurately, both factors must be considered. It's never one or the other, it's always both/and—the risk of loss set back-to-back against the percentage chance of gain. A big part of calculating pot odds is conducting a brutally stark analysis of how much emotion, time, and capital you'll have to invest compared to the size of potential return. If that ratio seems right, they play. If it's not, they'll fold and await the next deal. I completely agree with this approach.

If there's any trick to crossing the Swamp of Despair, it lies in being patient and learning to endure pain as you put one foot in front of the other, again and again. Your focus has to be evenly split between the reward ahead and the trials you face moment by moment. There's no other way. During this deeply uncomfortable passage, we must always remember that progress made by inches is progress nonetheless. Over time, those inches add up. In fact, those tiny steps are the only thing that ever carries anyone through the swamp to the opposite side, the Height of Success.

Michelle and I had set our sights on a new vision for WWE. We felt sure that our vision was correct. But getting there sucked. Whenever we thought we would win, boom! Another setback. And each time it did, it felt like every journalist in the country was right there, eager and waiting to do hit pieces on us.

George Barrios and Michelle Wilson have totally screwed up at WWE!

George Barrios and Michelle Wilson are idiots . . .

When will Vince McMahon fire these two?

Would the goddamn Swamp of Despair never end?

Apparently not. Because the biggest blow to our confidence was about to smash us right in the face.

***

In 2013, WWE's broadcast contracts came due. Michelle and I were convinced that this was the moment where all our hard work would pay off. We'd been crisscrossing the globe, telling the story of WWE's bright future to our business partners and the international media. We were using every opportunity we had to convince our media partners of the value proposition behind our repositioned content. Lo and behold, we began closing deals at higher rates than we'd ever enjoyed. And each time we did a deal, we announced it—and the world took notice.

In essence, we were saying, "See? Look here! These deals we're closing are bigger, more profitable than ever before. That's proof that our new vision of WWE's worth is accurate."

Michelle and I had also recommended keeping all of our new domestic contracts to five-year terms. This was considered unusual in an industry where ten years was the norm. Internally, we discussed our hope of the company seeing a 4–5x rise in the value of our domestic deals. But this didn't happen. At least not then. Instead, we got smacked in the face by Gates's Law.

Instead of a 4x rise in value, our new deals increased about 2x. This was the biggest increase in WWE history, but it was still short of our true value and less than what our investors expected. Which is why, the day we announced our domestic deals, WWE stock cratered in aftermarket trading. Down, down, down went the price of our shares. Frustrated, I stayed up all night brainstorming ways to deal with the impending fallout. I knew it would be a shit show. Investors losing their minds. Analysts gloating and pulling their knives out.

I remember it was five in the morning and our shares kept sinking in the pre-market. I was pacing my office from wall to wall. Suddenly, it wasn't just the financial media ripping me a new asshole; people inside WWE were joining them. I saw people's faces out in the hallway. Heard their whispers. Invented their words in my mind.

George and Michelle have completely fucked up. They said they would lead us but Christ, look at this! They took us inside an inferno . . .

This was the most painful moment I've ever had in my career.

Vince was out of the office that day, on the road producing *Raw* or *SmackDown*, I forget which. Fun fact: Vince McMahon isn't a morning person. His circadian rhythms run more or less nocturnal. When I first met him, he often worked until three or four in the morning before heading home and getting a few hours' sleep so he could walk back into the office at noon and do it all over again. That day, he called me at 6:30 am. He'd been tracking the stock price. Of course he had.

"How you doing, George?" Vince's voice was low and gravelly, like he'd been up all night.

"Hey, Vince. This fucking sucks."

He sighed and paused. Then he said something I'll never forget. "We're gonna get through this."

That was the moment I remembered who I was speaking to. One of the toughest, most dedicated, and most demanding men I'd ever met. A guy who'd gone bankrupt at least twice while building WWE after he'd bought it from his dad. Who used to laugh and say it had taken him more than twenty years to become an overnight success. It was vital for me to hear Vince supporting me right then. To know that this guy, who was decidedly not touchy-feely, was still giving me his vote of confidence.

"Don't worry," he told me. "We're gonna look back on this someday and laugh."

Turns out he was right. But right then it felt awful.

And of course, things only got worse after that.

***

As I write this, I'm recalling a presentation deck that Michelle and I built as far back as 2011. The same deck we used during presentations of our new grand vision for the company. One of the slides included a quote from an industry writer—I think he worked for *Forbes*. It was one of those quotes where the journalist basically said, Michelle Wilson and George Barrios are fucking this company up! Somebody needs to rein them in! They have no idea what they're doing!

As deck slides go, this one was a real attention grabber. Michelle and I would pull it up, then wait for laughter in the room to subside, at which point we'd reiterate our vision: We were foretelling the future of the media industry. This involved the unbundling of traditional networks.

"Nothing we're presenting here is supposition," I would say. "Make no mistake. This is all going to happen. Period. End of sentence. Within just a few short years, on demand will be the way people consume scripted and unscripted content. Everything except live content will be on demand. That goes for video, text, music, information of every variety—TV shows, movies, songs, books, news . . . it will all be out there, posted and waiting.

"And because of this paradigm shift, new players will enter the value chain. Consumers will access content however they want it, whenever they want it. Aggregators will certainly profit from their relationship with consumers, but get this: The people making the real money will be the differentiated IP holders—the companies that create content. It's the middlemen, traditional linear networks, who'll have a hard time in this new model. Also, counterintuitively, the democratization and proliferation of scripted content will make live content exponentially more valuable. Live content, which WWE specializes in, will be at a premium."

These days, people ask me, "How come you guys got so far out ahead of the curve? Why didn't other big media companies like Disney, for instance, do direct-to-consumer sooner?"

Go back to my conversation with Vince. It's not because companies like Disney or Time Warner didn't have smart people working for them. They did. It's because, in most cases, their CEOs could never survive such an aggressive business transformation.

Look at what happened with us. Our company had to go down in defeat before it could rise again toward victory. I'm always amazed how ancient cultures understood this principle. Witness the ancient Greeks. The heroes in their tales had to first endure katabasis, descent to the underworld, before they achieved anabasis, a rise to new heights.

I've already mentioned that Vince was WWE's controlling shareholder and, as I said, he believed in me and Michelle. If he wasn't an expert in classical business strategy, he was nonetheless wise. Vince understood that something can't come from nothing. That if we wanted to grow, a tithe would have to be paid. The journey to fulfill our vision would be rough, but he was willing to slog through the swamp to reach success. Show me the CEO or CFO of any other publicly traded company who would do that. Or wait. Don't bother. You can't. For good reason. It's like I told Vince. Rather than getting rewarded for being a visionary, they'd get fired.

The leading edge is the bleeding edge. Everyone wants to lead but nobody wants to bleed. You've heard that, right? There's an old saying in blues music, "Everybody wants to go to heaven but nobody wants to die." This is how disruptors take advantage of incumbents again and again.

Let's pause here and do a thought experiment. Think back about thirty-five years. Imagine you're telling people, "Guess what? Someday there's going to be this company called Amazon. It's going to be bigger than Walmart and it'll sell every good you can imagine . . . but through your computer. And here's the kicker. Everything you order will be delivered right to your door—the day after you order it!"

How would people have reacted? The smartest people would have laughed at you for several reasons, not the least of which was that at that point, Walmart was huge, too big to displace. These brilliant people undoubtedly would have leveraged one of the most overused but least understood terms in business: moat. Walmart's moat was just too wide and deep, they would have said. Did Walmart have the capacity to create a service like Amazon eventually did? Sure. But why would they disrupt their own business model? Walmart was making too much money, and nobody wanted to sacrifice that, least of all the CEO, who'd lose his job for rocking the boat.

Another example. How did Netflix become Netflix? Why, for instance, didn't a rival media outlet like HBO create the direct-to-consumer streaming business that Netflix ended up building? HBO was certainly better positioned to do so. Back then they were rolling in money. They had a great distribution model set up and they'd even blazed a new trail by expanding from distribution into content production with early hit shows like *The Sopranos*, *Deadwood*, *The Wire*, and *Oz*. So what went wrong?

Simple. Go back to David Carr's "long, dark hallway." Time Warner, which owns HBO, made too much money. They weren't about to twist their revenue spigots shut to transform HBO for the next stage of the journey, no matter how badly this was required. And on this point, let me be clear. It's not that HBO wasn't nimble enough, didn't have sufficient resources, or didn't have sharp enough minds at the helm. In my estimation, they just didn't view the required transformation as being in their best interest.

That's the reason we call these disruptions counter-positioning. Ultimately, the incentives aren't aligned for incumbents to change. But if you can counter-position an incumbent, you can disrupt them. Which means you can beat them.

***

Michelle and I kept plugging away. Years passed. Our relationship with Vince deepened. This was an amazing development and one I'm still thankful for. Mostly because it was so improbable.

Here I should add that Michelle's relationship with Vince is probably different from mine. Vince respected her, and she lived up to that respect. Over the years, more than a few people have told me that Vince took his cues from the way Michelle comported herself. That he felt he had to live up to her standard of being an executive. If that's true—and I'm willing to bet that it is—what a compliment.

For all that, Michelle and I share a habit of swearing like sailors. She and I use obscenities as a bonding ritual. To be clear, we don't swear all the time, but when we do, we're professionals.

Quick story. One time I was out driving with my daughter, Alayna, who must've been fourteen at the time. We were cruising down I-95, headed for Flushing to visit my mom, when Michelle called my cell. I routed the call through the car's speakers. Bad move. "Hey, what's up?" I said.

"You won't fucking believe what this fucking goddamn fucker journalist said about the fucking company!"

I shot a quick look at Alayna. Of course, she knew Michelle but only as my polished, professional colleague. For years, Alayna had watched videos of Michelle and me briefing high-level stakeholders and investors. In each of those presentations, Michelle came across as elegant and poised, the prototypical executive. But here? Dropping f-bombs all over the place? That was an eye-opening moment for my daughter, and one I felt guilty about. I should have told Michelle that I wasn't alone in the car.

I hope this gives you better insight into Michelle. She's a remarkably valuable character study. In many ways, Michelle is tougher than I am. But she's also more deferential to authority, so she and Vince didn't butt heads all that often. That honor was reserved for me. What can I say? You already know how I grew up. I can be difficult to get along with. I'm uncompromising. Hardheaded. I speak my mind, don't hold anything back. Now and then, this has ruffled some feathers. Okay, make that a shit ton of feathers.

In fact, on more than one occasion, Vince called me into his office after a meeting. "George," he said to me one time. "What you said to So-and-So. You can't do that. You were being disrespectful."

My defense was always the same. "I wasn't being disrespectful, Vince, I was disagreeing with somebody. There's a difference."

I remember another time we had a conference call in my office. There were probably six people participating. Vince called in from wherever he was, I forget where. In the middle of that conversation, he sort of snapped and said, "George, you have to stop yelling at me! You're getting agitated!"

Picture me half-shocked, half-amused. I wasn't getting agitated, I was excited. The two emotions might sound the same but they're not. Also, I have a pretty loud voice to start with. But when I get excited it gets even louder. I explained all this to Vince but he kept saying, "Please do not talk to me in that tone of voice."

One of the guys in the room threw the phone on mute and looked at me, mystified. "Vince outweighs you by . . . what? A hundred and fifty pounds? And all of it muscle? He's this tough guy on TV, chews tenpenny nails. Now he sounds like a little kid, telling you to stop making fun of him on the playground."

Fair point. When I met Vince, I think he was sixty-four years old, with a long and storied history of punching people who yelled at him. But I knew he was mellowing. The Vince McMahon I'd come to know was different from the Vince McMahon who, back in his forties, got so angry at an ESPN interviewer, he slapped papers out of his hands on camera. A lot of people thought that episode was planned. But I asked Vince about it one time. He shrugged and said, "I lost my temper. Shouldn't have done that."

What I'm trying to say is that Vince was always a puzzle to me. For one of the most introverted people I've ever met, he puts on a damn good show. When he meets you face-to-face, the man is all business. He'll shake your hand, look you dead in the eye, play the part he knows that you want him to play. But he's like some comedians I know. Onstage, he's loud and abrasive. The demon is in him. Offstage, he's the complete opposite, so quiet that some people get uncomfortable being around him. In a conversation among friends, he can barely get his words out. But all that frustration sort of erupts when he takes the stage. At that point he becomes this other version of himself. He's the Boss. He's Mr. McMahon.

The same man, I kept reminding myself, who once told everyone, in public, "George is the toughest motherfucker I've ever met."

For all our differences, we had a lot in common. There was the bond forged from our hard-luck upbringings. The fact that Vince is a tough guy, I'm a tough guy. We're both funny. We're also both prone to getting emotional, particularly when it comes to the subject of kids in need. I learned this early in my tenure with WWE.

At Vince's directive, WWE was a major supporter of the national Make-A-Wish foundation. For those who don't know, Make-A-Wish grants life-changing wishes to children with critical illnesses. I remember being at a wish reveal. This is a ceremony where an ill child is brought into the room and they're not really sure what's going on, so it's very exciting. During the ceremony, the child is told that their wish will be granted. At that point, they're often given a souvenir to whet their appetite for the experience they'll soon receive.

In this case, the child was a little boy. Let's call him Douglas. He was painfully thin with skin like milk, his skull hairless as an egg because of his cancer. But on that particular day, Douglas was smiling from ear to ear. Fascinated by NASA, he'd always dreamed of going on a flight into Earth's upper atmosphere. The foundation was going to make that happen for him. They'd made Douglas a toy rocket which they gave to him right there in front of everyone. A nice way of saying he'd soon take part in the aeronautical outing of his dreams with experienced NASA pilots. There wasn't a dry eye in the house.

I remember dabbing tears off my cheeks, asking myself if I was doing enough to make the world a better place. I had newfound wealth and prestige, but so what? What should I do with it? Right then and there, I determined to discuss the matter with Carol. I would argue that we should give more of our money and time to worthy charities. But was Make-A-Wish the right entity for us to sponsor?

You know what they say. Ask and ye shall receive. Knock and the door will be opened. As fate would have it, I struck up a conversation with the guy standing next to me. Told him how moving I found this wish being granted to Douglas. Imagine my shock when the man told me he was Douglas's father.

"We were thrilled when we learned that his wish would be granted," the man said. "Probably not for the reason you're thinking though."

"What do you mean?" I said.

He explained to me how there's something called the wish journey, the process of getting everything in order to grant a wish. Douglas's wish journey had been going on for months. "It's changed us forever," his father said. "I mean, sure, it's been great for Douglas. But also his siblings. My wife and me, too. See, all of a sudden, our lives weren't just about seeing the next specialist, getting to the next treatment, trying out the latest protocol, watching Douglas in constant pain." The father looked away like he was seeing something in the distance for which he held great fondness. A cherished home. "Suddenly, we had joy again," he said. "We had hope where, for so long, that had been denied us."

I was never prouder to be a part of WWE than I was in that moment. Doubly so when it turned out that for whatever reason—modern medicine, hope, or some combination of both—Douglas recovered. I resolved then and there to help Make-A-Wish however I could. I joined their national board in 2014, and later became its chairman. Carol also got very involved, probably more so than me. In addition to financial support, she gave her time on the front lines. As a volunteer, Carol takes children on their wish journeys. I'm not sure I could ever do that. I wouldn't be able to get through it.

By the way, guess which individual took time out of his busy schedule to grant the most wishes in Make-A-Wish history? That would be WWE wrestler-turned-movie star John Cena. Who, I'm happy to report, is hands down as stand-up a guy as he often appears to be.

But I wanted to tell you about Vince and me getting emotional. We were in a meeting once where we were playing a short video we'd created about WWE's partnership with Make-A-Wish. Imagine us sitting in the boardroom, facing a huge screen. The lights went down. The reel kicked off. It was two minutes long. When it was finished, the lights came back up. Vince and I had both seen this kind of stuff millions of times but there we were, dabbing our eyes and pretending we hadn't been moved.

Vince and I were never huggy-kissy with each other, but we didn't have to be. Vince consistently put his money where his mouth was. On aggregate, he was 90 percent supportive of everything Michelle and I were doing to transform the company. In fact, I remember him using this phrase with us so often it became one of our go-to management slogans. "Bet on yourself," he used to tell us whenever we proposed some new initiative. "If you're not willing to bet on yourself, no one else will."

Looking back, I'm so grateful he gave us that latitude, because little by little, things started turning around. Gradually, the voices of naysayers started to quiet. Supporters became more outspoken. Our revenue kept growing and our stock price kept ticking higher. The terms of our renegotiated contracts became more favorable. Meanwhile, the tone of all those people who'd once made it their mission in life to defy us started to soften. Became deferential.

The plan the three of us had created was working.

***

There's an old video of Steve Jobs. He was probably in his thirties when it was shot. He wasn't Steve Jobs yet, but you could sort of see that he would be someday.

In this interview, he said the most amazing thing. Something like: If you think about it, everything you see in the world has been made by other human beings. So you're basically living in someone else's creation. But it doesn't have to be that way. You can shift roles. You can be a creator. It can be you, if that's what you want.

After he'd spoken, the interviewer was silent. I don't think he got it. I understand this. During my Swamp of Despair at WWE, people told me daily, "George, you're waaaaaay off base on this one. We've been selling wrestling for thirty years, long before you got here. And we know better than you do what wrestling is worth."

No matter how badly I was hurting, no matter which doubts I was battling, I always made sure I replied the same way. "But why does it have to be that way?" In my mind, this was the pivotal question. The way I understand the universe, perception isn't truth, but it sure goes a long way toward passing for reality.

For instance, scientists tell us there's no such thing as color in the universe. What you and I call color is simply the way the rods and the cones in our eyes perceive light. Moreover, our eyes, which some people put so much stock in, can only perceive about .0035 percent of the full light spectrum. That's a little like going up to a door that's been mounted at the brink of the Grand Canyon and taking in that incredible vista by looking through the keyhole, then complaining that the view isn't everything people say it's cracked up to be.

Some people figure this out, of course. They straighten their backs, twist the knob, and open the door to see what really lies on the other side. But most people don't. They're more content with limited viewpoints. Calling them truth.

What I'm trying to say is that the value Michelle and I saw in WWE was already there. It existed, it was a thing—provided you had the right set of eyes to see it. This, to me, is an example of first principles thinking, otherwise known as problem solving from fundamental truths. You start with what you know is objectively true and break everything down until you're certain you're dealing with that which clearly exists. In my view and Michelle's, this was the value of WWE. From there, we had to build up again, had to prove why the value we saw was real.

Theoretically, it wasn't complicated. In our way of looking at things, aggregators in the sports entertainment sector weren't buying football, baseball, or basketball—they were buying live eyeballs. The sport didn't matter as much as the fact that people were paying attention to it.

Ask yourself, what's the value in the NFL? Does it have anything to do with the fact that players throw an oblong inflatable pigskin bladder up and down a hundred-yard field? Not at all. The value is that people love to watch it. They love it so much, they've habituated it, traditionalized it, and built a massive economy around it. If enough viewers tuned in to koala bears playing hopscotch, we would have sold that instead of wrestling.

Don't misunderstand me. I'm a huge fan of wrestling. What these performers do is an art form that's only matured as years have gone by. But first principles said viewers' interest was more valuable than what they were interested in. That's what Michelle and I worked from because that, to us, represented the pure physics of the situation.

First principles also told us that we couldn't change WWE using the same thinking everyone else was using. Albert Einstein once said, "We cannot solve our problems with the same thinking we used when we created them." So true. From what Michelle and I had seen, the entire sector was reasoning by analogy. This is a dangerous practice. Even some people in our camp were doing this. They were saying that WWE had always been in the lower-value tranche and always would be. Rather than looking for ways to break out of old patterns, they were doubling down on them.

This notion of seeing things differently calls to mind a quote from one of my favorite books, *Range: Why Generalists Triumph in a Specialized World* by David Epstein. Epstein makes many assertions that challenge conventional thinking. For instance, he argues that cultivating a broad experience base is more useful than depth of expertise. He champions diverse experiences and a concept he calls "desirable difficulty," taking on tasks that require great effort but choosing them in a targeted fashion to consciously develop skill and deeper learning toward a specific end.

Epstein offers this observation: "Big innovation most often happens when an outsider who may be far away from the surface of the problem reframes the problem in a way that unlocks the solution." Off the top of my head, I can't think of a more succinct way to describe the dynamic that led Michelle and me to approach changes at WWE the way we did. We were outsiders to that community. That's why we saw things differently, that's why we chose the actions we eventually did, and that's why we triumphed.

But again, this wasn't easy. What Epstein didn't mention in his book is the resistance reframers can face from people invested in the status quo. I mentioned how the possibilities that Michelle and I saw were theoretically simple. The truth is, in practical terms, it's hard to change anyone's mind about anything. You have to put in the grunt work, be willing to go against the status quo. Remember Gates's Law: What we begin today doesn't become a reality tomorrow. It could take months or years, maybe longer. And along the way, you must endure ridicule at every step. In so many ways, you have to have what religious people call faith: dead certainty in the reality of things unseen.

Most people don't do this. Or won't. Or they can't. In fact, I would estimate that 99 percent of the population accepts the reality in front of them. Why shouldn't they, when whole systems have been built to make that profitable for them?

***

Here's a funny story to drive home my point about seeing things differently. Just as our plan began to take off, we held an emergency meeting with our legal and digital teams. Turns out that a lot of our content was being pirated and reposted in China. This was bad because we had a network deal in China. Not a big one, but it was official and earning us revenue. More disturbing was how quickly these pirates were stealing, converting, and posting our content. Much faster and more efficiently than we were able to.

"How the fuck are they doing it?" somebody said. "These pirates are just kids but they're beating the pants off whole teams of people we've hired!"

Michelle and I were losing our minds. We got on the phone with Matt, the lawyer we'd hired to protect our IP.

"Matt, God damn it, we want all this fucking content taken down now!"

We could hear him scribbling notes on the other end of the line. "Okay, no problem. It'll cost money—"

"If we have to double what we're spending, do it!"

"Got it."

"Wait." While we were talking, I'd been looking over the data consumption numbers for pirated content. I saw that the pirates' posts were getting more views than we were. By a mile. And that's when it hit me. "If we add the hits we get on the pirated sites to our own, we can double the number of eyeballs we're getting in China." I turned to one of my analysts. "How much money are we making off China?"

Answer: not much.

I looked at Michelle, who nodded and bent to the speakerphone. "Matt?" she said. "New plan. Don't go after the pirates. We may want you to hire them."

That's how we rolled.

Again, the key to success is to look at things differently, and to have confidence in your viewpoint. Let me be blunt. Without the confidence quotient, success is never possible. Even with it, you might still fail, but at least you'll stay in the game, reexamining facts, going over old models, embracing new ones that seem to work better. Winston Churchill once said that "Success is stumbling from failure to failure with no loss of enthusiasm." I tend to agree, provided you're not just stumbling aimlessly. You have to have a plan.

This is the part where I tell you that Michelle and I both have huge egos. We always want to be right. But here's the crucial difference. When it comes to something that counts, we're both first in line to say, "Wait a second. I made a mistake. I see this differently now. I was wrong and I'm changing my mind."

It's like I was saying before about working the way professional poker players calculate pot odds. If I'm dealt a strong hand in Texas Hold'em, you'd better believe I'm going to pursue it. But if the flop turns against me, I won't stick around losing money on the turn or the river. I'm willing to fold and start all over again if I have to.

***

There were some dark stories during this period. Maybe the worst of them happened in April 2017. WWE was holding WrestleMania, our annual equivalent of the Super Bowl, in a stadium filled with about 60,000 fans. This was more than just a party. It was a marathon event attended by partners and sponsors where we gave presentations consequential for future business. Our entire board was in attendance for an exhausting week of work.

My perpetual lack of sleep conspired with an extra glass of wine to make me sluggish. I admit I wasn't my usual upbeat self. Apparently, this was noticed by some of our longtime staffers, a few of whom were always looking to curry favor with Vince. They brought the matter to his attention.

I never understood why Vince got so offended, but he did. To the best of my recollection, we barely ran into each other during WrestleMania XXXIII. Still, fueled by what people had told him, he called me aside not long after that.

"Were you drinking?" he said.

"Hmmm?" I said. "Yeah. I had a glass of wine or two."

"Well, I heard you were having too much."

"From whom?"

He didn't answer.

I said, "Vince, this is crazy. What are you trying to say? I was up all night, then I went to the event. I had wine, sure, but then, I think two hours later, I was up again to hop on the quarterly call and talk about our subscriber numbers. Which went very well, by the way."

He refused to engage me further. But two weeks later, he pulled me aside before we went into our board meeting. "George," he said. "When we go into executive session, I'm going to ask the management team to leave. I want you to stay and apologize to the board for what happened."

I remember feeling outraged, hurt, and more than a little betrayed. I also remember feeling stark terror. The thought of standing up before everyone, apologizing for something I hadn't done—that was awful. But Vince did everything just as he said he would. The management team got up and left and then it was just Vince and me and the board.

"Everyone," Vince said. "George has something he'd like to say."

I stammered. I stuttered. I wanted to die. It was one of the most humiliating moments of my life. But I gritted my teeth and did it. I apologized to everyone. Because fuck it. This wasn't the hill I was going to die on.

Walking out of that meeting, I remember thinking, *That's it. I'm finished at WWE. Finished everywhere. My reputation is ruined.*

The despair I felt was all the more dire and insufferable because Michelle and I had worked so hard for so long. And for what?

Turns out I needn't have worried. The board took everything in stride, almost like they knew the whole thing was being blown out of proportion. If anything, people were incredibly supportive. After that meeting, several board members made a point of coming up to me or reaching out over email. *Look*, they all basically said. *You're not the first person to land in a situation like this. We all know you're doing a great job. The important thing is that, moving forward, Vince has confidence in you. So don't let this drag you down. Get it together and get back to work.*

Looking back on it now, their generosity still overwhelms me. And I learned from that experience. Sleepless nights or no sleepless nights, wine or no wine, earnings call or no earnings call, I pace myself differently now. And nothing even remotely like that has ever happened again.

***

Now I want you to imagine the day that our stock hit $100 per share. I want you to imagine Michelle and me staring at each other across one of our work tables, realizing that all the time we'd spent—years' worth of time to unlock the secrets of Total Viewer Hours and their value—had finally paid off. Realizing, too, that our mental model was no longer mental. A figment. An idea. It was real. It was tangible. Solid.

Now I want you to imagine the same idiots who wrote that Michelle and I should be thrown out a window writing articles singing our praises. Saying that what we had done was one of the greatest transformations ever seen in the public markets. In fact, the very same writer whose fucking ridiculous quote we'd put in our deck just to show what we were up against . . . this selfsame son of a bitch fell over backward wailing hosannas at us.

I want you to savor the irony of that. I want you to feel the same vindication we did. Now imagine me getting voted among the Top Three Best CFOs in the Media Industry in a survey by *Institutional Investor*.

Not long after that, Vince officially announced that Michelle and I had been promoted to copresidents of WWE.

I've said this before and I'll say it again.

Sweet rewards.

***

About seven years after we began our campaign, Michelle and I were on a trip to Dubai. At that point, WWE was completely transformed. The stock price was 9x or 10x from where we started. Picture us: the rock stars of our company.

We were in the back seat of a hired car that was driving us around to a bunch of meetings. Out of the blue, Michelle said, "Did you ever really think we would do it?"

As my answer, I pulled up the app that I use to organize all my stuff. Then I pulled up the 2011 board deck we'd put together and showed it to her. "Read," I said. "It's all right there. Everything we planned to do. A direct-to-consumer business. The largest sport on social and digital." I paused. "We were predicting a 5x or a 6x leap. We made good on that, right?"

My voice was shaking when I said this. My eyes teared up. Because I was thinking about Steve Katz. Pete Peterson. Jeff Bewkes. Vince. I thought of my family. My aunts and my cousins. I thought of Abuelo. I thought of Mami and Papi. I thought about Carol, Alayna, Katrina, and Celia.

And that's when I realized how blessed I am.

But wouldn't you know it? In what seemed like the blink of an eye, the whole damn thing fell apart all over again.

Vince made me copresident of the company. And then he fired me.

CHAPTER TWELVE

Smackdown

Before I tell you what happened, here's a quick lesson from Business 101. Growth is always related to revenue, profits, and cash flow. By 2018, WWE was reaping mammoth rewards from the changes Michelle and I had implemented. The organization was no longer just a traveling road show obsessed with event logistics. We had entered a totally different game, the one I referenced when I quoted Reed Hastings, founder and CEO of Netflix. He said that his number one competitor was sleep.

What he meant was every minute every person spent watching Netflix was valuable. Because if people spent a lot of their time enjoying his service, then they would be willing to keep paying for it. Ideally, each eyeball would be turned to Netflix 24/7, and anything that got in the way had to be considered a competitor.

Despite how far we'd come, Michelle and I knew we weren't out of the woods. Word to the wise: When you're truly in business you are never out of the woods. We understood that further disruption was coming. Further balkanization of the media space was in the cards. That's how counter-positioning works. Once you disrupt a particular system, set your watch. It will happen again, and sooner than you think.

Metcalfe's Law states that the value of any network increases exponentially with every node added. The more users a network has, the more valuable it becomes. Because of this, the cost of adding new viewers is generally outpaced by the value they bring. This applies to stock exchanges worldwide, to social media networks, and yes, to passionate fan communities like WWE.

Michelle and I were chiefly concerned that when the next change arrived, WWE's organizational size might work against us. We envisioned scenarios where consumer aggregators—Netflix, Apple, Amazon Prime, Comcast, and the like—would start to consolidate as the battle between intruders and incumbents worked itself to a standstill. Regardless of how that shaped up, we knew WWE would retain value in the coming era. But big players wouldn't necessarily yield the same force as they had in the previous cycle.

The key point is that the value of eyeballs isn't linear. Consider a case where your organization has 500 eyeballs and my organization has 500 eyeballs. If we were to merge, our new combined viewership of 1,000 eyeballs might not represent a 2x leap. Rather, it might represent a 4 or 5x leap for the simple reason that no other organization might be operating at that scale. At the same time, organizations that stayed at the level of 200 or 300 eyeballs could see the value of those eyeballs decline. Why? Relatively speaking, they're too small to matter. That's how working at scale often operates, and it's perilous.

"We've got to stay nimble and open," I told Vince. "The media sector is still in the early stages of its latest transformation. We can't know for sure which way the world will evolve. At this point, what we can do is create options." Then I reiterated what I'd been telling him all along. "Down the line, we may have to start thinking about acquiring another company or being acquired. There are scenarios where that could be the best way to keep growing."

Whenever I said this, Vince would nod and we'd move on to the next topic.

***

We were opening new markets everywhere, but some of our best work got done in the Middle East. Michelle and I kicked off negotiations to have WWE become the first sports property to do a major event in the Kingdom of Saudi Arabia, population 40 million.

The senior official we liaised with ran the Kingdom's entertainment authority and reported directly to Crown Prince Mohammed bin Salman—MBS, as he's commonly called. By early 2018, WWE was close to closing a multimillion-dollar long-term agreement. There were problems, of course.

The Kingdom is a theocracy whose culture is different from ours. Historically, there were parts of the country that frowned on the sort of pageantry WWE offered. We faced all sorts of roadblocks getting our content into the country through traditional cable and broadcast TV. But this became yet another case where all the work Michelle and I had done began to pay off.

Our research showed that Saudi Arabia was the number one per capita consumer of YouTube videos worldwide. We had also heard that the Saudis were the number one consumer of whiskey per capita in the world—this despite the fact that the Kingdom had banned alcohol. Was that true? Who knows. All I knew for certain was that WWE had unlocked a ton of value precisely because we'd created the infrastructure to create and distribute our social and digital content.

Our negotiations dragged on because the Saudis are notorious hagglers. By 2018, despite having made great progress, we were still struggling to get the deal over the finish line. Complicating matters was the disappearance of Saudi journalist and dissident Jamal Khashoggi.

A vocal critic of Kingdom policies—and particularly the treatment of women—Khashoggi walked into the Saudi consulate in Istanbul, Turkey, on October 2, 2018, to secure certain documents for his upcoming wedding. He never walked out. Officially, he was declared a missing person. But the media began circulating rumors, including one where Khashoggi had been killed inside the embassy. That his body was dismembered with a bone saw and hauled out piece by piece in black plastic trash bags. Whether or not this is true cannot be stated definitively. As outraged as I was by what happened, I still defy anyone to argue they understand who was truly at fault. All I know is that on our end, Khashoggi's disappearance called into question our deal with the Saudis.

God, what a bumpy road that was. Vince, Michelle, and I spent a great deal of time debating the pros and cons of moving forward. Vince in particular was deeply uncomfortable with the uncertainty surrounding these events. I remember the three of us staying up late one Wednesday night. We were supposed to be preparing for the next morning's earnings call at 11:00 a.m.; instead, we again found ourselves debating the merits of moving forward at all.

In my opinion, we couldn't walk out on the deal. It was too worthwhile for WWE. But Vince kept shaking his head. "This thing with Khashoggi. Doing the deal could be the biggest risk we've ever taken with the company."

"Vince, listen to me," I said. "I understand how serious this is. But no one really knows what's going on."

Vince stayed quiet for long stretches. I could see he was contemplating our options. Michelle was sort of in the middle, I thought, seeing things from both perspectives. Finally, I felt that we had to shit or get off the pot. "I think we're wrestling with ghosts on this," I said. "We're inventing hypotheticals, ignoring reality. We can't walk away from a chance to partner with a country like the KSA." I closed my eyes and thought for a moment. Then I opened them again. "Remember the Saudis offered us their private jet? I say we use that. One of us should go over there tomorrow, iron things out, get the deal stamped, and be done with it."

A quick discussion followed. Who could we send? It couldn't be Vince. Sending the Boss would be tipping our hand. Besides, Vince wasn't our best negotiator. And Michelle couldn't go. As a woman, her presence in the Kingdom would pose certain problems.

"Fine," I said. "I'll do it. I'll go." Vince's assistant left the room to call our Saudi counterpart. He was delighted to hear from us and said he'd have the G6 gassed up and ready to take off the next morning from Westchester Airport.

That night I got home after midnight. I walked into my bedroom. Carol was sleeping. I used the dimmer to slowly turn up the lights. Then I started to pack.

"What are you doing?"

I turned around and saw she was awake, blinking the sleep from her eyes. "I'm packing," I said. "Flying to Saudi Arabia tomorrow morning after the earnings call."

She turned milk white. She wasn't the only one who was uneasy. My own head nearly burst when I saw the disclaimers I had to sign. One of them said, "The following infractions are punishable in the Kingdom by death: alcohol, shows of affection, pornography . . ." The list went on.

I remember thinking, *Jesus Fucking Christ!* Then amending that swiftly to *Allahu Akbar!*

Despite my unease, the die had been cast. I hopped on the plane with one of our analysts, let's call him Bill. At around eleven at night, we touched down at King Khalid Airport near Riyadh. From there, we were driven to our hotel where we spent the night and the next day waiting to be summoned.

Late the next evening, we received a call letting us know that a limousine was on its way to pick us up. The car drove us straight to a compound that was something out of a movie. Roving guards were everywhere. They carried machine guns and wore bandoliers of ammunition. The mood simmered with an air of casual menace. I have never been so uncomfortable before or since.

We were led into a building set up like a man cave on steroids. Six giant hundred-inch TV screens mounted on one wall were playing sports, YouTube, news, and yeah, they had wrestling on. These guys were hanging out watching our wrestlers!

The sheikh we had flown there to meet was sitting on a giant overstuffed couch across from the wall of TVs. A hookah right beside him. He was wearing shorts and a T-shirt. He looked up at me, exhaled smoke, and glared. Then he started speaking in Arabic. Loudly. I got the impression he was angry. His translator told me he thought WWE was asking for too much in our negotiations.

I remember thinking, *This cannot be happening.* What the fuck was I thinking coming here in the middle of the night?

After a few more rounds of loud talking, the sheikh seemed disgusted. He waved a hand dismissing me. His Number Two took Bill and me into an adjoining room to hammer out a deal.

We were given no privacy while we worked. The dudes with loaded machine guns and long black tactical knives hanging off their belts kept entering the room for no good reason. I remember one of them came in carrying an odd little ceremonial-looking box.

Aha, I thought. *That's what they'll put my body parts in once they've killed me and cut me in pieces.*

We worked fast and finished by one in the morning. Then we were led into another room filled with ornate decorations. A sumptuous banquet had been laid out. The sheikh, now fully dressed in his traditional royal garb, was already seated at the head of the table. The translator said, "His Royal Highness is pleased and invites you to join him for a celebratory dinner." I sat down next to the sheikh and we chatted amiably through the translator. The food was delicious. The whole night felt surreal. But the deal was done.

I asked Bill to make a call back home and inquire about the G6. He told me the plane wouldn't be able to take off for another twenty-four hours. I shook my head. "Uh uh. No way." I kept my voice low. "I want to go home now."

He nodded. "I figured you'd say that. There's a British Airways flight heading out of Riyadh a bit after four in the morning."

"Book it," I told him.

A car took us back to the airport. We made it through customs and got on the flight. I remember stowing my luggage in the overhead compartment. A flight attendant was in front of me and I tapped her on the shoulder. She turned around and before I could say anything, she gave me a warm smile. "I'll have a drink at your seat twenty-seven minutes after takeoff. We have to clear Saudi airspace."

She had read my mind.

***

A few months later, WWE's first live event took place in the Kingdom. I wasn't there for it, but I heard from my team that 40,000 people packed themselves into the stadium. Fathers and mothers with their children. Daughters dressed as boys, since at that point girls were forbidden to enter public places—though I hear this has recently changed. In fact, the Kingdom has loosened many of its cultural restrictions. There are grounds to suppose that some of that can be credited to WWE. For instance, consider the impact of having female wrestlers perform in public for a Saudi audience. Talk about shattering cultural paradigms.

I was told that a chant went up from the crowd as one of our female athletes took the stage. The colleague recounting this story said he turned to someone who spoke Arabic. "What are they saying?" he asked.

The translator smiled. "They are saying . . . 'There is hope.'"

Nowadays, WWE does multiple events in the Kingdom every year. I'm proud to report that lots of families attend them openly.

***

Once I got back from that trip, I spoke to Vince. The usual topic. Call it our elephant in the room.

"We just hit another home run," I said. "And we still have a lot of growth ahead of us. But like we've talked about, the big value unlock is through scale. Bringing more eyeballs under the same roof . . . that's the long-term play. So now's the time to dig into that. And again, we have two options. Do we buy someone, or do we sell WWE?"

Vince nodded to show he had heard me. His answer seemed clear to me. He was processing.

We had a few more discussions that year on the topic, but they never went anywhere. And right around here is where everything went to shit. Let me give you some background before I plunge in.

***

A large part of my compensation was issued as stock grants, none of which I had touched in the ten or so years I'd worked for the company. My financial advisor loved to tell me, "George, that's crazy! Cash out and diversify. Nobody keeps that much of their net worth in the company they work for."

Time and again, I replied the same way. "I don't just work at WWE, I run WWE." By this I meant that I believed 100 percent in the transformation we had begun. If the company prospered, as I imagined it would, WWE stock would be the best investment I could make. But I was also tacitly saying that if WWE suffered any setbacks, they would fall on my shoulders. Nobody else's. I was betting on myself.

Somewhere in here, Michelle and I started talking about what could come next. We'd worked very closely together for years and enjoyed how our talents complemented each other. It seemed only natural that we would share with each other the visions we had for our careers. Turns out that we both had the same dream of becoming CEO of a company. A job where we'd run the whole show without all the mishegas of having anyone else in the mix. Don't get me wrong. By this point, Vince had given Michelle and me broad latitude. However, we still had to run major decisions by him.

After eleven years on the job, I discovered I wanted a more unfettered environment to work in. Michelle told me she felt the same way. We both knew that we wanted a change, but we never discussed what that change might be. Looking back, it's clear that there were only two options, staying at WWE or moving onto other challenges.

In the meantime, life progressed. Business rolled on. The company kept doing well.

Michelle and I had no idea what was coming.

***

It was another late Wednesday night at the office. Another marathon session to prep for an earnings call the next day. This time, I remember, Michelle and I were working in her office. Once we had wrapped up business, I told her I'd made my decision. "I'm going to leave."

She just looked at me.

I took her silence for a question and explained. "I don't have a plan yet. But I know that running the company is too all-consuming to look for my next role at the same time. Carol and I are taking vacation next week. We've already discussed this. She's on board. So I plan to get through tomorrow's earnings call. Then I'll tell Vince."

Michelle leaned back in her chair and studied me. "That was my plan."

I think I said, "What?"

"I had the same plan. I'm also on vacation next week. I was also going to tell Vince I'm leaving. Right after the call."

Talk about weird. You know that feeling you get where the hairs on your forearms stand up? This was that. There was also the fact that Michelle and I rarely took vacation. And never before had our infrequent vacations coincided. It felt portentous—though of what, I had no idea.

"So . . . How does this work?" I said. "Do we tell him together? Or do it sequentially? I don't want him to think we're ganging up on him."

Michelle shrugged. "It's going to happen either way. My vote, we do it together."

So that's what we did.

The earnings call went well the next day. Once it was finished, we didn't wait. We went to Vince's office, which was beautifully appointed, very unique. Anyone can see what it looks like since we used that space in footage we shot for our programming. It was the set on which Vince played his part as Mr. McMahon, the Evil Overlord of Wrestling. Hilarious stuff. The whole thing was done up in the red-and-black color scheme Vince loves. I think it reminds him of the heavy metal he listened to back in the day. No surprise that a lot of WWE content borrows from that palette.

On one entire wall he'd hung this giant skull of a T. Rex. I'd always assumed it to be a replica, not an actual fossil, but who knows? I should have asked but I never did. The skull was a gift from his daughter and son-in-law. To me, it perfectly reflected Vince's public persona as the alpha predator.

He was sitting behind his desk, dressed impeccably as always in a tailored suit and tie. Michelle and I told him we were leaving.

"Don't do this." His voice came out scratchy. He dug a bit deeper and plowed ahead in full-on promoter mode. He began trying to make us see the wisdom in what he was saying, the reasonableness of it, the logic. Little by little, he got more emotional, started to well up. Michelle and I did too as what was unfolding became apparent to us all.

"You can't leave," Vince finally said. "I've spent thirty years of my life pulling people along, trying to get this business off the ground. The last ten years, it's been you two pulling me along. I could never have done it without you."

I was struck by the shift in his manner. Normally, Vince is a circumspect guy, very stoic. He never gets upset, never raises his voice no matter how difficult a situation might be. But here it felt like he was unburdening himself. Toward the end of that conversation, I couldn't help but notice the way he'd unknotted his tie and unbuttoned his collar. *This is hard for him*, I thought.

It was hard for all of us. The three of us had gone through so much together.

We stayed for two hours and it was awful, I tell you. Just awful.

"We can figure something out," Vince said. "We've got to figure something out."

By the time we left his office, it was eight or nine at night. We were the only ones left in the building. Michelle and I were walking back to her office to pick up our stuff.

"Maybe Vince is right," I said. "Maybe there's wiggle room for us to work something out. What do you think?"

"I think we should stick to the plan," Michelle said.

We spent about another hour in her office talking through what had just happened. "Maybe Vince is right," I said again. "There's still a lot to be done here. Why don't we think things through a bit more? There might still be a scenario where everyone can get what they want. If Vince could just pull back a bit more, let us have more autonomy. Governance with the board. This could still be a home run for everyone."

Going into that meeting, I'd been convinced that leaving WWE was in my best interest. Coming out of the meeting, I felt more open-minded. Seeing Vince shaken like that? Frankly, that rattled me.

Michelle thought for a moment, then shrugged. "I can give it a try, if he's willing to do it."

We left it at that, then left for vacation.

***

Two weeks later, Michelle and I were back in the office doing acrobatics with the company org chart. We were cooking up new ideas to pitch to Vince, all in good faith that we could find a new leadership structure that everyone loved. As Michelle and I saw it, nothing had to change fundamentally. If we were to stay, we would just like to have more decision-making power. Fewer situations where we needed Vince's sign-off. This, in turn, would free us up to optimize company operations.

I remember reflecting a lot on what Bill Gates did at Microsoft and Larry Ellison did at Oracle. Both men had founded their companies but they were also product people, and very hands on when it came to that.

When they decided to transition out, they stepped down from their roles as CEO and essentially became their company's chief product officer, a post from which they could mentor whoever had taken their place. Michelle and I agreed that something like this could work with Vince. More importantly, it would be to the ultimate benefit of WWE.

We floated this notion to Vince and worked for several weeks to hammer it out. We haggled, debated, and traded ideas. Little by little, I got the impression that Vince was hardening to the idea. The guy who had wept and asked us to stay was losing ground to the guy who preferred to get heavy with people when he felt threatened. I'll be honest, I started hardening too. I'm not sure how Michelle felt, but my patience was nearly exhausted. I was halfway out the door and I think Vince sensed that.

For instance, in early December 2019, Vince held a small group meeting in his office. When it was finished, everyone got up to leave, but Vince said, "George. Hey, stay for a second?" He closed the door and we faced each other, alone.

"What are you thinking?" he said. "I mean, for the future."

The question annoyed me. We'd spent weeks going back and forth on seemingly meaningless details without coming to a conclusion. Basically, as far as I was concerned, he had been kicking the can down the road.

I remember looking him in the eye and saying one word. "Nothing."

Vince didn't take too kindly to that. I saw that look come over his face. The one I'd seen many times before where he was pissed off but trying not to look pissed off. His posture shifted, his shoulders hunched, his upper lip twisted. I felt like I was no longer talking to Vince, I was talking to Mr. McMahon now. The Boss.

"I made you rich." His tone wasn't kind.

But his getting riled up didn't make me beg off. Instead, it got my spine up. "Actually, that's not true," I said. "For a CFO and copresident, I got a fair deal. But you didn't make me rich, Vince. I got rich because I bet on myself."

I remember catching a glint in his eyes. The glimmer of recognition that I had just used his own words, his own philosophy against him. Then I did something I'd never done before. Without another word, I simply got up and walked out of his office.

He and I never mentioned that incident. But looking back, this is the point where I decided I was done. It was clear to me that my relationship with Vince wasn't just strained anymore. It had severed.

At that point, as I saw things, I had responsibilities to WWE and I was committed to fulfilling them. This included unveiling a new three-year strategic plan for the company at our next earnings call, which was scheduled for February 2020. However, after that? I was convinced I'd be on to my next challenge.

***

Let me clarify something here. I wasn't out in the market looking for a new job. Even so, I got plenty of inbound calls. For instance, a private equity firm offered to have me come aboard as the president of one of their portfolio companies and transition to CEO within a year. Stuff like that. All very interesting. Even flattering. And yes, as everyone does, I had asked some of these people for more information, but did so more as a matter of course. And Mr. Stay-at-WWE was still holding out hope that Vince would come around.

My day-to-day work didn't change. Michelle and I were still busy architecting WWE's strategic plan, which outlined the company's three-year goals and the actions we'd take to achieve them. A big undertaking. If memory serves, the calendar had Michelle and me presenting our plan to the board on January 30. About ten days after that, assuming we earned the board's approval, we'd present our plan at the February earnings call. All part of the normal cadence.

January 30 rolled around. Michelle and I presented our plan to the board and I knew something was off right away. A very uncomfortable meeting. I confess my delivery was off, despite how excited I was about what we'd cooked up.

Once that meeting wrapped up, I left the building to decompress on a walk. Our corporate office was situated in the middle of a residential neighborhood in Stamford. As I strolled by a home with a For Sale sign on the lawn, I got a text from Vince's executive admin. "Hey, Vince wants to talk to you."

I texted back. "Be right over." It was 3:30 or 4:00 in the afternoon.

Ten minutes later, I walked into Vince's office. He was seated at his desk. When I came in, he stood up. "Look," he said. "We're done."

He hadn't wasted words so neither did I. "You know what, Vince. You're right."

"Let's do it today," he said.

I shrugged. "If that's what you want. But I gotta say, that's not smart. Our business partners, the markets, employees. When they hear we're leaving, they'll panic. A much better strategy, we lay out a runway. Announce our departure today if you want but give the markets, the business community six to nine months to digest it."

I'll never forget how Vince replied. "You know what, George? You get yourself into a bad situation, sometimes you just got to pull off the Band-Aid."

What followed was both emotional and immediate. One of those deals where you're escorted back to your office to pack up your shit under somebody's watchful eye before you get frog-marched out of the building. The people Vince tasked to do this were folks I'd worked with for over a decade. There was a woman from HR, for instance, an old and dear friend, who kept saying, "George, I'm so sorry about this!"

I told her not to worry and asked how her husband was doing. I knew he'd been ill.

There was an older guy, Rich, who was sort of Vince's fixer. He ran our security at the office plus our insurance programs. He came to me all choked up. "I can't believe you're leaving. It happened like this?!"

I assured him it was alright. Everything would be fine. I don't think he believed me.

I called Michelle as soon as I could and found out that Vince had axed her minutes before he'd fired me. And just like with me, he did it the wrong way, escorting her out of the building like she was a criminal.

After twelve years and all that we'd done.

Smackdown.

***

The official announcement came later that day. Michelle Wilson and George Barrios Ousted from WWE.

Vince gave this quote to the press. "I am grateful for all that was accomplished during their tenure, but the board and I decided a change was necessary as we have different views on how best to achieve our strategic priorities moving forward."

That night, the company's stock dropped 35 to 40 percent. Something like $2.7 billion went down the tubes overnight.

Michelle and I talked in the days that followed. She was pissed. I mean seriously, regally pissed.

She lambasted Vince. Called him names I won't repeat here.

I encouraged her not to look at it that way. In the theater of my mind, I kept replaying that awful morning where our stock tanked and Vince called me up to say we were going to get through it. I remembered him crying behind his desk like a kid who'd just been told that his best friend had died. The feeling in my heart for him then was warm.

"When the days were darkest," I said, "Vince was there for us."

"Yeah, but the way he ended things," Michelle said.

"I don't want to focus on how it ended," I said. "Let's not get stuck in a still shot of our last day at the office. Life's a movie, not a photo. We had a long, great story with WWE that just so happened to have a shitty ending. That's how I'm viewing it."

Michelle and I each got a decent severance package but here's a funny story.

By that point, I was serving as board chairman for the Make-A-Wish America foundation. Our CEO was Richard Davis, who had run US Bancorp, one of the most respected financiers in the world. Richard had recently taken the CEO role at Make-A-Wish, and the board had been very lucky to lure him in, as his leadership proved indispensable. After the WWE news broke, Richard called me and asked what had happened.

I gave him the truncated version. "It all blew up," I said.

He chuckled. "Well, George. At least now you know exactly what the market thinks you're worth. Two-point-seven billion dollars."

CHAPTER THIRTEEN

Taking the Fall

I don't care how long you've been in business, how often you've had egg on your face, or how many times you've had your ass handed to you, either in public or in private. Getting canned from a job you've worked at for more than a decade? Goddammit, that hurts. Particularly when, by all indicators, you did the job right, knocked the ball right out of the park.

Fuck modesty. Here's the objective truth: When I left, WWE was in a far better place than it had been when I signed on. Better still once Michelle joined the team. The financial press was saying we'd pulled off one of the biggest, most stunning transformations in sports entertainment history. And what did I get for all that? I got fired.

Remember that time when Vince asked me why incumbent companies didn't respond to emerging threats and opportunities? I told him that most executives knew they'd never survive such a transformation. The irony is, WWE made it through the Swamp of Despair to the Height of Success. And I still got fired.

At the risk of stating the obvious, WWE was Vince's company. He had every right to do what he did. But having the right to do something doesn't always mean it's the smart or the wise thing to do. The way the company stock fell seemed proof enough of that, and a harbinger of what was to come.

In my final assessment, Vince reacted emotionally rather than intelligently when I proposed a restructuring. For once, he seemed more invested in what he perceived to be his own welfare rather than what was good for the company. And he convinced the board to see things as he did. Which probably wasn't that hard. Let me repeat myself. Everyone likes their jobs. Most people follow the herd. And in this case, Vince was the cowboy running the cattle drive.

***

So now it was February 2020. Michelle and I were no longer at WWE. We were both excited about what the future held. What new challenges lay ahead. We called each other frequently and traded ideas about potential new ventures.

Meanwhile, the business community speculated over what had happened. That's just human nature, I guess. And sure, a few ignorant people cast aspersions widely and blindly. That's also human nature. Still, the vast majority of feedback I got told me that smart people—and therefore smart money—understood what Michelle and I had done at WWE. Furthermore, they understood how what we had done might've pushed some extremely sensitive buttons on the private control panel of one Vincent Kennedy McMahon. And they weren't put off by that. Because, deep down, the smart money knew how Michelle and I had fought for WWE's enduring growth and legacy. And they wanted to work with people like that.

Case in point. In early spring 2020, Michelle called to give me an update on what she was doing. As I'm sure you can imagine, when someone as talented as Michelle makes herself available, the phone never stops ringing. She'd already had a few high-level conversations and in fact had just been offered a CEO role by a legend in the entertainment industry.

"That's incredible!" I said. "Are you going to take it?"

"I'm not sure," Michelle told me. "It's an interesting job, a great offer, no question about it." She hesitated. "What about you?"

"I'm getting some traction," I said.

"Anyone I know?"

"Wade Davis."

"George!" Michelle said. "That's . . . whoa!"

Her reaction was understandable. Wade is another business legend and justifiably so. From his roots as an investment banker in the tech and media spaces, he'd joined Viacom, the goliath creator and distributor of film and television content. From about 2006 to 2019, he'd served in many capacities there, leading mergers and acquisitions and corporate strategy, ultimately rising to the role of executive vice president and CFO. Wade had been instrumental in leading Viacom through a pretty dramatic turnaround. He later founded and served as CEO of ForgeLight, a company built to acquire and operate companies in the space Wade knows best, media and consumer technologies.

Wade had called me about two or three weeks after I'd left WWE. At the time, he was serving as CEO of Univision, a company I knew very well. Univision was founded back in the early 1960s as the Spanish International Network. It had since blossomed into the largest provider of Spanish-language content in the United States. Think of it as TV for Latinos. If you speak Spanish, it's practically a given that you watch telenovelas, sports, reality shows, news programs, sitcoms, you name it. All on Univision. I'd grown up watching the network with Jorge and Abuelo. Couldn't get enough of it.

Wade told me he'd partnered with private equity firm Searchlight and Mexican media giant Grupo Televisa to acquire approximately a 60 percent stake in Univision for $4.8 billion. Under that deal, Univision's major programmer, Televisa, would retain an approximate 40 percent share in the company while continuing to provide content and serving as a strategic partner to the new owners.

"It's going well," Wade told me. "But we're trying to reinvent our digital side. George, what would you think about coming on board and helping us with that?"

I told him the truth. "That could take time, Wade. Transitions like what you're proposing aren't overnight deals. The bigger the ship, the harder it is to turn. And you're one of the biggest ships in the water."

I enjoyed our frank discussions, during which it became clear that I'd be a good fit for the company. I was a native Spanish speaker who had dived deep into digital media. I understood the media landscape and what was required to transform a company to a twenty-first-century infrastructure based on streaming rather than outmoded models. Long story short, I began consulting for Univision. But Wade soon made it clear he was thinking bigger than that.

In May or June, if memory serves, Wade asked what I thought about coming on board in a leadership role. Again, I told him the truth. I was tepid about it. "What I'm really looking for now," I said, "is a CEO position." Right then, that was the job Wade held.

"I get it," he said. "And I appreciate your honesty. Here's some in return. Truth is, this is the first step in building up my new private equity business. I won't be CEO forever. So how about this. What if you join the company as CFO? You get comfortable here. Learn the ropes for two or three years. When that's done, you'll be seasoned and ready to take over as CEO as I transition out of the role. What do you think?"

Wade was willing, of course, to put all this in writing. It sounded attractive. In fact, the more I thought things through, I couldn't imagine a better move for me.

"Let's do it," I said.

Wade was pleased and we set to work hammering out the agreement.

***

Right around here is when something remarkable happened. It was June, still early in the pandemic. Acting on a hunch, I texted Vince and asked how he was doing. I don't recall what I expected or if I expected anything. What I remember is being blown away by how quickly he responded.

"Doing well," he typed. And just so I'm being clear, for Vince McMahon, typing those two words was practically a manifesto on his current state of affairs.

I typed back: "Awesome. Michelle and I were talking. It would be great to catch up, find out how you're doing, tell you what we're up to. Dinner sometime?"

Again, he got back to me fast. "Sure."

To judge by the speed of his messages, you might never have known we'd just spent the past year on such an intense and, at times, antagonistic roller coaster. But I believed then—and I still believe now—that people are flawed. We make mistakes. And sometimes we learn from those mistakes. Which means we can change. Since you've already read this far in the book, you know that I learned this the hard way, pounding my head against life and its walls.

Once I'd checked with Michelle, I proposed that the three of us should have dinner at L'Escale, a place we all knew. For the record, L'Escale offers some of the finest examples of French cuisine available anywhere. It's located in the Delamar Hotel, right on the harbor in Greenwich, Connecticut. Happily, I can recommend everything on the menu, but if you go, try the chicken paillard. It's their signature dish and truly exceptional.

Vince accepted the date and time we proposed and just like that, we were on.

"What do you think this means?" Michelle asked.

Great question. We were now officially in strange territory. Vince had never been one to eat out. It's an open secret that he doesn't like business lunches or dinners. Whenever he did them, he seemed like a fish out of water. For instance, once a quarter, we'd have dinner with WWE's board of directors, a corporate obligation. Vince always attended. He was always polite, though I never thought he looked especially comfortable. It seemed clear that he couldn't wait to get back to his office and work alone until two in the morning. Whenever he did that, he would have dinner brought in. Sometimes sushi, sometimes steak. Back then, he seemed to favor low-carb options.

Complicating matters was the fact that COVID was rampant at that point. The world was in lockdown. I got the notion that home confinement as dictated by a federal government went against every individualistic, entrepreneurial bone in Vince's body—or maybe I was just projecting how I felt. And when it comes to individualistic, entrepreneurial bones, Vince McMahon's are very thick.

Still. He was willing to meet us. Seemed eager to do it. My curiosity was piqued.

"Let's just go see what happens," I told Michelle. "Vince and I spent twelve years together and the last time I saw him was pretty rough. I want a better memory. Best-case scenario? We mend fences."

Michelle agreed.

***

During all this, Wade and I had spent about two months hammering out a deal where I would join Univision as its president before ultimately transitioning to CEO. Which meant I would finally realize my dream. Moreover, I'd be CEO of a company that seemed like a perfect fit for someone of my heritage and professional trajectory. The icing on the cake was that Univision is headquartered in Miami, a city I love. Also, at that point, Carol and I were talking with Mom about moving her down there. It made perfect sense. Miami had dozens of places where Mom could be well provided for in an environment with deep Cuban roots. To our pleasant surprise, Mom seemed not only willing to make the transition, she was excited to do it.

During negotiations with Wade, I played hardball. I was at a point in my career where I had clear ideas about what I was worth and what I wanted out of my next job. If I didn't get what I wanted, I was willing to walk. In fact, I did this once or twice at key intervals in our talks. But Wade always called me back to the table and went the extra mile. He was being so patient. Such a gentleman. Doubly so because I knew that he had to represent my asks to Univision's other investors. Who, according to rumors, were not so inclined to grant my wishes.

People I talked to later said Wade's response was always the same when they balked. "I think we should give George what he wants. He's the perfect guy for this role. You won't regret it."

Remember that as I tell you what happened next.

***

On July 1 or 2, 2020, if memory serves, Vince, Michelle, and I sat down to dinner. A memorable occasion for many reasons. First, like I said, I've never had a bad meal at L'Escale. I mean ever. It's always a pleasure to be there. The service and the food are, to stick with their French theme, par excellence. Second, the place was empty. As I said, this was arguably the apex of the COVID shock wave, and a lot of people were sheltering in place. To say that we had L'Escale to ourselves is no figure of speech. It's fact.

The way dinner started, you'd never have known that only a few months before, Vince and I had been locked in our strange embroilment. It crossed my mind that this was probably the only occasion, outside of board dinners, where the three of us had socialized. There was also the not-so-insignificant fact that it was the first time we'd seen each other since Vince canned me.

At some point during that evening, the topic of my firing came up. Vince mumbled, "Yeah, I screwed that up."

I remember getting the impression that he regretted firing me, particularly since at that point the world seemed to be veering into such an awful place. It occurred to me that Vince looked lonely. Who wasn't back then? Everyone was working from home. Isolation was testing the boundaries of *everyone's* mental health. But here Michelle and I were taking a risk to meet with Vince personally.

I remember our conversation veered to how COVID had pounded a stake through the heart of sports and event businesses worldwide. Governments were forbidding people to gather in large venues, which meant that stadium competitions and large-scale events were out of the question. One casualty of all this was Cirque du Soleil. The company had been generating a billion dollars in revenue per year almost entirely from ticketing live events where thousands of people congregated to watch the world's best circus performers. No more. COVID hit Cirque du Soleil so hard, they had to lay off 95 percent of their staff and file for bankruptcy. This was on top of the fact that they were still carrying $900 million in debt from a leveraged buyout that took place in 2015. From a business standpoint, that was a template for total catastrophe.

On the other hand, look at WWE. Before Michelle and I signed on, it had a similar profile to Cirque du Soleil. Our revenue was largely drawn from ticket sales that depended on tens of thousands of fans packing themselves into live event spaces. Thank God we'd expanded beyond that, because now, while Cirque du Soleil and other sports businesses were shutting down, WWE was having its best year ever. It was raking in cash from the digital businesses and media rights that we'd built.

This wasn't just me saying it; Vince told us that.

He also told us he had a plan to weather the pandemic. Simple, really. He'd still produce shows but do it without any fans being present. He'd narrow the focus. Strip everything down to its bare essence—the wrestlers, the ring, the battle. In a controlled setting, he could film enough fresh content to keep audiences tuning in while simultaneously feeding them the universe of archived content we'd developed. A universe that, Vince reported, was still growing.

"Look," Vince said at one point. "I'll just come out and say it. What you guys did saved the company."

Michelle and I looked at each other. Neither of us said a word.

I mean, really. What could we say?

***

At one point during our meal, I got up to go to the men's room and bumped into John, L'Escale's maître d'.

I pulled out my credit card. "John," I said. "Do me a favor? Put dinner on me."

John had been at L'Escale a long time. He gave me a look and chuckled. "You think Vince McMahon is letting somebody buy him dinner?"

John was right. Rookie move on my part. I gave him an appreciative tap on the shoulder. "Fair point. Your family's good?"

"All healthy. And waiting for this to be over. You?"

"Pretty much the same."

"You got anything planned for the Fourth?"

"Just keeping it low key."

"Sounds like a plan. Good seeing you, George."

"Yeah, you too."

***

After dinner, I drove home and went to my office and sat in my chair. The Univision contract was sitting on my desk, ready to go. Wade's persistence had been amazing. Every single detail I'd demanded had been hammered out, enshrined in legalese. My new professional life was ready to begin. My dream of being CEO of a publicly traded company was about to draw one step closer.

Dad, I thought. *Hope you're proud of me. I miss you.*

I looked at that contract for a long time. It crossed my mind that I should read it again, take a victory lap of sorts before I signed it. But I didn't. Something felt off.

Instead, I left the contract sitting on my desk. Then I stood up and turned off the light and walked out of my office and shut the door behind me.

***

That weekend, Carol and I were hosting some old UConn friends for July Fourth—the COVID scare be damned. Tom and Kris were part of the McConaughy 16, one of those eight couples I mentioned who met and married out of our UConn group. Carol and I are close with them. They're like brothers and sisters to us.

So we had drinks. We grilled meat. We talked shit. It was summer. The world was in lockdown. Plenty to vent about. Lots of questions got posed that no one could answer. The topper, of course, was that I'd just been laid off from my greatest professional achievement, and in perhaps the most ignominious fashion imaginable.

"So Al," Tom said. "It was up to me, Vince McMahon could go fuck himself. Separate issue. But it's been a few months now. You got anything cooking?"

I told them about the Univision deal, describing what it would mean to my career, all the perquisites, the Latino angle, the Miami thing. "It's gonna be great!" I said. "I'm totally stoked for it. Really! I'm stoked!"

Except.

Later that night, mere minutes after Tom and Kris left, Carol staged an intervention. We were in our kitchen. I was at the sink, washing dishes. Hands up to my wrists in soapy water.

Tom's right, I was thinking. *Yeah. Fuck Vince McMahon.*

"They believed it," I heard Carol say.

I turned to her, working the sponge. "Whazzat?"

She was leaning against a counter, holding her coffee and watching me closely. "You've been telling me how great this deal is for months. The same way you told Tom and Kris. Like I said, they believed it. I don't."

I think I just stared at her, my hands dripping little white bubbles.

Carol shrugged. "Al, I know you. When you get excited about something, it's like you're on fire. The whole world lights up around you. But this thing with Univision? It's not that. You're not lighting up."

Christ, what a kick in the nuts. Suddenly, I felt like I was in an M. Night Shyamalan film. The main character's been cruising through scene after scene, doing things one way. Then comes the plot twist. Extreme close-up on the protagonist as he recalls certain events that he now views differently—the way they truly are instead of the way he wanted or presumed them to be.

The whole damn time I'd been telling Michelle how my talks with Wade were progressing. And she had encouraged me. "Great, George! Sounds great!" That's what I'd heard. But in retrospect, her voice had been flat. That telltale pause before she responded. More like "Great, George. Sounds great." See the difference?

Carol and I have known each other for so long, she feeds me back to myself. The more I mentally reviewed her behavior, the more clearly I saw that she hadn't been ecstatic. Excited? Well, sure. But she'd only been excited because I'd told her I was excited. In other words, Carol was being supportive, which is in her nature, something she's great at. But she'd also seen something I'd missed: that my excitement had seemed a bit forced. And she cared too much about me to point that out. So had Michelle, for that matter. Michelle, who knew my work ethic, personality, and goals as well as Carol did.

That's when I stopped looking outside myself and started looking within—where I saw something shocking.

All that fencing I'd done with Wade, pushing him for concessions, playing hardball, insisting on stuff that was—yeah, okay, I admit—it was over the line. Carol was right. That wasn't coming from me wanting to do the job. It was coming from someplace different. Someplace darker. It was like I wanted everything to be perfect because I knew, deep down, there's no such thing as perfect. In other words—and I can only say this with the benefit of hindsight—I was trying to sabotage the deal because I didn't really want it. That's when I knew what I had to do.

I called Michelle the next day and told her, "I've made a decision." I took a deep breath. "I'm not taking the Univision thing."

Imagine my amazement when she choked up. "George! Oh my God. This . . . this is the best call I've gotten in a long, long time!"

Over the next few minutes, it all tumbled out. Michelle confessed that, like Carol, she hadn't thought the job was right for me.

"It just . . . I don't know. The way you talked about it. It was like you were trying too hard to get excited. But you weren't. Not really."

"Why didn't you tell me?" I asked.

"George, come on. I couldn't do that. I want what's best for you. Didn't want to overstep my bounds. I'm sure that's what Carol was thinking."

I realized at once she was right. They were right. It would have probably ruined our friendship if she'd told me what I wasn't, at that point, willing to hear. God, that was humbling.

But it would have to wait. Because at that point, my marching orders were clear. I called Wade Davis and took a deep breath and told him how sorry I was. I was out.

Christ, what a goddamn mess. Wade, like me, had a reputation for being a bit of a hard-charger. Nonetheless, he stayed polite and even-keeled where I'd given him no cause to be either. "Wow. George," he said. "I worked really hard to get you everything you wanted. In fact, I don't mind saying I burned a lot of political capital to bring you on board." He sighed. "I'm disappointed. I'm just . . . stunned, George. I guess that's the right word. I'm stunned."

I mumbled, "I know, Wade. I'm sorry. I really am."

It was all my fault, and I felt like an ass. More so because this was the second time I had pulled this type of stunt. The first time, if you recall, was when I got passed over for the CFO job at the Times Company. I made a commitment to another company only to pull an abrupt 180 when the *Times* offered me their treasurer role.

Now look. You could argue—and trust me, I certainly did—that all's fair in love and war. And your career. Everyone's got to look out for themselves. And of course, you'd be right to say that. But it never feels good to me, acting in good faith only to end up leaving someone I respect in the lurch.

Disentangling myself from the Univision deal was one of the most embarrassing moments in a career which, as you've already read, has had other embarrassing moments. But this incident was made worse by the fact that my impetuousness ended up burning serious bridges. Or so I thought at the time.

Happily, I can report that Wade and I have repaired our relationship. And for those of you keeping score at home, this was the moment when my career, my life, my dreams, and my sense of self completely recalibrated.

CHAPTER FOURTEEN

Isos Means Equal

A week or two later, Michelle and I met at Prime, an open-air waterfront venue facing Long Island Sound in Stamford. This allowed us to keep good physical distance from one another while doing what we'd always done best. Brainstorming new ideas. Finding value where no one else saw it. Pushing each other to get more creative. By that point it was clear that we were both energized toward finding something we could work on together.

The restaurant was totally empty, just as it had been when we met Vince at L'Escale. The pandemic was making life more challenging by increments. Ah, well. Michelle and I knew it was temporary. We also knew that once COVID was over, those who'd worked hard throughout the ordeal and kept a sharp eye out for opportunities could profit handsomely. What kind of ideas did we discuss? At one point, we talked about raising money to buy Cirque du Soleil. Could we transform that business along the same lines we'd used to optimize WWE?

Within a couple of weeks, Michelle and I were talking every day over Zoom. Until she said, "I can't stand working through screens anymore. Let's get an office where we can sit together like we used to and let the sparks fly." So that's what we did.

By then it was August or maybe September 2020. We looked at a couple of places in Westport and wound up in a super-beautiful modern space, the Serendipity Labs on the west bank of the Saugatuck River. A perfect location for start-ups. Michelle and I started showing up there every workday, sitting across from each other, kicking ideas back and forth.

"We need a name for our company," she said one day. "Something meaningful, something catchy. Names are important. Any ideas?"

We both like the color blue and we both have a deep affinity for the ocean. We came up with Blue Mar but discovered that name was already taken. From there, we had a few more false starts. Naming a company is like naming a child. You agonize over it, only to realize later on that it probably doesn't matter.

Word to the wise. False starts aren't ever failures. More like a pointer to where you should really be heading. Like that old story about Thomas Edison. Someone asked him, "Isn't it true that you failed a thousand times to produce the electric lightbulb?" Edison responded, "I didn't fail a thousand times. I found a thousand ways that won't work." One of my all-time favorite reframes.

One day Michelle called me, excited. "I was helping my niece with her geometry homework. What do you know about isosceles triangles?"

I thought back to the book on mythology I'd been given as a child. "Isos comes from the Greek, meaning 'equal.' An isosceles triangle is a triangle with two equal sides."

"Exactly. We're the two sides and we're equal. Ergo: Isos Capital. What do you think?"

I thought it was perfect. We checked the name register and found that another company had taken that name, but they were defunct and the name could be purchased. So that's what we did.

So now we had a name for our new firm. The problem was, we still hadn't figured out our first move.

That was about to change.

***

In late 2020, some investment bankers we knew began reaching out to us. Most of them pitched us on the concept of SPACs or Special Purpose Acquisition Companies, whose use was spiking at that point. To give you an idea, in 2019, investors put $13 billion into 59 SPACs. In 2020, they poured $80 billion into 247 SPACs. A 6x increase in twelve months? Yup. I'd call that a spike. Or a bubble.

SPACs had been around for decades, but I confess that in my thirty-year career to that point I'd barely heard of them. Basically, a SPAC is a shell firm whose stated purpose is to acquire worthy private companies and take them public. To do this, a management group, called sponsors, raises money by selling shares of the SPAC on the open market through an initial public offering, or IPO. Since this is typically done before the sponsors have targeted an acquisition, SPACs are sometimes referred to as "blank check" companies. Investors often purchase shares with no idea how the sponsors intend to deploy their capital. Everything boils down to trusting the sponsors' backgrounds and sensibilities.

The financial media was writing a lot about SPACs, mostly casting them in an unsavory light. Contrary to the media's assertions, SPACs are not dangerous for investors. They have safety features built into them. For instance, when a SPAC's sponsors announce the business they plan to acquire, investors have the right to pull their capital out of the venture without any penalty. This mechanism is called a redemption.

More concerning to me was the fact that the uptick in SPACs—that 6x spike I mentioned—might reflect a certain level of irrational exuberance. In fact, SPACs weren't the only thing spiking. The number of traditional IPOs was also going through the roof. I kept asking myself, are there really that many private companies that are worthy of going public? Or has the investment community entered one of those phases where everyone is buying anything for no good reason? It's like the old story says. When the shoeshine boy starts giving you stock advice, it's time to be cautious.

Michelle and I debated the pros and cons of using a SPAC and decided the financial media was once again getting things wrong.

"There's nothing inherently wrong with a SPAC," Michelle said. "They're just another financial instrument—good for some investors, bad for others."

I agreed. "What I like about SPACs is how they empower sponsors to dramatically speed up the process of taking a company public. In the right hands, under the right circumstances, they can be a powerful tool for value creation."

We decided to enter the space. As our first step, we hired a business analyst who built us a data model with over 900 reference points. Then we took a deep dive into every SPAC that had been formed and every IPO that had kicked off over the past twenty years. We asked ourselves questions: How do we define a successful IPO? How successful are IPOs generally? How many successful IPOs came about through SPACs? Under what conditions do SPACs most often provide successful returns? And so on.

We were trying to get our mental arms around the odds of using a SPAC successfully. We figured that once we knew the odds, it would be easier to beat them. When our retrospective analysis was complete, we applied our model to each of the 300 or so SPACs that were then operational and sifted the data—parsing it, slicing it, dicing it.

"Whoa," I said. "Look at this."

Based solely on numbers, our model showed that more than 90 percent of SPACs from the most recent vintage were unsustainable. Bad risks. In other words, the so-called crowded field of IPOs was really anything but. Of the 300 SPACs pushing 300 IPOs, only thirty or so were likely to become what Michelle and I considered lucrative investments.

"I think this is great," I said to Michelle. "It means that we don't have to focus on 300 prospects. We only have to snag one of the good ones in the top 10 percent. This approach should completely obviate the current bubble in IPOs."

Michelle agreed. "The bubble is moot since the only companies we're interested in are bubble-proof. Great businesses with solid economics that can survive any market conditions. Our model will weed out the dross. And while everyone else is blindly swinging the bat, we'll only look at investments that make financial sense." She thought for a moment. "We should expect that a few other sponsors will also take this approach. How do we differentiate ourselves from them?"

"I thought about that," I said. "Right now, our model covers all things quantitative. Let's expand it to include qualitative elements. For instance, what if we operate under the premise that buyers and sellers in the SPAC space don't want to deal with low-quality sponsors? Only executives with great reputations and long track records of success. Let's build a model that ranks SPAC sponsors according to their bona fides, reputations, how well they've done in their careers, that sort of thing."

Michelle agreed with this approach. So we built a new model that showed us that of the 300 active SPAC sponsors, Michelle and I ranked in the top ten or twenty. That made us feel even better about our prospects.

"I think this is pretty compelling," Michelle said. "We good?"

I smiled. "We're *very* good. Let's do a SPAC!"

Creating the shell company was easy. Like all legal structures, it's just an endless amount of paperwork. Drawing up presentations was also easy. We had a good story to tell. Our materials laid out the case that our experience, network, and playbook put Michelle and me at the top of the sponsor list. In other words, we felt we were among the best people to help an aspiring company succeed in the public markets.

This was a very exciting time for us. On one hand, we were capitalizing our SPAC, taking meetings with interested institutional investors. In the end, we capped our raise at $250 million even though we had demand for 7x that amount. Not a bad position to be in. I think our success reflected both the current state of the market and the attractiveness of the plan Michelle and I had developed.

Once the money was raised, we began taking pitches from some of the biggest banks in the world. Morgan Stanley. Goldman Sachs. UBS. JP Morgan. Michelle and I were pleased to find that all the preliminary work we had done allowed us to move through the pitches very quickly. We knew immediately which companies fit our model for a compelling acquisition—and, more importantly, which didn't. We were looking to build a long-term sustainable public company that could generate value for decades, perhaps generations to come.

Michelle and I ended up sitting through dozens of presentations on electric vehicle manufacturers, flying taxi company start-ups, and pick-and-shovel plays for forthcoming fusion technologies, all of which sounded attractive. For instance, I personally have little doubt that within thirty years or so, flying taxis will be as normal as gold and red leaves on a sidewalk in autumn. Still, these ideas were too far out there for our purposes. They needed time to come to fruition, and quite frankly, Michelle and I couldn't find places to add any value to their operations.

The pitches kept coming. To call some of them breathless would be an understatement.

"Listen to this!" people told us. Or "Read this! We think it's a pretty good opportunity!"

Pretty good? I thought. *Who gives a fuck about 'pretty good'? Pretty good is bullshit. It's normal. Michelle and I have no interest in that.*

"No," we kept saying. "Thank you but no."

No. No. No. No. No. No. No. No. No.

We were only interested in one thing, an opportunity we could knock straight out of the park.

And then we found it.

***

It was March 2021. By running our process, one name kept popping up: Bowlero, the largest bowling center owner and operator in North America. We took a few Zoom meetings with the company's founder and CEO, Tom Shannon, and his CFO, Brett Parker. Man, were we impressed with these guys.

Now let me clarify something. I don't consider myself a bowler and have no special affinity for bowling. Didn't matter. Our model told us this company was golden. Let me try to explain Bowlero the way Michelle and I saw it.

We learned that bowling is a location-based turnstile entertainment business featuring one of the largest participatory sports in the country. About 70 million Americans bowl each year. That's almost a quarter of the US population, a hefty market. Now think of the nuts and bolts of the business.

Customers enter a facility called a bowling alley. Once it's built, lasts basically forever. The equipment is niche but hardy; it hardly ever requires repair or replacement. All this is important because these factors limit the business's capex (capital expenditure) requirements: Less money is needed to maintain the company's physical assets. Low capex is excellent, very attractive when running a business. Operating costs on bowling alleys are also low since most bowling alleys only need a few employees to run them. This again feeds wider profits. Are you with me so far?

Now think for a moment. What happens once your customers enter the bowling alley experience? You charge them for games, shoe rentals, food, beverages, music selections on the jukebox, video games, and so on. All of which you offer at a high markup without any competition. I mean, it's not like people can go outside the bowling alley to rent someone else's shoes for a little less money. And as anyone who's ever been near a bar business knows, the markup on draft beer is gorgeous.

But here's something else we found interesting. Bowling has great unit economics. What that means is that once you're in the bowling alley, every game you bowl gives the business a 100 percent profit margin. And the data shows that most customers stick around to bowl multiple games. The result is a business that can generate, under most circumstances, a very healthy profit margin.

Michelle whistled. "Who knew bowling was such a great business? I like this. I like this a lot."

I nodded. "Bowling alleys are basically machines that gush cash. I love it."

But there was more. When we looked at its business, Bowlero was valued at north of $1.5 billion. Back then, they had about 300 alleys under ownership, or nearly 8x the number of alleys owned by their closest competitor. And this left between 3,500 and 4,000 independently owned alleys nationwide—mom-and-pop joints that were just waiting to be acquired, rolled up, and improved using Bowlero's time-tested methodologies.

Our analysis told us that more than 20 million people on average had bowled at a Bowlero center annually. Also that the market for US bowling had grown 50 percent over the last decade to a hefty $4.5 billion, while the global market had nearly tripled during that time to $11 billion. We had ample reason to speculate that the bowling industry was set for a massive rebound as the country emerged from lockdown and people started venturing outside their homes to resume group activities.

I remember being amazed by all this. "Holy shit!" I told Michelle. "What do you think?"

She narrowed her eyes. "Bowlero fits our model almost perfectly. Tom Shannon lives in Miami. You and I are going to Miami next week to speak with investors. Let's call Tom right now and set up a meeting and win this deal."

So that's what we did. One of the many things I love about Michelle is her bias for action. Once we've decided on a path, she moves. And word to the wise, better not to stand in her way.

I picked up the phone and called Tom and told him about our plans. He seemed interested and maybe a little surprised. There weren't a lot of face-to-face meetings happening at that time. Tom gave us some dates that worked for him. Michelle and I flew to Miami and I remember that trip very well, since apart from the pilots and flight attendants, she and I were the only people on that Boeing 737 MAX.

COVID is decimating the airline industry, I thought. *I'm really glad we did what we did at WWE.*

***

If memory serves, Michelle and I met Tom for coffee, then breakfast the following day. We knew we were in a crowded space, negotiating against other interested SPACs. But our talks proceeded so well that Tom put us in touch with his banks, who began passing us Bowlero's financials, business models, projections—all typical stuff when laying the groundwork for a prospective deal.

Since this was our first post-WWE project and we were still road-testing our process, Michelle and I wanted to dig deeper. We asked to spend time with the head of Bowlero's financial planning and analysis, or FP&A.

Brett Parker viewed our request as odd. "Why would you want to do that?" he said.

It was completely understandable that Brett would view this as odd. In merger and acquisition transactions, it's typical to interact with a company's senior management team—in other words, their CFO. Meaning Brett, rather than his direct reports.

"Look, I get it," I said. "What can I say? Michelle and I love digging into stuff."

"What are you looking for?" Brett said.

"Not sure, but we'll know it when we see it. Your FP&A guy built your financial model, right? I'm guessing he'll have the details I need."

I had already come to respect Tom and Brett as incredibly detailed, thorough businessmen. But I'd also learned that when Michelle and I look at things jointly, we often see things that even the brightest people tend to miss.

Brett chuckled. "George, that's a lot of data. But if you really want it . . ."

"I want it."

"Then you've got it."

A few days later, Bowlero's FP&A guy came to our office in Westport. He was about forty years old and remarkably bright. Let's call him Kwan. Kwan plugged his laptop into the big-screen TV in one of our conference rooms. The three of us spent that whole day poring over his spreadsheets line by line. I remember leaning over his shoulder and pointing. "What's hidden under that column? Can you expand that?"

"That's the column for quarterly data," Kwan said.

"Right. I want to see monthly."

"Monthly is . . . sure . . . okay . . ."

"And then weekly," said Michelle.

"Uhm . . ."

"What's up?"

"It's just . . . uh . . . nobody's asked to look at the data like that."

"Sure, we get it. That's cool. But can we get that view, please, Kwan?"

"Sure thing."

Talk about rising to the occasion. In no time flat, Kwan got in the swing of things. It was clear that he was a consummate professional who knew his own model inside and out. In fact, the more we demanded of him, the more excited he got. He started jigging and jumping like a show pony put through its paces, happy to show off his skills—which were ample. I also considered it likely that due to COVID, it had been a long time since he'd spent quality, in-person, professional time with other human beings. Now that he found himself in a room with people who worked him hard over eight hours, he was in heaven. Michelle and I were impressed.

That day ended up being a very enriching experience. Michelle and I confirmed our gut suspicion that Bowlero was a company worth acquiring. Kwan even had a couple of aha moments about the model he'd built. At the end of our marathon session, he said, "George, I've been at Bowlero five years and I've never had anybody dig in like that. You did it in eight hours and you picked it all up so fast."

Michelle and I high-fived each other, then high-fived Kwan. "This is who we are, this is what we do," I said.

A few days later, Tom called to advise us that Bowlero had selected us as their SPAC sponsors of choice. But there was an issue. Part of the deal he was seeking required $470 million as a minimum cash condition. At that point, we only had $250 million in our SPAC. We also had to assume that we'd have redemptions once we announced Bowlero as our acquisition target. On that point, we had no illusions. By then, plenty of SPACs were getting 100 percent redemptions.

Bottom line, we needed more capital.

"What do we do about that?" Michelle asked.

"Only one thing we can do," I said. "Bring in PIPE investors."

***

PIPE stands for Private Investment in Public Equity. In a nutshell, these are investors who provide the slug of capital needed to get a deal over the finish line in exchange for certain ownership rights. Bringing in PIPE investors is a common phase of the SPAC process and one where, it turned out, Michelle and I were fortunate.

Before we'd dug into SPACs, we'd met with Apollo, a blue-chip American investment firm with over $500 billion in assets under management. The folks at Apollo were people Michelle and I knew from working at WWE. They'd already greenlit a commitment of $75 million to whatever project we found interesting, sight nearly unseen. When we walked them through Bowlero's fundamentals, they got excited and upped their pledge to $100 million. Michelle and I then took meetings with other investment groups, some of which we knew from our days at WWE. Many of them also saw value in Bowlero and offered commitments.

This became an intense and ongoing process. Constant meetings. Constant footwork. At one point, some of our employees expressed their concern that I was working too hard. At another point, I was on vacation with Carol and some longtime friends in Nevis, a beautiful island in the

Caribbean. Each day I would pause our festivities two or three times to do Zooms with prospective partners.

"Al, come onnnnnnnnnnnnnn," groaned one of my old college buddies, Josh. "You're supposed to be relaxing. The bocce court's open!"

What could I tell him? There's an old saying in the investment world: Each deal dies ten thousand deaths. So true. Putting a deal like that together was like grabbing a fistful of very fine sand. The more of it you thought you had clutched in your hand, the more it kept slipping through your fingers. Without getting into specifics, the situation was precarious. On top of which, I knew my limitations.

I saw myself as an operator, someone who *ran* businesses. That's what I'd done for the past thirty years. Maybe the folks who'd done deal work for the same amount of time had grown inured to the kinds of ups and downs I was facing, but I wasn't. I knew I had to keep pushing. The way I saw things, the deal wouldn't be done until it was done.

In the end, we raised an additional $370 million, which, combined with the fact that Tom eventually lowered his cash requirement, got us over the finish line. Or should have. At any rate, at that moment, the way forward looked clear.

"Nice," Michelle said, once we had everything arranged. "We're playing in the big leagues now."

I gave her another high five and said, "You're fucking right we are."

***

While all this was going on, I checked in with Vince now and then. Quick texts like, "Hey, did you see what's happening over at [insert name of company here?] Looks like an opportunity. You guys on it?"

He would text back and thank me for pointing it out, then comment in general terms about how WWE was doing.

Why was I spending any time thinking about WWE? The truth is, because I cared about the company. I cared about Vince. You don't pour in blood, sweat, and tears like I did without caring. You don't spend twelve years working with someone without respecting them. I wanted WWE to soar to even greater heights. That's why I reached out.

The rest of the world would probably have found this odd. By that point, word on the street said that Vince had fired me because he got tired of me. In fact, I heard through channels that this was precisely the story some core-cadre WWE employees were pushing to people in the business community. But there were dissenters. Through different sources, I heard another version of the tale—Vince had tried to keep me but couldn't find a way to do that, so that's why he let me go.

Shrug. Yawn. Whatever. Sometimes you have to let people think what they think. Truth is, they're going to do that anyway, right?

***

The Bowlero deal had been moving along nicely enough, but then it hit the expected retrading phase. Retrading is when a buyer or investor renegotiates the terms of their purchase or investment after those terms have been locked. This usually happens when new information comes to light such as market fluctuations, appraisal inconsistencies, problems in financing, that sort of thing. However, it also happens when one party to the deal reassesses their position. For whatever reason, they feel that they are due more from the other party, and so they request new terms. This happened to us in November 2021.

The deal was nearly done. We'd entered the eleventh hour when I got a call from one of the investment banks. Let's call the guy on the phone Larry.

"Hey, George," he said. "So sorry, man, but we're still a few million dollars short of the minimum threshold and somebody is going to have to kick in." His clear implication was that Michelle and I should dip into our pockets to get the deal over the finish line.

"George, we're so sorry," Larry kept saying. "But look . . . if we can't work this out . . . the deal's dead in the water. Okay? It won't move forward."

Up until that point, I'd been involved in plenty of deals. And yes, I'd retraded a few of them when it came to light that information we'd been given was false. But never to simply gain advantage. Never to fuck someone over. For whatever reason, I'm just not built for that. I simply don't bother with nickel-and-diming my partners. For one thing, I don't enjoy it. For another, it sets up a bad reputation that can follow you the rest of your career.

Now that I've done this for a while, I recognize certain tactics for what they are. Back then, however, I admit I got agitated. "I'll get back to you," I said, and hung up.

I immediately called Michelle. "That's it," I told her. "I'm done. On a relative basis, you and I have given up more than anyone else to get this deal done. We shouldn't be the ones they're calling now. Let somebody else dig into their pockets. Now at the eleventh hour, they're calling us? Fuck this! I say we give them a hard no. Be crystal clear. We're willing to walk away."

Michelle agreed. "You're right. Total bullshit. Just call him back and say no. If they call me, I've got your back." I had followed Michelle's lead earlier in the process when we made our first concessions. Now she was following my lead.

Minutes later, I called Larry back. Let me preface this by saying that I liked Larry. Still do. Up until that point, we'd had a good and productive relationship. But there I was, pacing my sunroom with my phone welded to my ear hearing Larry talk shit at me, clearly to get me to blink. He kept saying the deal would die if we didn't pitch in and I kept saying no, we'd agreed to the terms and the deal was locked because that's what agreement means. Like, check the fucking dictionary, dude.

"George," Larry said. "Come onnnnnnnnn, man. Do you really want to kill your very first deal over a couple of points? How's that gonna look for you guys?"

The son of a bitch was threatening me.

I said, "You know what, Larry? We've had dinner a few times, spent time together and whatnot. Just so you understand, I'm always flexible. That's how I got this far in life. But when I get a hint that somebody's being an asshole, game over. I shut them off. So I'm telling you now. You guys want more? Go get it from somebody else because you're not getting it from us. And if anyone's killing this deal, it's you. Read the papers. They'll tell you what I'm worth. I don't need this deal and I damn sure don't need the headache. Think it over but get back to me fast, we're on a goddamn fucking deadline."

I hung up the phone before he could answer and called Michelle back and told her what happened. She said, "Perfect. Let's see where it goes."

Good thing we spoke. Because right away she got a call from Larry who clearly thought he could end-run me by talking to Michelle.

He couldn't, of course. Michelle stood firm. "I don't know how you did it," she told Larry, "but you really pissed George off." She made me the bad cop. Smart thing to do. "If George told you no, that's our answer, he's working the numbers. No. What's that? Larry, I just said no. So I'm clear, if George isn't in, then neither am I."

Twenty-four hours after he spoke with Michelle, Larry called me back and said, "All good. The deal will go through."

In the final assessment, we merged Bowlero with Isos Acquisition Corp. to create a combined entity valued at roughly $2.6 billion. Our projections said that company revenue would reach a healthy $859 million in 2022. Which we exceeded.

Compare this with other IPOs and SPACs from 2021. The data is clear. That was one of the worst vintages ever for SPACs and traditional IPOs. Most companies that went public that year saw their share prices decline by 40 to 50 percent in the first twenty-four months. Whereas, at its highest point, ours increased almost 70 percent. In other words, not only were we at the front of the SPAC and IPO pack, we outperformed the overall market.

All this was a harbinger. Bowlero was the first deal Michelle and I did together. It was profitable, it was enduring. By and large, it was fun. It was also just the beginning.

***

Late November 2022. By this point, Carol and I had moved Mom to the Palace at Coral Gables. She was ninety-eight years old. I was down in Florida, paying a visit. I was sitting with her in the main lounge. Remember? Scroll mirrors. Marble statues. Hand-woven carpets. Chandeliers dripping with crystal.

Happy hour had just kicked off. The grand piano was humming and the player was singing a Celia Cruz hit while waiters brought butlered hors d'oeuvres and we waited to be seated in the dining room for a Cuban feast of Pan con lechón.

Jesus Christ, I remember thinking. *We've come such a long way from the rattling streets of Flushing, Queens. Zip code 11354.*

My phone started buzzing. I checked the screen, which said VINCE McMAHON. My surprise must have shown on my face because my mother narrowed her eyes at me. "¿Quién es?"

I tilted the phone and she looked at the caller ID. "¿Por qué te esta llamando?" (Why is he calling you?)

"Yo no sé."

You know the rest. We've come full circle.

The lounge was too crowded, so I went into the library, closed the door, and thumbed the call through.

That gravelly voice on the other end of the line. "Hey George. How you doing?"

"I'm good, Vince. You?"

"Remember how you used to say that thing?"

"In order to grow, the company's either got to acquire somebody else or be acquired?" I said.

"That's it. Listen. . . . I've decided I want to do this. . . . I only get one shot at it, so I want to do it right. I need the A-Team. . . . Would you think about it? If you need time . . ."

"I don't need any time, Vince. Let's do it," I said.

The line went quiet. I think Vince got a little choked up. I surprised myself, too, getting teary-eyed.

"How about Michelle. You think she'd do it?"

I shrugged. "If you're asking me what my gut says, I'd be shocked if she wouldn't come back."

"Do you want to talk to her first?"

"Sure."

"Alright. Talk soon?"

"You got it."

I clicked off.

What did I tell you before, at the start of this book? Everyone's the hero of their own tale. And sometimes, if we're lucky, life gives us a chance to rewrite our unhappy endings. And if there's a chapter to your story that ends on a low note, you can change it.

One more time I'll say it. It's all up to you.

CHAPTER FIFTEEN

It's On

Vince had resigned as CEO of WWE in July 2022. He understood how complications in his personal life could intrude on WWE's business, and he refused to let that happen. The company's stock price rose when he left, which surprised me.

However, six months later, in January 2023, Vince returned as executive chairman of the board of directors. He could do this because he was WWE's controlling shareholder. And he brought Michelle and me with him.

Wouldn't you know it? The stock price rose on the news of our return. And yes, I know how self-serving this sounds, but I heard from many people who all said the same thing. *If George and Michelle are coming back to WWE, the future looks very bright indeed because they do not fuck around.*

Back in the driver's seat, Vince kicked off a sweeping campaign of changes. He also had the board announce publicly that WWE would review its strategic alternatives, including the possibility of a sale. The financial media went nuts when they heard this. The global investment community went into a tizzy. Suddenly, no one could talk about anything else. In all the commotion, no one cared to discuss Vince's personal life. There was too much money at stake.

On that point, speculation abounded. People were wondering, How much is WWE really worth? Who will step forward and tender a bid? How much will they offer? What form will the organization take moving forward? All great questions.

Everyone watched and waited as the process rolled forward.

***

The first board meeting Michelle and I attended was held in the same building we used to work in, WWE's iconic Fortress of Doom. Also known as Titan Towers, it served for years as the company headquarters. Picture a black glass, oblong, rectangular building featuring four parking levels and four floors offering 100,000 square feet of office space. If you're driving down I-95 through Stamford, Connecticut, you can't miss it; the fortress shows up clear as a mountain on the landscape. It always had two flags flying over it—a black banner with white lettering that said WWE and a massive American flag, since Vince considers himself a huge patriot. That American flag was so big, the company had to get a special zoning ordinance from the city to fly it.

Walking back into that building felt bizarre and perfectly normal all at once. As best I could calculate, I'd spent something like 4,000 days working away in the Fortress's hallways and offices. It was the home that I had been banished from in disgrace. But now I was back, returning as a hero. And of course it made it all the more sweet to have Michelle at my side. If there was a soundtrack to this segment of the film version of my life, it would have been "We Are the Champions" by Queen.

Michelle and I took the elevator up to the top floor. Vince met us as we stepped off the elevator. He'd grown a pencil-thin mustache Clark Gable would have envied. I remember being shocked. In the first place, I'd never known Vince to wear facial hair of any type. In the second place, I'd grown a goatee since being let go from WWE. Prior to this moment, Vince had teased me about it mercilessly during our Zoom meetings.

He's aping me, I thought. *This is some kind of joke. He's sending me up.*

But I soon saw he wasn't. Something else was at play here. Something in Vince had shifted. At that point, I couldn't tell what.

There were hugs all around. Then Vince pulled back and gave us a serious look. "Welcome home." He was tearing up. Could barely get the words out. Michelle and I teared up too. All three of us, there in the elevator vestibule on the top floor of the Fortress of Doom. Dabbing tears from our eyes.

Finally, I stood up straight. "Can we just get to work, please?"

Vince nodded and gestured toward the boardroom. "Right this way."

***

Any confusion that might have lingered over me being ousted from WWE was at that point put to rest. The meaning of my return was incontrovertible. Why would Vince McMahon ask someone he'd fired, ostensibly because he couldn't do his job, to come back aboard? Doubters, haters, and naysayers in the business community were forced to recalibrate. *Oh!* people started thinking. *We must have gotten that story wrong the first time. And George and Michelle hit it out of the park with that Bowlero deal. Maybe George wasn't so bad after all . . .*

The vindication I enjoyed was something that doesn't happen often in business or in life.

Did I savor it? You'd better fucking believe I did.

Once Michelle and I officially joined the board, a team was put together, tasked with guiding WWE through the strategic review process. JP Morgan was on this team—no surprise there, they'd always been WWE's primary banker. Jeff Sine was there, too. Jeff cofounded Raine, a powerful, nimble boutique media group that provides M&A services while guiding companies through capital-raising campaigns. Jeff had been working with Vince throughout the six months or so that he was gone from WWE. Later in the process, the board brought in Moelis & Company, a global investment bank that's justifiably famous for handling restructuring and recapitalizations for governmental and corporate clients. We were all there to explore what was the best path forward for WWE.

As part of this mandate, the team was estimating the worth of WWE's business. This is standard procedure for any number of potential transactions. From our place on the board, Michelle and I were pleased to lend our insights into where WWE might drive additional value in markets both tapped and untapped worldwide. I'll never forget the conversations, the arguments, the back-and-forth for hours and days and weeks on end. It was all great fun and a tremendous learning experience to work with colleagues of such remarkable caliber.

Each member of the team was crucial to the process in their own way, but I felt that Jeff Sine was our linchpin. This went far beyond how well-known and well-respected Jeff is. I just couldn't help but notice how easily and gracefully Jeff made overtures to potential partners, the way he comported himself at all times as though he not only enjoyed his work but felt privileged to be able to do it. Watching Jeff work—the genuine care and fellowship he exuded in every moment, through every gesture and word—was something I'll never forget.

***

Since I'd been away from WWE a couple of years, I wanted to bring myself up to speed on where the business stood. I dove into my analysis as though I knew nothing about the company, full circle engagement, no assumptions, using the same process that, by now, I hope feels familiar to you. Reams of data. Stacks of binders jammed with information. I read these compilations over and over again, and something kept coming up. Something odd. So I picked up the phone and called the then CFO, Frank Riddick.

Frank had been on WWE's board for ten years during my tenure with the company. We had become friends and I viewed him as my mentor—then and now. Talk about a guy with an interesting pedigree. He'd worked for decades in industrial businesses—JMC Steel Group, Formica Corporation, Armstrong World Industries. These are people who make things. He'd also served in a variety of executive finance roles at Merrill Lynch. When I called Frank, he wasn't just serving as CFO of WWE, he was also company president. He's superbright and tremendously self-deprecating, which puts you at ease right away.

"Frank, check me on something." I flipped pages in a binder. "Am I reading this wrong? About 99 percent of the current revenue comes from deals that were put in place before I left."

Frank didn't hesitate. "No, that's correct, George. Congrats!"

It was a typically kind thing for him to say. Frank was confirming that the business Michelle and I had built was essentially the same business we were, at that point, preparing to sell. The same business that had continued to grow by leaps and bounds despite our absence, despite COVID, despite six thousand other potential impediments.

I remember hanging up the phone and staring out the window for a long while. It took me a minute or two before I realized I was smiling. "Well," I said out loud to my empty office. "How about that?"

***

Once the worth process was complete, our team presented a potential road map to Vince. This is how we could set things up, we said. This resource will do this while that resource does that. This is when we'll solicit offers. Here are the things we're hoping to see in an offer. Here are the criteria we consider red flags. Here's how we'll sort through the offers, weigh them, and stratify them. Here's the reply process we'll use. And so on.

Vince listened to all this attentively. I could see him filing everything away.

Once we were finished explaining, I said, "So? What do you think? Any questions?"

Vince thought about that. "Yeah," he said. "I just realized. Have you two seen the new building yet?"

Michelle and I looked at each other. Shook our heads.

"Thought not." Vince picked up the phone. "Well, let's take care of that right now."

***

Two years before I'd left WWE, it became clear that the company had outgrown the Fortress of Doom. Back then, we had too many locations. The Fortress was our headquarters, but we also had a video production facility in another part of Stamford, plus another space we were leasing across the street from the Fortress. Having operations so spread out made little sense from both logistical and financial standpoints. Michelle and I had imagined putting everyone under one roof. So we led an initiative to buy the old UBS trading floor building in downtown Stamford.

Built in the 1990s, the building sits on a twelve-acre complex. Its main tower offers 400,000 square feet of office space. The floor itself is large enough to house 1,400 traders and 5,000 computers. To help you picture the scale, the trading floor is nearly as large as the flight deck of the USS *John F. Kennedy*, the world's largest aircraft carrier. Picture two football fields placed side-by-side. Or twenty-and-a-half basketball courts. Or forty-four singles tennis courts. *The Guinness Book of World Records* once listed UBS as the largest trading floor in the world. It was destined to be a leading light of the financial community, but after the financial crisis of 2008, the complex had sat vacant. Michelle and I thought it would make a perfect new headquarters for WWE. So we bought it, all in, for somewhere between $150 and $200 million. On top of which, we kicked off a massive and expensive renovation campaign that Michelle and I never saw completed.

Some of you might be rereading that last paragraph, thinking, *$200 million? That's a high price for an infrastructure purchase!* Not really. By that point, WWE was doing a billion dollars in revenue and was worth multiple billions. And the company was still growing faster than anyone had dared to imagine. We viewed it as an investment in the future.

Now look. I'll be the first person to say that COVID made the timing of that purchase problematic. We bought a massive office complex at precisely the moment when three-quarters of the world's labor force was forced to hole up and work from home. Yikes! But no matter. As was eventually proven, it was still the right thing to do. That building is now the new headquarters for WWE, a beautiful gleaming space offering enough room for the company to grow for the next twenty to thirty years.

Talk about irony. When Michelle and I entered the UBS complex, we were met by Rich the security guy. Yup, the same guy who, almost two years before, nearly wept while he escorted me out of the Fortress of Doom.

I'll never forget the look on Rich's face when he took us inside that massive hall and showed us around. His eyes were gleaming. His grin was enormous. "So?" he said. "What do you think?"

What did I think? We were standing alone in that massive, gorgeously appointed space. I think I blurted out, "God, it's just . . . it's amazing!"

Rich nodded. Then, very quietly, he said, "You made this possible. This is yours."

It was a wonderful thing for him to say—in fact, the perfect thing—and one more bow that got hung on the incredible comeback Michelle and I had made.

***

Today, people ask me, George, how much work did you do for the WWE deal? Was it easy or difficult?

Let me put it this way. I became so entrenched in what I was doing that I did what, for me, was at that time unthinkable. That spring, UConn's basketball team made the Final Four championship. And of course I had seats. But I ended up not using them. Because while the Final Four was going on, WrestleMania was being held at SoFi Stadium in Los Angeles.

There were so many things that had to be done to finalize the company sale, it made more sense for me to be out in LA, on-site. Carol and I made a sort of working vacation out of it by renting a place on the Strand that faced the Pacific in Manhattan Beach. We invited Chris and Josh to join us. Their daughter lived nearby, north of Los Angeles, and they got to visit her while they were there.

I remember one evening I worked through the night to get a particularly important segment of the deal done. Exhausting, but totally worth it. The next day, I went to WrestleMania, which was attended by 60,000 fans. There was a big party being thrown for all of WWE's business partners.

This will always be one of my finest memories: walking into that room and having everyone—all these people I'd worked with for so long, people I respected—turn my way and smile. Some of them clapped softly as they looked my way.

I remember thinking, *Papi, wherever you are, I want you to know. That Lincoln Continental is yours. That, and so much more.*

***

The deal team's infrastructure was in place. We were ready. We opened the phone lines. Offers began to pour in.

We got plenty of bids but the most attractive by far was tendered by Ari Emanuel, CEO of Endeavor Group Holdings, one of the biggest players in global entertainment. Endeavor companies include William Morris Endeavor, which represents artists in every field: authors, actors, directors, producers, musicians, fashion icons, professional athletes, you name it. It also owns some of the choicest enterprises in film production, fashion talent, and sports entertainment. As it happened, Ari had also served for years as Vince's personal representative.

Endeavor was already buying up properties in the sports entertainment space. In July 2016, it purchased the Ultimate Fighting Championship franchise for $4.025 billion as part of a larger buying spree that included the Barrett-Jackson Auction Company and the Miss Universe organization. UFC is the largest producer of mixed martial arts (MMA) events worldwide. Endeavor's purchase price reflected the largest acquisition in sports entertainment history—until they offered $9.3 billion for WWE. If memory serves, this bid was 15 to 20 percent higher than any other offer we received. And it was really just the beginning.

Endeavor saw the parallels between UFC and WWE. Both organizations sell the drama of combat to audiences worldwide. The fact that one offers scripted combat content while the other offers unscripted, actual combat was largely irrelevant. WWE and UFC had been high-level individual players in the sports entertainment space. The proposed deal would merge the two to create a new public company called TKO Holdings, a powerhouse in the sports and entertainment world.

TKO would have hundreds of millions of fans worldwide. That's rare. In fact, as I write this, only a handful of sports media platforms can boast that scale, including FIFA, NBA, and NFL. Since WWE and UFC had similar infrastructures, both companies could operate more efficiently together than apart. Everything that Michelle and I had built for WWE could be used by UFC. The industrial logic of the merger was compelling.

But it kept getting better. WWE and UFC had key contracts with NBCUniversal, FOX, and ESPN set to expire in the near term. As the new big kid on the block, backed by the full force of its viewership,

TKO would be positioned to renegotiate the highest prices on the market for TV and streaming rights. Distributors like Apple, Amazon, Netflix, NBC, CBS, you name it, would pay these higher prices because they all wanted access to TKO's viewer base.

Of course, these distributors would keep doing business with the NFL and NBA. But where some sports have always struggled to cross geographic boundaries, combat sports—be they scripted or real—harken back to humanity's primitive past. The art and rite of fighting is part of our species' evolution. It doesn't matter what culture you come from, what religion you practice, or what language you speak. When two warriors climb into a ring, everyone knows what's going to happen next. The fighters square off, the excitement kicks in, and the whole world is hooked.

My father understood this. You'll recall that he was a boxer and a boxing fan. Why else had he made such a teachable moment out of those bullies who'd given me trouble back at the Glen-Ora?

***

The icing on the cake for the team was the value this deal would create for WWE shareholders, including Vince, who still had a sizable portion of his net worth in WWE stock. Endeavor's offer valued WWE at $106 per share, or approximately 16 percent over the stock's mean share price at that time. Staggeringly, it also represented a 73 percent premium over WWE's valuation since Vince, Michelle, and I returned to the company. Once the deal closed, Endeavor would own a 51 percent controlling stake in TKO, with WWE's shareholders owning the remaining 49 percent. Endeavor would appoint six of the eleven board seats while WWE appointed the remaining five. Vince would serve as executive chair of TKO's board, which meant TKO could benefit from Vince's experience. He'd be in a prime position to guide the new organization, his pupa, through its earliest stages as a butterfly. For all parties concerned, we felt this was the best possible deal.

When I started with WWE, the company was valued at less than $1 billion. Selling the company for $9.3 billion meant that Michelle and I had basically 10x'd the company over fourteen years. It was a great source of pride for us and confirmation that Vince had been right to bring us back.

Post-merger, and traded on the public markets, TKO would hit a valuation of more than $21 billion. From there, the value would double over the next twenty-four months. Why? Go back to the industrial logic of the deal. Bringing WWE and UFC together created a behemoth that wielded significant leverage in the sports and entertainment ecosystem.

In January 2024, seven months post-merger, WWE completed a deal with Netflix to stream *Monday Night Raw* beginning in January 2025 for ten years at a price tag in excess of $5 billion. This was especially telling since three years prior to that, Netflix had gone on record stating they would never pay for live sports. Too expensive, they said. Of course, they also said they would never sell advertising on their platform, but we all know how that went. Here's another rule of thumb I've learned in business: Never means never—until circumstances change and you find that you absolutely have to do never right now in order to keep growing.

When the Netflix deal was announced, I was in my office. I usually have CNBC on, and they carried the story. The first thing I did was call Michelle. She hadn't seen the news yet and she was stunned. We reminisced about meetings we had taken back in the day with Ted Sarandos, who would become Netflix's co-CEO. Robust discussions about the potential value of *Raw* and *SmackDown* to Netflix's content slate. Ted wasn't ready to commit to live sports then, but my guess is that the seed we planted eventually bore this fruit.

Friday Night SmackDown, which we had shifted to FOX, found its way back to USA Network while WWE's monthly premium live events continued to go out over NBC's Peacock streaming service. All of which is to say that today, WWE is thriving. I know I speak for Michelle when I say how proud we are to have played our part in that.

But maybe the biggest change was this. The sale of WWE effectively ended control of that organization by the McMahon family since the company's founding in 1953. Vince served as executive chairman of TKO for something like seven months before he resigned to attend to some personal matters. Soon after that, he began selling his stock. If what I hear is correct, he's now liquidated his entire position.

That's hard for me to wrap my head around. Vince being completely out of the business? Almost impossible to fathom. Vince McMahon and the WWE I knew were always synonymous in too many ways to list. But the more I think about it, the more excited I get for him. A guy that talented, that astute, that driven thrives on new challenges. Whatever he puts his mind to next, I have no doubt he'll accomplish it.

Was our relationship a bumpy road? Sure. But bumpy roads are often the ones that lead us to the best, sometimes hidden destinations. And along the way, they give you what most people search for all their lives. A grand adventure.

Vince, if you're reading this, thanks for the ride. And what's next?

***

We've come to the end of this book, which means it's time for me to recap what I hope you got out of it. It's also time for me to clarify something that might be a major misconception.

The title of this book is *Sometimes Wrong but Never in Doubt*. Some readers might interpret this as a recipe to be cocky. It most certainly is not. If you recall, the title comes from a phrase a manager wrote about me in one of my early performance reviews. I remember reading this review before our meeting and thinking, *Oh that's just great. I'm fucked because this guy thinks I'm too goddamn arrogant.*

In fact, when we sat down face-to-face for my review, he promoted me! I was confused and couldn't leave well enough alone. So I asked him, "What does this mean, what you wrote here? Never in doubt? Why did you put that in there?"

He told me it was a phrase he'd read in Atul Gawande's book of essays, *Complications: A Surgeon's Notes on an Imperfect Science*. Gawande wrote it while working over 100 hours a week at Harvard University's Brigham and Women's Hospital. To say that he pulled back the curtain on how the medical industry operates would be a grand understatement. He yanked the goddamn curtain right off the rod.

A key point he touched on again and again was how great surgeons *must* have confidence. Without it, they'd likely become overwhelmed by the complexities of each case and never move forward with lifesaving treatments. Yes, of course there's a tipping point. An edict like this can be taken too far. But a wise person gets their confidence from their abilities, their preparation, and their expertise. Let's establish that baseless confidence is arrogance. But as my manager said to me that day, "George, you do so much work on every project you touch, it's like you reinvent it in your own mind. *That's* what gives you the confidence to move forward. Never lose that."

This struck me as not only true but well observed. It's an approach I feel comfortable passing along with this caveat. Remember that Jerome Lawrence quote I gave you back at the beginning of this book? Here it is again:

> It's the loneliest feeling in the world—to find yourself standing up when everybody else is sitting down. To have everybody look at you and say, "What's the matter with him?" . . . I know what it feels like. Walking down an empty street, listening to the sound of your own footsteps. Shutters closed, blinds drawn, doors locked against you. And you aren't sure whether you're walking toward something, or if you're just walking away.

I won't bullshit you. There's a price for pursuing your vision. Being the hero of your own story can suck. Extras get to hide in the wings and pray that people will forget about them. Heroes have to dream big, then go on a quest that turns their dream into a reality. Along the way, they must face the demons of doubt, the monsters called Ridicule, foes called Failure. They must battle these enemies who will kick the living shit out of them. That will feel awful, but just remember this:

Getting knocked down isn't a sign of failure. It's a sign that you're on the right track—so long as you get up again and keep going. Success in life is as simple as that. Success is always a hard-won battle, but the hardest battle you'll ever end up fighting is with yourself. So cultivate confidence. Be willing to blaze your own path. Bet on yourself when no one else will. You will wade to your neck in the Swamp of Despair and suffer the slings and arrows of outrageous fortune. But you must keep going, keep moving forward, repeat, repeat. No matter what.

Not everyone will understand why you're sometimes wrong but never in doubt. I offer these next words lovingly: Fuck them. Remember what Henry Ford once said: "Whether you think you can or you can't, you're right." Translation: Your view of the world is the view that matters most. Never forget that. Never run from it. Uphold it. Fight for it. And share it.

At the same time, read between the lines of this book. Smart people know how important it is to cultivate relationships with people who honor, value, and trust you. For instance, everyone should have a Carol in their lives, a life partner who always has your back and provides you with beautiful, talented kids, unflinching assessments, the truth, and a home. If more people had their own version of Carol, I can say without hesitation that this world would be a much better place.

They should also have a Michelle—a friend and the best business partner anyone could ask for. Michelle and I are successful because we complement each other. If a wise person must be intimately acquainted with their own strengths and weaknesses, business partners must be doubly so. Thankfully, Michelle and I have differences and similarities that both serve our common good. We also share the same work ethic. We have the intellectual capacity to figure things out, no matter how complicated they seem at first, and the emotional fortitude to push through any obstacle as we deepen our search for the truth. This means that we're always willing to dig in and see the world differently, even when—perhaps especially when—the whole world is saying, "You're wrong!"

Everyone should also have inspiring, challenging counterparts like Vince McMahon. Never run from the people who push you to be better. Embrace them for the great life partners they are. For all our ups and downs, I can say that working with Vince, and people just like him, has made me a better leader, a more creative thinker, and a deeper human being. You can't put a price on that.

Finally, I want to say this. Wherever you go and whatever you're doing, look for the value that's probably already there in whatever endeavor you're undertaking. Embrace it. Take responsibility for it. Make it your own. Then add to it from your unique way of looking at the world and give it back better than you found it.

This is the only work worth doing in life, and if it scares you to think about doing it, good. That's a damn good sign that you're on the right track.

Remember, no one gets scared unless they're on the edge of a breakthrough.

Epilogue: Still in the Ring

My original idea for ending this book was to close with my triumphant return to WWE. Who wouldn't want to finish a story on that high note? Turns out, life had other plans. You've been on this journey with me, so I thought I'd close the circle and share a little more with you.

In February 2024, my mother celebrated her hundredth birthday. In the few years since I'd left WWE, she'd been living in Miami. I'd visit her monthly and I was with her on her hundredth birthday. At that age, she was as sharp and spry as anyone could imagine. We celebrated at the Palace at Coral Gables where she lived, and she had a blast.

I know Mom adored those monthly visits I made. What I failed to realize was just how important they were to me. Each trip served as a reminder that success isn't just about the deals you close or the companies you build. It's about showing up for the people who matter most.

Two months later, in April, Carol and I were away with four other couples from the McConaughy 16. We were staying at a beautiful, brand-new resort in St. Vincent and the Grenadines. Partly this was a vacation, partly it was helping Carol research a book she's writing about her paternal grandmother's family. On our last day there, we got a call from the Palace at Coral Gables in Miami. Mom, they said, had fallen ill and been taken to the hospital.

Carol and I flew home the next day and went immediately to see her. We learned that Mom had developed a serious infection. Over the next couple of weeks, doctors managed to get it under control. We thought she'd dodged a bullet but, sadly, she never really recovered. On June 4, 2024, while in hospice, she passed away peacefully in her sleep.

I feel incredibly fortunate that Carol and I were both there when Mom finally left us. We'd been taking turns traveling back and forth to Miami, making sure she was never alone, but on that particular day, we were both there. It was like Mom's final gift to us, one that I'll always treasure.

Looking back, how could I be anything but grateful? I was a sixty-year-old man who'd enjoyed the great fortune of having his mother stay with him until she was 100. I think, in some ways, the trauma of losing my father early only amplified the role Mom played in my life. All the sacrifices she made on my behalf. Her unwavering support of me, even when it was unwarranted. What would I do without those now? Losing Mom was especially painful for me. Still is. A little piece of advice: If you're lucky enough to have a parent still alive, cherish them.

Around the same time, Michelle and I were excited to push forward into the next chapter of our professional lives. We came out of the WWE merger energized, ambitious, and eager to build on our partnership. We had no idea what that would look like, and so we explored different opportunities that included advisory, venture capital, and laying the groundwork for a sports private equity fund. Some of these experiments clicked and some of them didn't.

As satisfying as this work was, what I remember most about this period was the pressure of trying to build something new while facing serious personal challenges. My mother's passing. A family crisis. An illness of my own, which sidelined me for months. I weathered all these while enduring unforeseen business setbacks. In the end, I realized I had to scale back. Twice, I had to let people go, and I hate that. It hurts me to let people down. All these things combined were enough to make me question whether I'd lost the thread.

I was back in the Swamp of Despair. The part where you've climbed up out of the muck, you're exhausted, you're filthy, you realize you've barely survived, and the road ahead looks steeper and lonelier than ever. No matter how many times you go through this, the only question that goes through your mind is *Should I keep going? Or call it a day?*

Fortunately, I remembered what someone once told me. The person who succeeds is the person who is willing to fail just one more time. I chose to keep going.

That persistence paid off. In 2024, Michelle and I partnered with CVC, an international private equity powerhouse, to create Global Sport Group, a $14 billion holding company built to own and grow the world's most iconic sports assets.

CVC could've chosen anyone to help them architect this incredible entity so that it could scale value across iconic properties like La Liga, Ligue 1, and Six Nations. They chose Michelle and me. We spent the next eighteen months shaping the vision, positioning the portfolio, authoring the value creation playbook. Our efforts were immensely enjoyable, and so effective that Michelle and I were asked to join the GSG board and continue as strategic advisors. We were thrilled!

GSG is the most ambitious project I've ever been part of. It's bigger than Bowlero. Bigger than WWE. No one has a crystal ball, but I see amazing possibilities for this incredibly talented team. The vision to build the most successful sports holding company in the world is something I feel so fortunate to be a part of. Michelle and I won this opportunity by doing what, by now, I hope you've come to expect from us. Getting into the details, reimagining the status quo, and relentlessly overdelivering.

As my work with GSG took off, my venture investing accelerated as well. I brought on a great partner, Kunal Mehta, who now leads that business. Kunal and I continue investing in a portfolio of early-stage companies while helping their founders navigate the Swamp of Despair. Helping others push through their doubts and overcome their obstacles is one of my most rewarding roles.

So here we are. In some ways, everything is different. The businesses have changed. The sector has evolved. The stakes are higher. I'm older. But one thing is the same. I'm still in the ring. I'm still sometimes wrong but never in doubt. And I wouldn't have it any other way.

Remember that Joe Walsh quote from the dedication? While you're living life, it feels like pure chaos. Random events smashing into each other without any rhyme or reason. In my case, that meant losing my father at age nine, struggling in school, getting fired from WWE, watching my mother pass at a hundred, dealing with family crises and business setbacks.

But when I look back on all of that now, I don't see chaos. I see what Walsh called the finely crafted novel. In hindsight, it's obvious to me how my father's early passing made my mother's role more crucial in my life. How every job I took prepared me for my next challenge. How getting fired from WWE positioned Michelle and me perfectly for the vindication that followed. How personal struggles taught me lessons that no business school could provide.

At the time, it sure didn't feel like a novel. It felt like surviving one crisis after another. But Walsh was right. Hindsight is everything. Now I see the threads connecting it all, the way each seemingly random event was actually preparation for what came next. How they forged the person I am today. And I'm so grateful. I'm just so grateful.

Papi, that Lincoln Continental is still yours. But now I understand something I didn't before. The real prize was never the car itself—it was the drive to keep going, to keep building, to keep believing in possibilities even when, perhaps especially when, they seem impossible.

That drive doesn't end with any single transaction or achievement. It's what gets you up in the morning and keeps you moving forward, no matter what life throws at you.

And life, as I've learned, always has more to throw at you.

You know what I say? Bring it on.

Lessons Learned

I didn't write this book because I had all the answers. I wrote it because I've taken enough hits, made enough calls, lost enough sleep, and seen enough cycles to know which lessons stick—and which you can only learn the hard way.

But more than that, the act of writing this—of forcing myself to sit with the story—helped me clarify and distill what I actually believe.

The following twelve points aren't meant as a blueprint. More like a distillation that I hope anyone reading this book will profit from. It may help you to think of these points as mantras snapshotting poignant, powerful lessons. Each lesson has earned its place here not because it sounds good, but because it's been battle-tested—in business, in life, in the mirror. I share these lessons not as doctrine, but as orientation points. Use them. Challenge them. But above all, make them your own.

1. Do the Work, then Move with Confidence

Confidence without the work is bravado. We've all seen it. We know what it looks like. And it never pans out. Not for long, anyway. I'm going to assume that you've built deep expertise, pressure-tested your thinking, and truly understand the problems you face. But doing the work isn't enough. You have to actualize your work with confidence. Success comes from the marriage of the two—work and confidence. To do anything of consequence, you have to have both.

2. You Are Your First Zip Code

The places and circumstances you grew up in tend to hardwire your early operating system. Mine was built on scarcity, pride, hustle, and loyalty—not as virtues, but as necessities. That code shaped how I first viewed risk, trust, money, and power. Take a hard look at how your first zip code made you who you are. And if your formative experiences don't seem to lend themselves to success, you're probably not looking deeply enough. Take heart, because there's a nugget of gold buried in every pile of soot. Remember that people are not immutable. We can evolve and we can transcend. Just remember that your first zip code never really logs off the system that governs you. Keep checking in with yourself.

3. Pain Is the Entry Fee for Growth

Growth rarely feels like growth when you're in it. It feels like pain, something to avoid, which is why so many people *do* avoid it. Remember, no one gets through life without getting at least a little banged up. Getting fired. Losing my father. Being left behind. None of that felt noble in the moment. But each time I experienced pain, it cracked something open—and that crack let the clarity in.

4. Clarity Is the Ultimate Leadership Trait

Life can be a carnival of big stakes and bigger egos. A leader's job is to cut through the noise. Clarity isn't just about communication—it's about thought, focus, direction, and action. The best leaders make complexity seem simple, human, and real. In other words, they lead with clarity—and they deliver it with authenticity and conviction.

5. Loyalty Isn't a Tagline

I was raised to value loyalty like oxygen. But the higher you rise in business and in life, the murkier the air seems to get. In business, for instance, loyalty gets tested, twisted, and sometimes traded. Some people value it, others weaponize it. But real loyalty is earned through time, scars, and action—not slogans, promises, and hollow duty. Look for true loyalty, which is based on principle. Value it. Reward it. Practice it yourself. Especially when it's hard to do.

6. Original Thinking Is Lonely—Until It's Not

I've had moments where I saw the pattern before anyone else did, and I've had to live in the discomfort that comes with that—being misunderstood, doubted, sidelined. Isolated because no one saw what I saw. Most bold ideas don't show up looking obvious. They look wrong, arrogant, or even dangerous—until they prove themselves otherwise. Be willing to weather the loneliness of your ideas. Don't focus on the lonely part. Focus on bringing them to reality.

7. The Business Model Is the Strategy

Strategy doesn't start with a spreadsheet; it starts with understanding a system. Questions you should always ask yourself include: Who creates value? Who captures it? Where does the leverage lie? What's core and what's extraneous? You can only move your business forward, and make choices that matter, once you've mastered the system in which it operates. That's the business model. If you don't understand the model, you're just guessing. Don't do that. Make the shift from internal to systemic thinking. From focusing only on yourself to understanding your place in the overall industry. This small shift can change everything.

8. Storytelling Is a Leadership Skill

Strategy lives in the model; belief lives in the story. If you can't explain what you're building and why it matters, you'll never bring others with you. Storytelling isn't decoration. It's how leaders shape and create momentum.

9. Focus on Finding the Right Question, Not the Right Answer

It's human nature when confronted with a problem to jump right in and try and solve it. Unfortunately, doing this means you miss the opportunity to understand the true nature of the problem. Remember that great answers are always available, they're like copper. But the right question is as precious as gold and equally difficult to mine. At WWE, Michelle and I spent the bulk of our time figuring out the right questions. Try it. You'll see what I mean.

10. Invert. Always Invert.

Assumptions are powerful foundations. They form the bedrock of our thinking. But beware. Assumptions can also imprison our thinking. Remember what happened when WWE's content was pirated in China? We were furious. We spent all our time and energy trying to stop it because, as a content company, we assumed that piracy was bad. And it usually is. However, when we flipped the assumption, we realized that our enemies could become our allies. It required nothing more than inverting our assumption about piracy, and it yielded great results.

11. Know When to Leverage First Principles over Comparisons

People reason by analogy. It's a shortcut, a rule of thumb—and it usually works. One of the most common analogies people use is the past. That is, if something is happening now, or has happened before, it will happen again. Here too, they're usually right. But not always. Rather than rely on existing views of the game, Bill James broke baseball down to its atomic elements and built new strategies for winning from those first principles. Michelle and I did the same when we repositioned WWE. When you operate from first principles, you stop playing everyone else's game—and start creating your own.

12. Strategy's Just Talk Until You Execute

I've seen billion-dollar strategies die in the PowerPoint. Why? Simple. Execution isn't the follow-up, it's the main event. Clarity of thinking, enthusiasm, discipline, and adaptability—that's the grind that consistently drives transformation. Anything else is just dabbling. I've seen this time and again. Everyone agrees on the strategy, but then they're unwilling to commit their time, money, and reputation to implement it. Here's my advice. In life, don't dabble. Pick your battles. Commit. And win.

My last words on all this. Life has taught me that experience doesn't make us wise, reflection does. I hope I've inspired you to reflect on your life, decide what's important to you, and move forward with purpose.

Now go on, get out there.

And win.

GB